Christopher Schmitt

Designing CSS Web Pages

New Riders

800 East 96th Street, Indianapolis, Indiana 46240
An Imprint of Pearson Education
Boston • Indianapolis • London • Munich • New York • San Francisco

Designing CSS Web Pages

International Standard Book Number: 0-73571-263-8

Library of Congress Catalog Card Number: 2001099566

06 05 04   7 6 5 4 3

Interpretation of the printing code: The rightmost double-digit number is the year of the book's printing; the rightmost single-digit number is the number of the book's printing. For example, the printing code 02-1 shows that the first printing of the book occurred in 2002.

Printed in the United States of America

Trademarks

Warning and Disclaimer

Publisher
David Dwyer

Associate Publisher
Stephanie Wall

Production Manager
Gina Kanouse

Managing Editor
Kristy Knoop

Senior Acquisitions Editor
Linda Anne Bump

Acquisitions Editor
Todd Zellers

Development Editor
Laura Loveall

Senior Marketing Manager
Tammy Detrich

Publicity Manager
Susan Nixon

Copy Editor
Karen A. Gill

Indexer
Cheryl Lenser

Manufacturing Coordinator
Jim Conway

Book Designer
Alan Clements
Christopher Schmitt

Cover Designer
Alan Clements
Christopher Schmitt

Composition
Gloria Schurick

To Mom

Contents At a Glance

Table of Contents

Part II   Using CSS   53

Part III Advanced CSS   161

Part IV Launching Progressive Design with CSS:
Deconstructions   203

About the Author

 **Christopher Schmitt**, an award-winning web designer and developer, has been on the Internet since 1992. In 1997, he graduated with a fine arts degree with emphasis on graphic design from Florida State University, where he was asked to design the first incarnation of the department's Web. While Christopher was an undergraduate, he interned for both David Siegel and Lynda Weinman, wrote for local newspapers about Web sites of interest, was an editor for his local newspaper, and won the prestigious High Five award for Web site design.

After graduation, Christopher worked for such firms as Studio Verso in San Francisco, was President of Media Collective, and was Senior Design Technologist leading the production of award-winning Web site projects for a multimedia ad agency in Orlando.

Christopher has written for *New Architect*, *A List Apart*, *Digital Web*, and *High Five*, and he has contributed four chapters to *XML, HTML, XHTML Magic* (New Riders Publishing, 2002). In 2000, he led a team to victory in the Cool Site in a Day competition, where he and five others built a fully functional, well-designed Web site for a non-profit organization in eight hours.

Christopher also created the Web Design Pad, a mousepad sporting the first-ever look of Web-safe colors in a true color wheel arrangement that was widely sold throughout the U.S. and abroad.

Christopher shows his true colors and most recent activities on his personal Web site (Christopher.org). He is the list mom for Babble (Babblelist.com), a mailing list community devoted to advanced Web design and development topics.

Currently, Christopher resides in Orlando where he is Project Manager and Idea Generator for the new media publishing company, Heatvision.com, Inc. He also continues to write about Web culture and design.

About the Technical Reviewers

These reviewers contributed their considerable hands-on expertise to the entire development process for *Designing CSS Web Pages*. As the book was being written, these dedicated professionals reviewed all the material for technical content, organization, and flow. Their feedback was critical to ensuring that *Designing CSS Web Pages* fits our reader's need for the highest-quality technical information.

Porter Glendinning has spent the past several years designing and developing interfaces to Web-based applications for an Internet consulting company in the Washington, D.C./Baltimore area. He lives in Olney, Maryland, with his wife, Laura, who puts up with his obsession with the Internet; and their very large yellow lab, Arrow, who eats his socks. Porter can be found online at www.glendinning.org and www.cerebellion.com. He also co-administers the Babble mailing list, a forum for discussions on advanced Web design topics of all sorts (www.babblelist.com), with Christopher.

Nathan Woods is the director of the Web design firm NextStepDesigns (www.nextstepdesigns.com), which specializes in revamping outdated sites for small companies. He has worked in architecture for more than 15 years and has recently reeducated himself in Web design to better integrate project extranet technologies into the construction environment. He can frequently be found lurking in various newsgroups and discussion forums involving the Web, out on the slopes of Southern California flying RC Sailplanes, or spending time in the backyard with his wife and two children.

Acknowledgments

This book has gotten to where it is today with a lot of help along the way.

First, thanks to Linda Bump for helping to get the project rolling by helping me refine the idea that would become what you see before you.

Thanks to Molly Holzschlag (http://www.molly.com) and Eric Meyer (http://www.meyerweb.com) for their enthusiasm for this book, which fueled me through the whole process.

A great deal of respect and thanks go to the book team, for helping to bring an idea to reality and, along the way, making me appear a lot better on paper than I know I do by myself: Linda Bump (again), Laura Loveall, Porter Glendinning, Nathan Woods, Todd Zellers, Aren Howell, and Ginny Bess.

A mighty thanks to Porter Glendinning (http://www.glendinning.org) for long chats at all hours of the day and night about web design theories, CSS and HTML specs, how to best shape the ideas for the book when the right words failed to find their way to me and, most importantly, having fun at my expense while doing it.

Special thanks go to the interviewees: Steven Champeon, J. David Eisenberg, Jeffrey Zeldman, Greg Roelof, and Håkon Wium Lie.

Thanks to Miles Tilmann (http://www.webhole.com) for his simple, but powerful illustrations.

Special thanks to the contributions of Mark Newhouse (http://homepage.mac.com/iblog), Jason Fried (http://www37signals.com), and Mat Gaver and Brook Pifer at Gen X Images (http://www.genximages.com).

In my life, I'm fortunate to learn from talented communicators: Lori K. Mirrer, Gail Rubini, David Seigel, Lynda Weinman, Jeffrey Zeldman (again), and Molly Holzschlag (again).

Thanks to Gail Rubini (again) for use of her office when I needed to finish a couple of chapters while I was away from HQ.

Thanks to my friends for putting up with me during this book and helping me with advice along the way: Tony and Stephanie Chen, Dee Lalley, Linda Sierra, Kristi and Matt Repstien, Andrew Watson, and Ryan Yordan.

Thanks to the members of the Web design mailing list, Babble List.

And, most importantly, thank you, the reader. I worked hard to make this a book I would want next to *my* computer while I coding my designs. I hope this book serves you well.

Tell Us What You Think

As the reader of this book, you are the most important critic and commentator. We value your opinion and want to know what we're doing right, what we could do better, what areas you'd like to see us publish in, and any other words of wisdom you're willing to pass our way.

As the Associate Publisher for New Riders Publishing, I welcome your comments. You can fax, email, or write me directly to let me know what you did or didn't like about this book—as well as what we can do to make our books stronger.

Please note that I cannot help you with technical problems related to the topic of this book, and that due to the high volume of mail I receive, I might not be able to reply to every message.

When you write, please be sure to include this book's title and author as well as your name and phone or fax number. I will carefully review your comments and share them with the author and editors who worked on the book.

Fax: 317-428-3382

Email: stephanie.wall@newriders.com

Mail: Stephanie Wall
            Associate Publisher
            New Riders Publishing
            800 East 96th Street
            Indianapolis, IN 46240 US

Foreword

As someone who knows a little bit about Cascading Style Sheets, I often see questions from people who want to know how to use CSS more effectively. "What's the best way to lay out a page?" is a popular one. "How do I control font sizes?" is another. These are the kinds of questions that come up again and again, as more and more people discover CSS and its incredible power and flexibility.

There are three basic ways to answer such questions. The first is to simply answer it in a terse manner. This is helpful, but doesn't really help the inquirer understand the implications of the answer, let alone how it can be generalized into other solutions. The second is to spend a few paragraphs (or pages) talking about the theory behind the question, a short history of the Web's evolution, and alternative approaches—and *then* you get to the answer. This is boring. By the time the answer comes up, the reader has already fallen asleep. The third way is to give an answer, preferably with examples, and a little bit of theory and explanation as a way of annotating the answer. This gives the inquirer what they need, but also shows them directions for further study, should they be so inclined. It marks the location of the oasis, while also giving pointers to other oases and rivers of knowledge.

Personally, I feel the third way is the best of the lot. It's the way of the veteran bush guide who does his best to help explorers navigate unfamiliar land, pointing them to new areas while helping them avoid injurious (or fatal) mistakes. In this, I can think of few CSS guides more qualified than Christopher Schmitt. He's a frontline troop, an in-the-trenches guy, a day-to-day Webmaster like so many of us. He has to deal with unreasonable design requirements, pressure from clients and upper management, browser flaws, and all the rest. Despite his youth, he's been doing it for a long time—longer, I think, than almost anyone I know, including me. And I'm dangerously close to being an old man in this business.

Rather than simply throwing examples at you, or plodding through page upon page of CSS theory, Chris takes the time to place the use of CSS in its context. Instead of just focusing on HTML and CSS, this book looks at CSS and how it can be used with other technologies—SVG, PNG, and

HTML among them. The text doesn't act as though CSS exists in a vacuum. Instead, Chris shows us how CSS is more important and touches on more of the Web than we may have realized, and how it can be used to make Web design easier, from the first conceptual sketch to the last design tweak. He's talking as much about what to do, and why you should do it, as he is about how to do things.

I'm glad to see that guides like this one are coming out, because it means that we've finally outgrown the legacy of the browser wars and are getting on to the interesting stuff. I'm even more glad that Chris has stepped forward to share his experience and wisdom, not to mention a bit envious of his readers. They'll be getting the kind of guide I wish I'd had, way back when I started.

Eric A. Meyer

www.meyerweb.com

August 2002, Cleveland, Ohio

Introduction

My first contact with Cascading Style Sheets (CSS) came in late 1996. Like most Web developers, I learned on my own by tinkering, sharing knowledge with others, and then tinkering some more. And after going through some CSS techniques for styling Web pages and learning with others about its potential, I took a couple of things away from the learning experience during that time in the 1990s.

One thing I learned was that style sheets possessed a great ability to deliver the visual presentation of a Web page. Instead of forcing HTML to deliver both content and presentation in the same document, sooner or later CSS *would become* a moving factor in the design of Web sites.

The other thing I learned was that style sheets' implementations in browsers weren't ready for prime time. Only Microsoft's Internet Explorer at the time was making the first major steps—although shaky to say the least—to support the technology. You could do quite a lot with IE's CSS support, but you could also wind up with potentially violent presentations in Netscape's Navigator, which still had the major market share, if you used what was fully available in IE.

Today, we find ourselves with fresher browsers—and even viable browsers from companies other than Microsoft and Netscape (now owned by AOL Time Warner)—and CSS support is more robust in browsers than it was in 1997. Also, I've learned a lot more about CSS as well as other Web technologies and design practices that relate to designing for a better Web. That's where this book comes in—to help Web designers and developers learn to design better for the Web.

Håkon Wium Lie:
The father of CSS

To be honest, I can't think of a better way to introduce this book about designing Web sites with CSS than to have a brief interview with Håkon Wium Lie, the father of CSS.

Lie graduated from MIT Media Lab. In October of 1994, he proposed style sheets (see his proposal at `http://www.w3.org/People/howcome/p/cascade.html`) and was in charge of their development at the World Wide Web Consortium (W3C) (`http://www.w3.org`) until 1999. Currently, he is the chief technology officer for Opera Software (`http://www.opera.com/`), the company that makes the Opera browser. One of Håkon's primary goals as Opera's CTO is to make sure their browser has the best support for W3C standards while remaining small and fast.

Christopher Schmitt: How did you come to the notion for what would be CSS? What methods or technologies inspired CSS?

Håkon Wium Lie: Around 1990, when the Web was developed at CERN, I wasn't there. Instead, I was at the MIT Media Lab working on personalized newspapers.

The idea was to select content based on the background and interest of the user. Also, we wanted to make systems that presented news in a way the user preferred, e.g., on a big screen like a broadsheet paper or a smaller screen like a tabloid newspaper. Trying to combine the interests of the newspaper, the content, and the user was high on the list of goals. This is the background for the "Cascading" part of CSS.

CS: What problems do CSS solve that traditional Web development methods don't?

HWL: CSS let you express the presentation of a document, while HTML (or XML or any "ML") expresses the content and the structure. By making that separation, you can create pages that scale to fit different devices. You don't need to have a PC screen with exactly 800×600 pixels. Also, the presentation will *look* better!

CS: **Are you happy with the way things are going regarding markup and CSS? Any thoughts about SVG, SMIL, Flash?**

HWL: Most pages use CSS these days, but most often it's not used to its full potential. You will find pages that continue to use tables for layout and then—as an afterthought—sprinkle the page with CSS to achieve certain effects.

This is partly due to browsers not implementing the more advanced features until recently. Also, Web developers—those who make pages—are increasingly conservative and stick to what works in Netscape 3. I think it's time to change!

CS: **Do you think the main problem with CSS seems to be with browser implementations? Browsers are getting better support for CSS, but it seems like it's a slow journey.**

HWL: Yes, it has been a slow journey. With hundreds of millions of Web browsers out there, it takes time to upgrade.

In the early days, people upgraded their browsers whenever there was a new version of Mosaic—or something—available. The Web is moving slower with all the new users, and the journey, therefore, is slower.

Buggy browsers are also a problem. The CSS support in Netscape 4 was a disaster. Microsoft's initial work was good, but as soon as they overtook Netscape in the user statistics, they stopped caring about standards. Only by strong involvement from the user community have they almost completed their support for CSS Level 1.

CS: **If someone wants to learn CSS, what tips would you give them?**

HWL: Buy a good book. Then, try writing simple HTML pages accompanied by simple style sheets. Write everything "by hand" to get that hands-on experience. Doing the simple stuff is very simple and the advanced stuff is only moderately hard.

CS: **What do you see for the future of CSS?**

HWL: CSS will be around for a while. It will be implemented in TVs, printers, and phones. There will also be revisions to the specification to add functionality that people request. The CSS group in W3C is working on CSS3.

> **CS:** **What do you see for the future for the Web and Internet technologies?**
>
> **HWL:** I plan to spend the rest of my life on the Web, so I hope it remains a place for open exchange of information. The greatest threat to the Web is a Microsoft ice age. I, therefore, encourage people to use software from other vendors, including Linux, Mozilla, and Opera.

Who Should Read This Book

This book is for Web builders who want to get rid of the old techniques that made their content viewable in only one or two browsers, thereby locking out other types of Web browsers. When a new browser version hit the market, you had to redesign the site. Or maybe you had to build a completely different site for this new batch of browsers. This book attempts to point you in the right direction and give you a new set of tools for a new millennium.

This book also aims to serve those who have a print design background and might be familiar with style sheets. We hope this book serves you as a gateway to learn about CSS and how to better design for the Web.

In addition, this book is for developers and designers who are familiar with HTML but not with how to use CSS. This book will serve as an introduction to CSS—as well as other Web technologies—allowing you to spring into your own projects and learn more detail about CSS.

About the Content in this Book

Designing CSS Web Pages is divided into five Parts:

- Part I, "Starting Out," looks into the issues that are associated with starting a Web design project and preparing to design with CSS.

- Part II, "Using CSS," starts out covering the basics of CSS so that you can see how CSS is a part of Dynamic HTML.

- Part III, "Advanced CSS," is dedicated to creating different style sheets for the same page.

- Part IV, "Launching Progressive Design with CSS: Deconstructions," is about deconstructing Web pages to see how CSS was used to make the designs.

- Part V, "Appendixes," contains four appendixes. One appendix has formatting exercises that you can use as a sort of visual design swatch. The three other appendixes have reference material for CSS 2, HTML 4.01, and a conversion guide for HTML to XHTML.

About the Book's Companion Web Site

Change is the only constant. By the time this book hits the shelves, Web standard specifications will be revised, browser software will be upgraded, and there might some new CSS tricks discovered that need to be shared.

To keep up with these changes, my company, Heatvision.com, has set up a companion site to this book to help out. The companion Web site located at http://www.cssbook.com/ hosts downloadable code samples that were used in this book, more recommended reading (suggested books, Web sites, and online articles), and reviews of CSS and HTML authoring tools.

Conventions

Every computer book has its own style of presenting information. As you flip through this book, you'll notice that it has a layout with a few conventions that you should be aware of as you begin reading.

One of the most important layout conventions is the way that the code is treated. A lot of the code falls under a numbered listing, like this:

Listing 1.1   Example of a Code Listing

```
.byline {
  background-color: inherit;
}

.comment {
  position: relative;
}

.widget {
  margin: 0.5em 0 0;
}
```

continues

> **Listing 1.1　Example of a Code Listing　(Continued)**
>
> ```
> .widgetImage {
>   margin: 10px 0 0 10px;
> }
> ```

These code listings are available for download from this book's companion Web site, which is located at `http://www.cssbook.com`. Information about this and other New Riders books is available on the publisher's Web site at `http://www.newriders.com`.

You'll also see that the book uses two different types of asides. Following are examples of both.

Note

These are short notes that give you the extra information that you need.

You'll See These, Too

These are longer asides that provide more details than the short Notes do. Had this sidebar been shorter, it probably would have been a Note and not a sidebar. Because it is not that short, it's actually a sidebar providing more background. However, we have a number of sentences to put here. Thankfully, this should be the last one. Or is this the last one? Well, maybe not.

This sidebar is an example. The sidebars used in this book really do contain information that is germane to the topic of designing with CSS for the Web. Trust me: We wouldn't want this sidebar to go on any further than it absolutely had to.

This book also follows a few typographical conventions:

- A new term is set in *italics* the first time it is introduced.

- Program text, functions, variables, and other "computer language" are set in a fixed-pitch font—for example, `spacer tag` and `blockquote`.

Part I

Starting Out

Chapter 1

Planning and Structuring Content

Sometimes, people and businesses get lucky on the Web. They create a Web presence that garners exposure and a high volume of traffic. Their Web presence then goes beyond log files or hit meters to connect with people. A site becomes a destination when it connects others with personal stories—a respectable place for instant social commentary or the most respected brand for online shopping for everything under the sun and then some.

However, without proper planning, any site that does become successful will not be able to leverage that kind of luck for long. In fact, you are more likely to achieve the success you want online through hard work, planning, and structuring of your message than a lottery ticket of a Web site. To ensure that your Web site meets its goals to become a success, it's important to strategize as to the rationale behind its existence.

In this chapter, we will look at factors that will help you reach your intended audience with your message before you put pen to paper for sketching out designs or code markup between a body element. Afterward, we will look into how to get your content ready for Web delivery and the application of design, the presentation of your message, through Cascading Style Sheets (CSS).

Know Your Audience

Design consists of more than visuals, graphics image formats, sound files, and typography. Design requires planning, and one rule binds print designers, architects, movie directors, car manufacturers, politicians, and Web designers. That rule is: "Know your audience." Because one kind of person doesn't make up the millions of Web surfers, not one manner of Web site design can reach this audience.

When a client hires you to build a Web site, you should solidify the goals the client has for their site. Determine the site's intended functionality—the client's needs against his wants—so that you can examine your client's competitors. Examining competitor sites in this context is an expected exercise of design strategy. Exploring how a client's competition reaches its audience is a good way of determining the status quo for doing business in your client's industry. However, if you apply a similar design to a client's site as a competitor, you are shortchanging the client. Doing so means that you are failing to differentiate the client's brand and to attract the competition's customers. In addition, you might just be adding to the stockpile of bland Web sites. In essence, you are wasting money and time instead of approaching the Web site's design from the audience's point of view.

People make judgments in the way they communicate with others, from wrongful discrimination to giving genuine courtesy. Their perceptions of whom they are talking to dictate interactions, such as conversations (or the lack of conversations) in every part of social life. First impressions are important in every occasion from job interviews to blind dates. The same can be said for how you craft the message for your Web site. If the design does not reach out and inform at the start, it's not effectively doing its job. To quote Jan V. White's *Color for Impact: How Color Can Get Your Message Across or Get in the Way* (Strathmoor Press, 1997), "'First-glance value' is not just a catch phrase. It is the very kernel of functional communication, given today's frantic competition for attention… Content and form are one. Design is a lubricant for ideas."

Print designers, architects, film directors, and Web designers, for example, work through a design problem like a consummate negotiator who is trying to create paths for understanding the material. By negotiating a compromise between art, function, and experience, designers and developers work on the visuals, content, and backend portions of a Web site, which make up the inherent experience of surfing the Web site. (This isn't your father's graphic design job.) The kinds of visuals and tools that designers use to successfully bring that experience to users depend on with whom they are going to communicate on behalf of their clients.

Customer Types: Tomāto or Tomäto

Even when an audience shares similarities for two competitors in business, their Web site designs and development produce two different types of sites. For example, both Barneys New York and Target share an audience that is interested in purchasing consumer goods (see Figures 1.1 and 1.2).

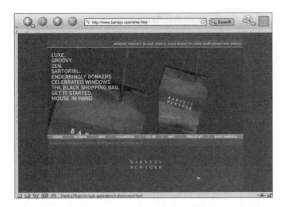

Figure 1.1

To view Barneys' e-commerce site, you need a high-end computer and a fast Internet connection to handle the presentation.

Figure 1.2

Target provides a Web site that almost all Web-enabled computers that have a current generation browser can reach.

Both Target and Barneys New York have physical "brick and mortar" stores that sell their products to customers. What separates the businesses is the type of customer each is targeting.

Target aims for the bargain shopper customer type, or the sensible, middle-class society. It has a wide selection of everyday and every-so-often goods (such as snack items, drinks, contact solution, and so on, as well as stereo equipment, fake Christmas trees, Halloween costumes, and the like). Barneys of New York targets and markets to the richer segment of society, or the full ticket price customer.

These differences in types of audiences are easily identified in the companies' respective Web sites. Barneys New York has few HTML-based forms on the site, but it almost exclusively uses a multimedia experience with Macromedia's vector-based tool Flash. To get the full experience of Barneys's Web site, users need to have fast Internet connections to handle the large file sizes, and they need a high-end computer system to render the Flash presentation. Target's site, on the other hand, has a simple, straightforward design that targets the majority of American Web surfers. On Target's site, people can shop for reasonably priced goods without interruption on a fairly low-powered computer with one of many available browsers.

Figure 1.3

Informing the world unlike its print counterpart, which informs only the United States. The aim of this site is to inform its readers about the latest in national and international news.

Reader Types Versus Customer Types

Knowing your audience isn't just based on customers, regardless of what the talking heads on financial networks and television shows say about new media. Believe it or not, people surf the Web for information. (There's a reason that the Internet is referred to as the information superhighway.) These people are reader types. They can check out *USA Today*'s Web site for coverage of American-centric interests (see Figure 1.3) and compare the news with what's in their local newspaper's Web site as well as other national or even international news sites. Although the online publication of *USA Today* reflects the content of its print counterpart, the site also supports online-only content and publishing updates that occur five days a week.

Web sites that reach out to customer types need to provide a different type of atmosphere from those that cater to readers. With shopping sites, they need to provide a sense of trust with your credit card information and timely fulfillment of your order. Sites that cater to reader types are concerned about meeting publishing deadlines on a regular schedule to retain and grow their readership. Having something original or interesting to say is also a good idea.

The American right to freedom of the press does not belong only to people who can buy a printing press. Justin Hall's Links site, an independent online publication chronicling his life in his own words, images, and programming, is an example of a one-man publishing empire (see Figure 1.4). Established in 1994, Justin covers the convergence of new media and society, and his audience is anyone interested in things that matter to him and those that get caught up in the journal of an expressive person. Justin's publishing schedule is his own. (Usually, it's a once-a-day writing schedule.)

Figure 1.4

Justin Hall's personal site is an easy-to-read personal journal of one man's perspective through technology and its effect on culture. Yes, it has ad banners, too.

Experience Types

Surfing the Web is an experience unto itself. Users can engage in online artwork that only exist on the Web. And although they can burn art pieces onto CD-ROMs, the delivery of the artwork is the Web. Instead of going to a museum to experience artwork in person, the art is available wherever a person can go online to find it. Web artist Richard Grillotti's PixelJam takes full use out of a browser's capability to stretch images and the animation specifications in GIFs (see Figure 1.5).

Museums, on the other hand, are leveraging the power of the Web to advertise their shows (see Figure 1.6). Although the museums might have shows for their electronic artwork, the user has to physically go to the museum to click a mouse, tap keyboards, or use other input devices that the artist has created to interact with the artwork.

However, both SFMOMA and PixelJam are out to create a unique surfing experience for their visitors. Grillotti's site is the experience, whereas SFMOMA's is an attractive marketing ploy that tries to lure paying visitors to their museum (and stop in the gift shop on their way out).

Figure 1.5

Richard Grillotti's PixelJam uses the nature of GIF animations that are small and then stretches them like a canvas over a browser frame. In short, it's Web art.

Figure 1.6

The San Francisco Museum of Modern Art (SFMOMA) tries to convince visitors to check out their "brick and mortar" art museum.

Through audience types, we realize that various types of sites are available. For your site development, you need to realize up front if you're building for one, two, or all three of these site types for your audience. It's not just a matter of knowing the audience, but building the right type of site for your audience.

Liberation Through Audience Limitations

If you don't know who you are talking to, will your audience know what you're saying through your Web site? Probably not. Your audience will probably be as lost and confused on the site when they reach your home page (see Figure 1.7) as you are. Without thinking about the audience for your Web site, the people who do show up to see your Web site won't be catered to effectively like they would be at a site that was built from the ground up to help them.

Figure 1.7

Starting a Web project without defining your audience leads to a Web site without a beneficial purpose.

One of the great things about taking an audience-oriented design approach is that you are actually reducing design possibilities, or the options that would be fruitless. You don't take unneeded steps. Instead, through research and strategic thinking, you can determine what the best ways are of *not* wasting time, money, and other resources at your disposal (see Figure 1.8).

Figure 1.8

By boxing your audience, you can put them under observation and testing to determine their likes, dislikes, and what they want from a site like the one you are going to build.

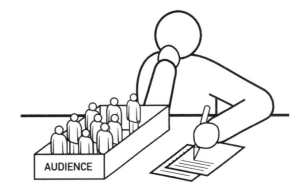

It is also important for you to know who *isn't* part of your audience. Sometimes, the best way to determine the best solution is to eliminate what obviously *won't* work for your Web site. Eliminating different groups of audiences allows you to narrow in on your audience (see Figure 1.9).

Figure 1.9

Getting rid of audiences that don't serve your mission brings you a step closer to bringing your message to the right audience.

With an audience-centered approach, you won't spend time trying to reach millions of Web surfers. Instead, you'll be able to focus on the people who matter to your project being a success. Just because a million people could potentially visit your Web site, the likelihood of your ISP's servers melting down from too many users won't happen without careful planning.

Of course, serving a specific audience at the beginning of the project does not imply that you will be serving the same audience at the end of the project or during the maintenance and content updates. During the development phases of a Web site, a client or a project manager will add his opinions about how to improve the Web site. Take these opinions with a grain of salt. These opinions are coming from one person's perspective of Web surfing and what he thinks is "cool." By adding only this client's/manager's philosophy of approaching the functionality and design, chances are that you are cheating the audience instead of making the site a quality environment.

Of course, blindly ignoring the person who is paying for the Web site (and therefore you) isn't a good thing either. If possible, you need to reach a consensus about the best way to approach the project. Remember: You've researched the best way to build the client's Web site so far, and you can back up your claims. Ask the client to do the same for any change or modification that doesn't seem to help. See what the client has to say and reach compromises.

Gathering Content

Web builders should always determine the who, what, when, where, and why before writing a sentence of copy or applying the most basic of Photoshop's filters to an image. By approaching the project as set of questions that need to be answered, the final product will be better. You'll have fewer questions about what the site should be and should do at the end of this kind of Q&A. You will have a road map to getting the right content before you design. However, the content, the essential part of the Web site, has a strong chance of being mishandled at the expense of trying to land and turn around business.

If you build a Web site for yourself, either as an independent publication like an e-zine or homage to the *Superfriends* television show, the burden of filling up Web pages with content falls to you. You manage the content flow and publication schedule. However, when a client hands over his time and money to you for a Web site, he wants his intended audience to use his Web site and he wants his super-heroic message conveyed.

Where Things Go Wrong

Typically, Web design studios are still vying for a project when the design of Web site is determined. This usually happens when a client is presented an image of what his new Web site will look like. The image is called a *comp*, which is a concept artwork depicting what they see a client's site could potentially look like if they hired the designer or designers. Regardless of what this artwork turns out to be, the comp is still an artist's rendering, a weather forecast that always shows a beautiful day.

The goal from the developers' perspective is to get the client's business, and if providing eye candy will get the job, so be it. The effectiveness of the site depends on how well the designer or designers who are working on the initial artwork are at forecasting the content requirements for the project.

This method of creating Web sites could be satisfactory for sites that are destined to stimulate art pieces at the whim and desecration of the designer. Firms, boutiques, or freelancers who build the sites are usually paid to fulfill real business objectives and reach intended customers.

I am not implying that clients just grab the Web designer with the best knack for keen eye candy. A client typically will want to ensure that the project can be handled correctly. Most clients will approach their Web site with a clear head and have a list that is a mixture of wants and needs for their business to succeed online. However, if a client is presented a comp, he forms preconceived notions of how the site will look and be structured.

Instead of the audience being the approach to the end product, the Web site shown in the artistic rendering becomes the approach. If a client chooses a design presented to him (and likes other aspects of the job proposal), the Web site studio wins a check and signed contract. The work of "strategic development" begins then.

The tasks in strategy development include competitive analysis, content development, strengths/weaknesses assessments, functionality reports, and maybe even target demographics. You should address these missions to answer key questions at the start of a Web project so that you can have a pure understanding of where the design of the site should go.

Additional Resources

For more reading about the process of Web development and client relationships, I recommend these books:

- *Collaborative Web Development: Strategies and Best Practices for Web Teams* by Jessica R. Burdman. (Addison-Wesley, 1999) ISBN: 0201433311.

- *Secrets of Successful Web Sites: Project Management on the World Wide Web* by David Siegel. (Hayden, 1997) ISBN: 1568303823.

- *Web Redesign: Workflow That Works* by Kelly Goto and Emily Cotler. (New Riders Publishing, 2001) ISBN: 0735710627.

In the place of an appropriate site is an appropriate mess. The once beautiful site that the client signed off on (see Figure 1.10) now will have been produced and then diluted to fit the content and functionality. In time, the site will grow into a monster of links, badges, and animations that will override any key messages that the client wants to convey (see Figure 1.11).

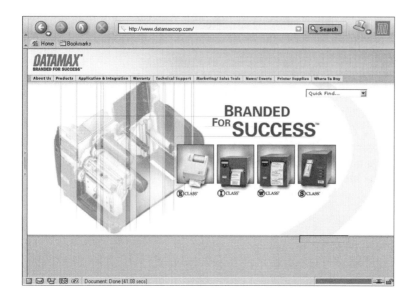

Figure 1.10

In this redesign for Datamax Corporation, the layout is clean and simple.

Figure 1.11

A few months later, the home page for Datamax Corporation is awash in links to various subsections and graphics elements that conflict with each other for the user's attention.

These types of sites are often hard to navigate, long to load, and lacking in key content. The content that *is* available will miss the intended target audience. As if an underperforming site is not enough, the client then spends even more money and time to the same designers to "fix" the problem with a new redesign. Thus, the cycle begins anew with a new comp to land the redesign.

Additional Information

For more information on the subject of evolving tools, see Stewart Brand's book, *How Buildings Learn: What Happens After They're Built* (Penguin USA, 1995). The books tells you how buildings adapt to the owners of a home or an office.

To have a successful Web site, your visitors need to feel that they "own" the site. You can do this by reaching out to them by continually asking for ways to improve the site or asking them to participate in discussions on the site. You can draw a parallel to people who move into a brand new house. The architect might have an idea in mind for how this house would be best used: an environment for a mother, father, and their 2.3 kids for the rest of their lives. However, what happens to the house when a single parent who has a child of her own and several foster kids moves in? The house changes to the new needs and wants of that family. The house changes on the inside and outside, but the framework stays the same. For example, rooms that were designed to entertain houseguests are transformed into ad hoc bedrooms, and the backyard garden turns into a mini football field.

You can avoid having a house that changes often by making sure you are building correctly for your audience. Of course, it's not the end of the proverbial world if you realize that your Web site isn't making the most of its resources. Simply think of yourself as a live-in architect: re-examine your message and ask your audience for input on how to make the house better.

Getting the Content Right: I've Learned This Lesson Before, But Never Like This

Then there's the pesky task of acquiring the content. If you have worked in the industry, you know how hard it is to get content from the client. Working on content with a client is one of the hardest things to do. If content management does not share a mention in your proposals to client, make the importance of crafting the content to fit the audience a focus from now on in your pitches to clients.

Several metaphors emphasize the point that structuring is extremely important. Here's a list of some of them I've used or have heard others use:

- **You wouldn't build a house without blueprints. You plan the size, shape, rooms, utilities, and materials and get the best contractors *before* you start construction.**
- **You wouldn't buy a car your crazy Uncle had "just thrown together one day." You want to buy a car that has been planned, assembled, and tested.**
- **You wouldn't run for a high-level political office without making sure that you have enough money to campaign.**
- **You wouldn't just show up in Orlando for vacation without having decided where to go for lodging and outings.**

Now here's one more:

- **Designing a Web site without predetermined content is like making a Twinkie with the wrong filling.**

After several years in Web design and development, I've seen lots of white in customers' and project managers' eyeballs who roll their eyes when I'm evangelizing about the importance of content. Somehow, bringing up points using Ford cars, blueprints, and hypothetical vacations to Orlando bores people to tears. Or maybe it's the thought that producing copy is less attractive of a proposition than judging a beauty contest of potential Web site designs.

Regardless of the reason, it is vitally important to iterate the importance of content before the designing and building phases, and I do that by using the Twinkie metaphor. Because a Twinkie is small, inexpensive, and after several hours of troubleshooting Web production errors into the midnight hours, even downright desirable, the lesson tends to goes down faster with the Twinkie metaphor than with auto parts. And just like a sweet, high-fat Twinkie, I hope the point I'm trying to convey goes down easy, but sticks with you long after you sample it.

The Mistake of Design Before Content

If you look underneath a Twinkie, you will see three spots of cream filling. Hostess has a mechanical process of inserting cream filling into the cake shell. The outer cake shell is made first, and then the cream is filled into the Twinkie (see Figure 1.12).

The cake shell is like the comp that the designer creates for the client. By selling the visual first, the designer hopes to get the creamy content from the client to put into the Twinkie. The problem is that the content rarely fits into this pre-made shell. The designer might not realize that the client's filling is made of artichokes and sun-dried tomatoes. For a Web design firm to be good at selling Twinkies as Web sites, the firm needs to automate the process. Although a developed site will be available for the client and visitors to see, the real success from the site will come as a surprise rather than any serious planning and calculated risks.

Let's say we were to take Twinkie sites as a way of doing business. To make a substantial profit with "Twinkie sites," you would need to hone your craft into an automated assembling line. Just like Hostess does not make one Twinkie at a time, you shouldn't be going after one client at a time. Hostess makes several hundred Twinkies at once—they're not individually and lovingly hand-crafted.

In the Web development world, such businesses already exist. For example, VerisignSites, which VeriSign owns, allows customers to buy a domain name, pick a Web site template, and edit the content in their browser (see Figure 1.13). As another example, at Yahoo!'s GeoCities site, people can build Web sites if they don't need a vanity Web address (see Figure 1.14).

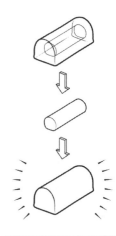

Figure 1.12

In a perfect world, you could build the cake shell and then insert the right amount of cream filling to make the perfect Twinkie.

Figure 1.13

VerisignSites is a one-stop place for buying a domain name, selecting a design, and filling it with content. That's good news if you find a site that matches your content perfectly—you'll have a successful Twinkie site!

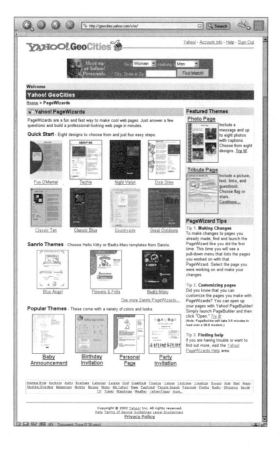

Figure 1.14

The GeoCities site offers free Web site designs. It even has a page design for birthday invitations.

In these situations, clients are stuck with the Twinkie shell, regardless of their recommended diet. And because you're filling your content into a prebuilt Twinkie cake shell, your content *must conform* to the inside of the shell, not the other way around. If you force the content into the preformed shell, you will get weird Twinkies (see Figure 1.15).

Figure 1.15

What happens when you have a Twinkie cake shell, but you really want to talk about carrots and broccoli? Your site becomes a Frankenstein–a sugar covering with a healthy center.

Ensure Proper Communication

Because most companies and clients do not have the resources to hire a copywriter full time—much less a freelance job—the act of writing will come from someone in the company who occasionally writes better than anyone else. When you finally receive the content from the client, you likely will need to rewrite or at the least revise some part of it.

You will need to go through the copy as if you were a site visitor. You need fresh eyes, as if you have never heard of this product or service. Although the Vice President of Product Development will no doubt understand his product inside and out, he probably won't be able to educate someone about the product who hasn't heard of it.

Guide, Don't Tell

Most companies who are attempting to stretch their marketing dollar will repurpose marketing copy from print collateral (print pieces such as business cards, stationary, envelopes, and so on) that carries the company's image by publishing it directly to the Web without revisions. This leads to an inability to capitalize on the inherent strengths of the Web medium: the linking of documents at related junctions, which is the nature of hypertext. At the very least, content that is destined for online distribution should take full advantage of what the Web has to offer.

When reviewing content that you have written or obtained from your clients, make sure to look at it from a descriptive angle, leading the user to the different sections of the site. Web sites need what is termed "guide copy," allowing for access and understanding of what is contained within the site and leading users deeper into the site experience.

A Web site's written content can and should be more than simple marketing fluff. Using the content to guide the site visitor toward the intended destination is an important element of any process.

Structured Markup Is Why We Are Here in the First Place

Yes, believe it or not, the Internet wasn't designed to make Amazon.com a household name. Rather, the Internet was built primarily to share scientific papers with scientists. The Internet was initially established in 1962 by the Defense Advanced Research Projects Agency (DARPA) (see `http://www.arpa.mil/`), and they held a public demonstration in 1972. Tim Berners-Lee announced the Web as an academic exercise in 1990 at Conseil Européene pour la Recherche Nucléaire (CERN), the high-energy particle physics laboratory in Geneva, Switzerland.

The building block of the Web, Hypertext Markup Language (HTML), was simple enough for the focused and scatterbrained individuals to encode their work in simple tags. When a headline was marked with the `<h1>` `</h1>` container tags, it flowed through on its own line with the text in bold and larger than text marked in p. A headline that was wrapped in h2 usually would appear to be larger than a headline text that was wrapped in h6. Also, if a passage of text was quoted from another source, then the `block-quote` tag could be used to create a passage of text that was indented.

With such a low barrier to publishing material, more than scientists got in on the action. People from all walks of life soon joined the online world.

HTML Terrorists

When the precursor to Netscape's Navigator, NCSA Mosaic (see `http://archive.ncsa.uiuc.edu/SDG/Software/Mosaic/`), came out with its HTML extensions, such as the `font` tag, the `blink` tag, and the ability to change background colors, Web builders started using them. In doing so, Web designers were slowly becoming HTML terrorists while they were thinking they were simply doing their job.

David Siegel's *Creating Killer Web Sites* (Hayden Books, 1997) was the first book that approached Web design as a serious issue. That's when the abuse on structured markup became common practice. If you told designers in the late 1990s that they were hurting instead of building a strong Web, they acted puzzled and asked if you had seen their portfolio lately.

Designers took appearance as a paramount issue (which is their job) in making Web sites successful. Following are some typical Web designer thoughts of the time:

- **"Who cares if we indented text with** `blockquote`**? Of course people will know I'm not quoting the entire Web page. That's downright silly. Who thinks that?"**
- **"Tables are to be used for numerical information? What does that mean? If I couldn't use tables for placing my images and text, the browser wouldn't let me do it, right?"**
- **"I need my designs to be pixel perfect, just like they are in Photoshop. I used to use single pixel GIFs as spacers, but now I use Netscape's** `spacer` **tag for that."**

I won't even mention what happened when Web builders discovered when Netscape began to support the animation part of the GIF specification.

However, to be fair to the designers (especially because I was once an HTML terrorist, too), sometimes the designs called for visual presentation. Web sites for Hollywood movies that dealt with images and were time sensitive, for example, could not achieve marginal success if they didn't break the rules of structured markup.

Blame the Browsers

The browsers in the late 1990s were poor in their support for Web standards. Both Netscape and Microsoft, the companies that own the major portion of the browser market share through their respective browsers, were big companies. And big companies are used to getting their way. Why would they want to stop making their own extensions to the Web?

Well, thanks in part to a group of developers and designers who make up the Web Standards Project (WaSP), the builders of the Web started demanding that sites perform to the recommendations made by the World Wide Web Consortium (W3C), which was founded by Tim Berners-Lee. Although it was okay for browser vendors to promote their extensions to HTML, WaSP members argued, they should adopt the standards that the W3C set forth. Slowly, the major browsers came to use the angle of standards support in future releases as marketing material. This was the start of the change in how Web design was accomplished, but something terrible happened.

The initial browsers that implemented CSS did so poorly. What killed designers' and developers' early adoption of CSS is that the initial browsers that supported CSS did not work well enough to have meaningful use. The marginal benefit from using CSS that didn't affect rendering was mostly selecting margins for the entire body page and requesting fonts. We wound up getting ways to get rid of the `leftmargin`, `topmargin`, `marginwidth`, marginheight, and `face` attributes for the font tag.

If you want to incorporate CSS into your Web pages and be conscious of how your designs appear in as many browsers as possible, you can include only a few CSS rules. Listing 1.1 is an example of a "Web-safe" snippet of CSS code that will work in almost any browser in which support for CSS is vague, to say at best.

This snippet is given as a sign of the weak implementations in browsers. With the current generation of browsers taking over the share of the browser market, we now are able to make more use of CSS capabilities.

Listing 1.1   Web-Safe CSS

```
body  {
   /* Gets rid of margins in space around page's content */
   margin: 0;
   /* Selects font for the page */
   font-family: Verdana, Arial, Helvetica, sans-serif;
   /*Selects color for body text */
   color: #333;
   /* Selects the background color of the page. */
   background-color: #CF0;
   }
p, td  {
   font-family: Verdana, Arial, Helvetica, sans-serif;
   }
```

CSS: Terrorist Rehabilitation

Because the browsers took an early adoption to CSS, designers have plunged to use the power of this technology in Web design. That's a good thing. Due to the shoddy implementations of CSS, practical use was years away until today. Now we can start shedding the old habits thanks to standards-based browsers from the major browser vendors, but you will need to know a couple of things:

1. Forget how you used to develop Web pages in the traditional "HTML Terrorist" fashion.

   Just so there isn't confusion, this is what you will be giving up for contemporary Web design:
   - Single pixel GIFs for positioning
   - HTML tables for page layouts
   - Non-breaking spaces for leading, propping table cells
   - The ability to put important text into images
   - Framesets

2. If you've built for the Web before through traditional "HTML terrorist" methods, you will need to reinvestigate HTML.

3. Your content shall be clean of excessive markup that's purely for visual presentation, such as slicing images and placing them into an HTML table.

4. Take the time to learn CSS. Buying this book is a good start; however, you must also try reading the specification that the W3C set (see http://www.w3.org/Style/CSS/) or Eric Meyer's *Cascading Style Sheets 2.0 Programmers Reference* (McGraw-Hill Professional Publishing, 2001).

5. Validate your markup against the spec during the development of your Web site. Valid code will allow your content to be compatible with browsers that follow standards and for browsers that haven't been released yet.
   - For CSS validation, see http://jigsaw.w3.org/css-validator/.
   - For HTML or XHTML markup, see http://validator.w3.org/.

HTML, the markup language that was used to make most of the Web pages in the 1990s, is actually an implementation of SGML. To the average Web designer, SGML is not that all that interesting. Designers should know that SGML depends on having documents be very structured. The root in HTML is structured documents. Just because you can code malformed documents doesn't mean it's the right way.

Why bother with structured content? Well, forward compatibility is one reason. *Forward compatibility is* the ability to mark up your content in a manner today so that it will ensure proper display in future browsers.

If you use W3C recommended markup, *in theory* you won't need to fear browser vendors' extensions. As Web builders, we generally hope that the W3C and browser manufacturers keep backward compatibility as a primary goal as they work on refining and creating Web technologies. It's not a perfect situation to be in, but your Web sites will be in a better predicament for following W3C recommendations than not.

By following W3C recommendations, you will save time and money in future redesign costs. If properly set up, revised CSS will automagically update your site's appearances faster than a competent text editor can search and replace.

Also, remember the Twinkie sites? With preformed cake shells that are common in such sites, you run into another problem. Often, you will need to place "body copy" into text-area form fields (see Figure 1.16). The inherent context of marking up the content in HTML is lost when you're using systems like these. The integrity of the site is at the hands of the people who might not know how best to maintain the site.

Figure 1.16

Yahoo!'s GeoCities page builder asks for content through a Web form.

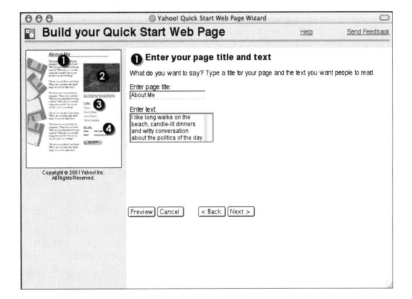

In addition, by producing your content in valid HTML or XHTML and applying the style through CSS, your pages will be more accessible to people who have disabilities. If you run a Web site for an American government and an American-funded agency, it's more than a sensible approach to your Web site project to follow the Americans with Disabilities Act and its Section 508. It's the law in the United States.

Content that is trapped in HTML that has been marked up in traditional Web design methods will not be able to be leveraged down the road when changes in browsers or Web technologies occur. In theory, structured content that takes advantage of CSS will be able to take advantage of these changes, like future versions XHTML or CSS allowing for greater control of the page layout and style. By using Web standards, you have a way to update the content more easily than if you have used single-pixel GIFs, GIFs for text, or numerous nested tables.

Content Structuring Exercise

Notice in Listing 1.2 that I've declared the document type through the DOCTYPE tag in the first two lines of markup. A valid, well-structured document will declare what version of HTML the document type definition (DTD) is using.

Listing 1.2   Sample of Properly Marked Up Content

```
<!DOCTYPE HTML PUBLIC "-//W3C//DTD HTML 4.01 Transitional//EN"
"http://www.w3.org/TR/html4/loose.dtd">
<html>
  <head>
    <title>Web Design Pad - a better mousepad by design for Web designers,
    developers, and builders</title>
  </head>
  <body>
    <h1>Web Design Pad</h1>
    <p>A better mousepad by design for Web designers, developers, and
    builders</p>

    <ul>
      <li><a href="benefits.html">Benefits</a></li>
      <li><a href="faq.html">Frequently Asked Questions</a></li>
      <li><a href="press.html">Press and Testimonials</a></li>
      <li><a href="https://secure.designpad.com/order.html">Order Today!</a></li>
    </ul>

    <h2>Benefits</h2>

    <p>Not just another mousepad. We packed this unique mousepad with functional-
ity by placing those sacred Web colors in an easier and faster to comprehend
arrangement. And the Web Design Pad looks awesome on anyone's desk.</p>


    <h3>The Designs Go Faster on Color Wheels</h3>
    <p>The color wheel format presents colors in an orderly progression, enabling
the user to visualize the sequence of color balance and harmony. Precise hexadeci-
mal values are printed directly on each of the colors. The RGB=HEX conversion
scale is wrapped around the edges of the mousepad. This helps Web developers
choose compatible Web-safe colors and reference correct hexadecimal coding
instantly.</p>


    <h3>Keep Tabs on Your Colors</h3>
    <p>Ever try to find a simple shade of green in other Web color devices? We
did on several occasions for a recent Web project. What took seconds with the Web
Design Pad took us ages on other mousepads and Web editors.</p>


  </body>
</html>
```

This code allows a browser that is rendering the page to know how to properly render the page. Remember that we are breaking away from traditional design, and one of the things we have to do now as Web builders is ensure that our Web pages validate. To validate our code, a validator like the one at W3C (see `http://validator.w3.org/`) needs to know what HTML specification you are coding in. The same goes for the browser. As the browser tries to render your Web document, it uses the DOCTYPE tag as a guide for tips on how to render your content.

The current generation of browsers actually has two rendering engines. These browsers render out a page in two modes: Strict or Quirks. If you use the DOCTYPE for current flavors of HTML or XHTML, you are going to get your content rendered in the way that's more closely spelled out in Web standard, even if HTML hacks stop working. This state of rendering content is called Strict mode, or Standards mode.

On the flip side, if a browser doesn't understand the DOCTYPE, the rendering engine goes to Quirks mode—a state in which the browser renders content in a manner that Web developers are used to seeing from older browsers, warts and all.

For More Information

For more information about how DOCTYPEs turn on a browser's Strict mode or Quirks mode, look at these Web pages:

- DOCTYPE grid showing which mode occurs in browsers (IE, Navigator, and Mozilla) with a specific DOCTYPE. See `http://gutfeldt.ch/matthias/articles/doctypeswitch/table.html`.

- Microsoft's documentation about implementations in IE 6. See `http://msdn.microsoft.com/library/default.asp?url=/library/enus/dnie60/html/cssenhancements.asp`.

- Mozilla's documentation about DOCTYPE sniffing. See `http://mozilla.org/docs/Web-developer/quirks/doctypes.html`.

Knowing the DOCTYPEs to use becomes important when considering how we want browsers to render our content. Here is a listing of valid DTDs for HTML 4.01:

- **This DTD contains recommended HTML elements without the deprecated elements, such as FONT:**

```
<!DOCTYPE HTML PUBLIC "-//W3C//DTD HTML 4.01//EN"
  "http://www.w3.org/TR/html4/strict.dtd">
```

- **This DTD contains the deprecated tags (see Appendix C, "HTML 4.01 Reference"):**

```
<!DOCTYPE HTML PUBLIC "-//W3C//DTD HTML 4.01
Transitional//EN"
  "http://www.w3.org/TR/html4/loose.dtd">
```

- **If you use a frameset, this is the DTD you want to use:**

```
<!DOCTYPE HTML PUBLIC "-//W3C//DTD HTML 4.01 Frameset//EN"
  "http://www.w3.org/TR/html4/frameset.dtd">
```

For XHTML, which requires stricter markup syntax, these are the valid DTDs:

- ```
  <!DOCTYPE html PUBLIC "-//W3C//DTD XHTML 1.0
  Strict//EN" "http://www.w3.org/TR/xhtml1/DTD/
  xhtml1-strict.dtd">
  ```
- ```
  <!DOCTYPE html PUBLIC "-//W3C//DTD XHTML 1.0
  Transitional//EN" "http://www.w3.org/TR/xhtml1/
  DTD/xhtml1-transitional.dtd">
  ```
- ```
  <!DOCTYPE html PUBLIC "-//W3C//DTD XHTML 1.0
  Frameset//EN" "http://www.w3.org/TR/xhtml1/DTD/
  xhtml1-frameset.dtd">
  ```

To check whether the code validates, download the file from the book's Web site and see http://validator.w3.org/. Better yet, if you have your own Web site, run your Web pages to the validator.

Include Navigation

After you have marked up your content, you need to provide the page navigation. Do not confuse this with site-wide navigation. This page navigation allows users who can't skim over the navigation menu a chance to skip through the repetitive site-wide menu that's on every page.

A page typically consists of a header, some content, and a footer. In your content, you might have subsections of information besides the main content. Main content could be an article, whereas subsections of content could be a subscription form for a newsletter, advertising banners, or related links to the main content. The footer contains the copyright information, links to privacy policy, and other legal information.
  ```

Page navigation should fit into a page layout in this manner:

1. **Header**
2. **Page Navigation**
3. **Site Navigation**
4. **Content**
5. **Footer**

A page navigation contains the following links:

```
<div class="pagenav">
  <ul>
    <a href="#content">Content</a></li>
    <a href="#navigation">Navigation</a></li>
    <a href="#footer">footer</a></li>
  </ul>
</div>
```

We apply the following anchors to the previous markup along with the page navigation (see Listing 1.3).

Listing 1.3   Applying the Page Navigation to the Web Document

```
<!DOCTYPE HTML PUBLIC "-//W3C//DTD HTML 4.01 Transitional//EN">
<html>
  <head>
    <title>Web Design Pad - a better mousepad by design for Web designers,
    developers, and builders</title>
  </head>
  <body>
    <h1>Web Design Pad</h1>

<p>A better mousepad by design for Web designers, developers, and builders</p>

<li><div class="pagenav">
  <ul>
    <a href="#content">Content</a></li>
    <a href="#navigation">Navigation</a></li>
    <a href="#footer">footer</a></li>
  </ul>
</div>


    <a name="navigation"></a>
    <ul>
      <li><a href="benefits.html">Benefits</a></li>
```

continues

Listing 1.3   Applying the Page Navigation to the Web Document   (Continued)

```html
    <li><a href="faq.html">Frequently Asked Questions</a></li>
    <li><a href="press.html">Press and Testimonials</a></li>
    <li><a href="https://secure.designpad.com/order.html">Order Today!</a></li>
  </ul>


  <a name="content"></a>
  <h2>Benefits</h2>

  <p>Not just another mousepad. We packed this unique mousepad with
functionality, by placing those sacred Web colors in an easier and faster to
comprehend arrangement. And the Web Design Pad looks awesome on anyone's
desk.</p>

  <h3>The Designs Go Faster on Color Wheels</h3>
  <p>The color wheel format presents colors in an orderly progression,
enabling the user to visualize the sequence of color balance and harmony. Precise
hexadecimal values are printed directly on each of the colors. The RGB=HEX
conversion scale is wrapped around the edges of the mousepad. This helps Web
developers choose compatible Web-safe colors and reference correct hexadecimal
coding instantly.</p>

  <h3>Keep Tabs on Your Colors</h3>
  <p>Ever try to find a simple shade of green in other Web color devices? We
did on several occasions for a recent Web project. What took seconds with the
Web Design Pad took us ages on other mousepads and Web editors.</p>


  <a name="footer"></a>
  <p>Copyright Christopher Schmitt. All rights reserved.</p>

  </body>
</html>
```

Figure 1.17 shows Listing 1.3 on a Web Design Pad.

Figure 1.17

An example with page navigation in place.

Now that we have the page navigation in place with working anchors, let's hide the page navigation from the visual display by declaring a style (see Listing 1.4).

Listing 1.4   Declaring a Style

```
<style type="text/css">
  .pagenav  {
    display: none;
  }
</style>
```

Now we separate the areas of header, content, and footer (see Listing 1.5).

Listing 1.5   Separating the Header, Content, and Footer

```
<!DOCTYPE HTML PUBLIC "-//W3C//DTD HTML 4.01 Transitional//EN">
<html>
  <head>
    <title>Web Design Pad - a better mousepad by design for Web designers,
developers, and builders</title>
  </head>
  <body>
```

---

continues

Listing 1.5   Separating the Header, Content, and Footer   (Continued)

```html
    <div class="header">

      <h1>Web Design Pad</h1>

  <p>A better mousepad by design for Web designers, developers, and builders</p>


      <div class="pagenav">
         <a href="#content">Content</a>
         <a href="#navigation">Navigation</a>
         <a href="#footer">footer</a>
      </div>


      <a name="navigation"></a>
        <ul>
          <li><a href="benefits.html">Benefits</a>
          <li><a href="faq.html">Frequently Asked Questions</a>
          <li><a href="press.html">Press and Testimonials</a>
          <li><a href="https://secure.designpad.com/order.html">Order Today!</a>
        </ul>


    </div>

    <div class="content">

      <a name="content"></a>
        <h2>Benefits</h2>          <p>Not just another mousepad. We packed this unique
  mousepad with functionality by placing those sacred Web colors in an easier and
  faster to comprehend arrangement. And the Web Design Pad looks awesome on any-
  one's desk.</p>


        <h3>The Designs Go Faster on Color Wheels</h3>
        <p>The color wheel format presents colors in an orderly progression,
  enabling the user to visualize the sequence of color balance and harmony.
  Precise hexadecimal values are printed directly on each of the colors. The
  RGB=HEX
  conversion scale is wrapped around the edges of the mousepad. This helps Web
  developers choose compatible Web-safe colors and reference correct hexadecimal
  coding instantly.</p>


        <h3>Keep Tabs on Your Colors</h3>
        <p>Ever try to find a simple shade of green in other Web color devices? We
  did on several occasions for a recent Web project. What took seconds with the
  Web Design Pad took us ages on other mousepads and Web editors.</p>
```

```
    </div>

    <div class="footer">
      <a name="footer"></a>
      <p>Copyright Christopher Schmitt. All rights reserved.</p>
    </div>

  </body>
</html>
```

Figure 1.18 shows Listing 1.5 on a Web Design Pad.

Figure 1.18

An example with page navigation in place, but hidden through CSS.

Review Content for Design Possibilities

After you have marked up the content, it's time to take a look at the markup look for visual design. Instead of beginning with the design as a means to get to the content, stylize the information you are trying to convey in terms of visual presentation by examining intensely at the message that got to you this point. Look at the tone of the material you have and how a visual design will best serve your client, your client's audience.

Note

For more examples of proper versus improper content structure through HTML, go to the "Incorporating CSS Ideally" section in Chapter 3, "Setting Up Style."

After you have the content marked up structurally, you can look for CSS to design the content for visual presentation a number of ways (see Figure 1.19) without having to rearrange your content. No more will we have to mess with single-pixel GIFs, relying on HTML tables for layouts, or putting up with the FONT tag.

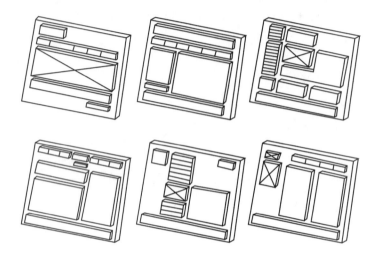

Figure 1.19

Potential design possibilities for one Web document, leveraged through the power of CSS.

In the next chapter, we will look into what makes up contemporary Web design and how to better approach our Web designs.

Designing for the Unknown

It's no wonder that designers seem to wear black all the time: They are in a state of constant mourning. For designers, building for the Web is a terrible experience. As page layouts break, colors shift and crisp images have to be reduced in quality for download speeds; their picture-perfect designs are trampled by buggy browsers on a plethora of platforms that surf the Web.

This chapter examines the prime dilemma of Web design: As builders of the Web, we must realize that we do not have control over how an audience views our work. We must realize that in this unknown, the audience can still make changes to how they view our work by changing various options in the browser software.

The best way to approach this kind of "unknown design" is to prepare our designs for flexibility. We will need to give up precision for flexibility to better communicate. From Web-safe colors to the types of possible page layouts, this chapter covers Web page building approaches to better facilitate that communication.

Web-Safe Colors

Developed by programmers who were writing the Web browser software, the Web-safe colors were the 216 common colors that both Netscape's Navigator (then called Mosaic) and Microsoft's Internet Explorer used.

Specifying Web-Safe Colors

An easy way to code Web-safe colors is to use the numbers listed in Table 2.1. RGB color values are made up of three individual values, each representing an amount of red, green, or blue. Take the three values for color and put them into the markup where you apply code.

For instance, the color for blue in hexadecimal code is #0000FF. That's because the first two digits represent red, the next two represent green, and the last two represent blue. It goes in RGB order. The initial two sets of colors—red and green—are set to the lowest value, which means they don't show up while red is set to display all red. For a full green, the hexadecimal code would be #00FF00.

Table 2.1 **Conversion Chart for RGB, Hexadecimal Pairs and Percentages**

RGB	Hexadecimal Pairs	Percentage
0	00	0
51	33	20
102	66	40
153	99	60
204	CC	80
255	FF	100

If you had a computer system that could only spit out 256 colors, any color that was not in those limited numbers would undergo a process of banding or dithering. The colors that your computer could produce would be used to help simulate the other colors. Colors that were specified in HTML, such as a background table cell, tended to shift to the nearest Web-safe colors, whereas colors in images tended to dither in images.

With the knowledge of the Web-safe color set, you could create images. These images were geared primarily to large areas of flat colors in the GIF format because they used a lossless compression scheme; image quality didn't deteriorate after multiple resaves. JPEGs, whose format is geared toward photo-realistic images, weren't used because their compression scheme meant that color shifts occurred every time you saved an image into JPEG. So, although you might have started out using Web-safe colors in an image that was destined for JPEG save, the color shifting occurred as a byproduct of the lossy compression algorithm. Every time you saved an image in JPEG format, information was stripped from your image, creating a loss in quality.

Back in the mid-1990s, most of the computer systems shipped with 8-bit graphics display (256 colors). On the flipside, most designers had powerful (for their time) displays that allowed for millions of colors. Now such computer displays are common in computers that the major computer manufacturers ship.

Using Web-Safe Colors

Do you need to worry about using Web-safe colors? No, not really. Like I mentioned earlier, today's computer systems come with the ability to display millions of colors. You might want to consider picking Web-safe colors for Web-based projects as a base and build off to other, non–Web-safe colors just in case you want to make sure you are reaching the maximum audience effectively. Alternatively, when you're designing for handheld devices or other interesting gadgets with screens, it might be necessary to fall back to the Web-safe palette. Until such time, feel free to pick colors outside of the cube.

HTML Tables for Layout

One of the practices that made the design of good-looking pages possible was the use of HTML tables for grid layouts (see Figure 2.1).

Figure 2.1

Builder.com makes extensive use of HTML tables to achieve page layout.

Note

A *pull quote* is an extract from an article, often enlarged and embellished with some other design elements, to draw the attention of the reader or break up the monotony of a large amount of text. It's a common designer tool.

Tables have long been used to create multicolumn, grid-style layouts— structures ranging from simple to complex with headers, footers, navigation bars, and more. In more complicated layouts, designers even nest tables inside of other tables to do things like present a pull quote, embed a complex Web form, or slice one large image into several smaller pieces that can be arranged individually.

The original purpose of an HTML table was for tabular data. *Tabular* simply describes data that is organized in a table arrangement. Each row in a table represents an entity, and each column represents a property of that entity. An example of tabular data is material used in scientific research, such as in Figure 2.2.

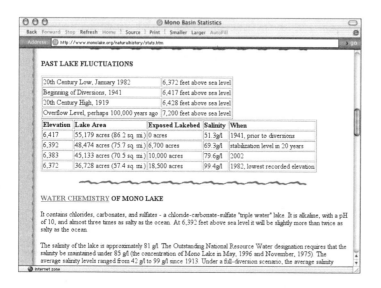

Figure 2.2

Statistics presented as tabular data.

Another example is a calendar—often illustrating a month with a top row for the name of the days and the proceeding rows the dates of days (see Figure 2.3).

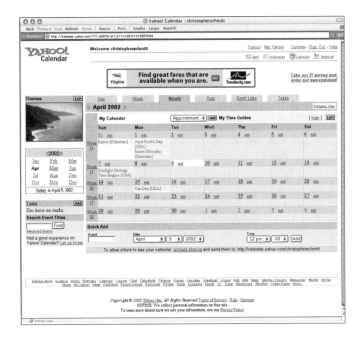

Figure 2.3

Here's an example of extensive use of tables for a calendar service.

On the design-oriented end of the spectrum, tables often hold images that are sliced and hold them together. Designers use tables to wrap navigation bars, columns, and sidebars (among other elements) in tables to achieve success in their designs.

Sometimes, tables are clearly appropriate in page designs, such as for tabular data (see Figure 2.4).

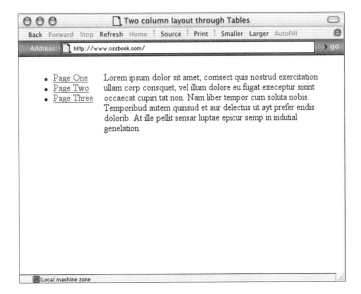

Figure 2.4

Tabular data without percentages, decimal points, plus signs, or minute signs.

Sometimes, HTML tables are inappropriate, such as when slicing a large graphical design and putting the images into multiple table cells—or using tables for columns (see Figure 2.5).

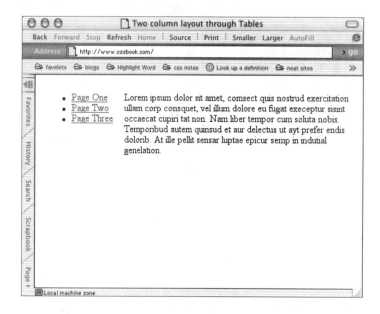

Figure 2.5

Two-column layout through HTML tables including navigation.

And sometimes it's subjective as to the best way to use tables (see Figure 2.6).

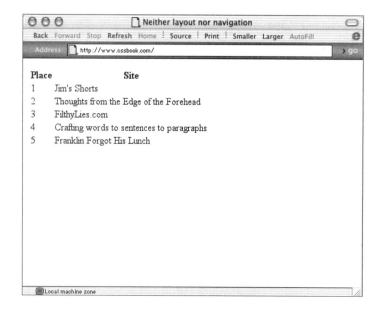

Figure 2.6

Tables for content presentation (that's not a column layout or navigation).

For example, when you want to put up a thumbnail gallery of images in a grid arrangement, how do you approach the Web production? Do you use HTML to lay out the images? Or do you attempt to use CSS and multiple `div` tags to pull it out?

In this scenario, you have data, but not in the traditional "coming out of a database" sense. If you want your grid structure to be backward compatible with older browsers (or browsers that do not render CSS), then tables might be the best way. Really, no matter what you decide, it's a subjective call that you have to make on a case by case basis.

Types of Web Page Layouts

In newspaper design, you have the constants of printing on the same size paper and manual of style for laying out copy and images. In graphic design, print pieces can range from menus to CD-ROM labels. In broadcast design, you have the standard aspect ratio of 4:3, or 16:9 for wide screen.

However, Web design is not newspaper design, graphic design, or broadcast design. The Web is a medium in which the only constant is the lack of constants. People can and do view the Web on different devices with varying capabilities and settings.

When approaching a Web page layout, you have a few options: solid, liquid, and a mixture of the two, which is called *suspension*. A suspension is a mixture of solid matter floating in a fluid. In suspension designs, you have solid elements floating in a liquid design.

Solid Designs

Solid designs often come from Web builders who want to account for the exact placement of all items on a Web page, similar to traditional print designers. The column widths, fonts, and images are set in pixels, which is the unit of measurement for screen displays.

Although solid designs help reduce design headaches for the Web developer, it's often a tunnel vision view. The designer doesn't think of the Web as being a fluid state with various browsers and monitor resolutions. Instead, the Web that is shoved into a print-design practice causes massive amounts of white space or real estate to appear if a user has a high-resolution display (see Figure 2.7). On the other hand, if the user has a machine set to 640×480 display, he might be able to see only a portion of the fixed layout at a time.

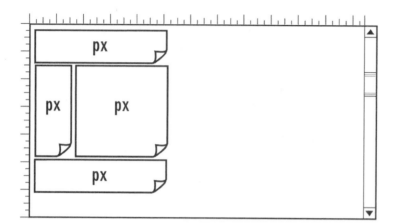

Figure 2.7

Fixed designs stay
in their own space.

Liquid Designs

In liquid design, you place your content into expandable shells. By using relative units, such as percentages, these shells can fill up the extra available browser real estate in the same way that a fluid takes the shape of its container (see Figure 2.8).

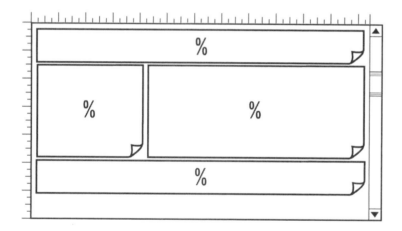

Figure 2.8

Relative designs adapt
to the environment like
water that takes the
form of its container.

Liquid design eliminates the excessive white space caused by fixed design when the user has a high-resolution monitor. When used appropriately, white space can be a good thing; on the Web, however, trying to achieve the right portion of white space is a tricky thing. People often resort to white space that padding the sides of columns provides.

When you allow your text to expand to the size of the browser window liked those allowed in relative designs, this increase in line length makes it hard for people to read comfortably. Designers should try to keep their lines below 400 pixels to make the text easier to read for their visitors.

Suspension Designs

The combination of relative and fixed designs is called *suspension design*. A suspension design is accomplished with a combination of fixed width elements and percentage width elements (see Figure 2.9). This might be the best way to design for the Web because it allows you to have certain content marked off in a confined area while filling up the browser viewport with other "liquid" content. A common variation of this design might include a left or right column in a fixed width, while the main column fills the remaining space.

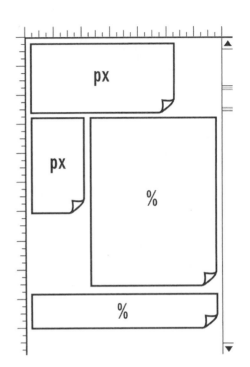

Figure 2.9

Fixative design layouts are a compromise between fixed width and relative designs.

Problems Attempting to be Exact on the Web

When you try to exert absolute control of designs through fixed measurements or all portions of your design, your designs break. Type sizes can be adjusted so that they grow beyond limiting column widths. People who surf with their monitors set to a low resolution cannot successfully view designs that are built for 1024×768 resolutions.

Figure 2.10 has two problems with it. One problem is that the fixed width leaves a lot of real estate unused. This leads to users who have high resolutions seeing an ocean of white space, far more than any designer would want visitors to see. The other problem is the running of the main column over the sidebar. This is caused by not properly nesting correctly and testing your pages in different browsers and platforms.

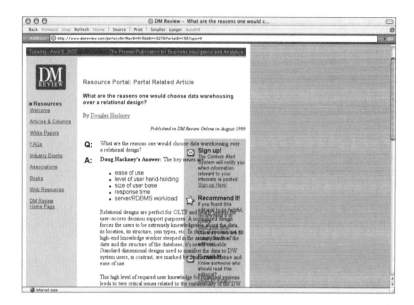

Figure 2.10

If you're not careful, this could happen to your Web page.

Lynx is a text-based browser for the Web (see `http://lynx.browser.org/`) that runs on Windows, many UNIX flavors, and other operating systems (see Figure 2.11). To aid in a user's surfing experience, it's a good thing to make good use of the img's `alt` attribute. First, it's necessary to include an `alt` tag for img's so that you can create valid HTML markup. However, to make good use of an `alt` attribute, you need to include a descriptive value for the `img` `alt` attribute or leave the value blank so that the browser can skip it altogether.

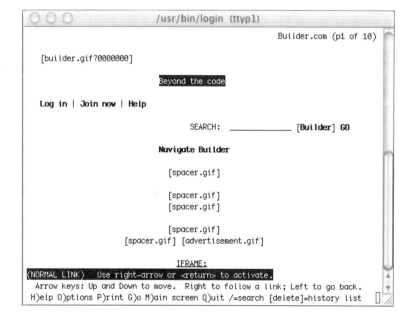

Figure 2.11

Here's a view of Builder.com through Lynx, a text browser.

There are some devices available today on market for you to buy—devices that might make you wonder why they were built in the first place. Like this one—a device such as digital cameras that can surf the Web as well as create, edit, and upload Web pages (see Figure 2.12). From start to finish your image is on the Web. Your Web site might show up in the viewport of these types of devices as a photographer surfs from his trusty camera.

Figure 2.12

Bored taking pictures? You can surf the Web on your camera. How will your site look on a digital camera?

Some people have a tendency to be finicky with the fonts they interact with. People with poor eyesight might wind up canceling their newspaper subscriptions and resort to getting their information from other media, such as radio or television, if they cannot read the printed word. On the Web, rather than canceling and looking for alternatives, users can control their viewing environment and thereby manipulate the default size of the typeface.

In Internet Explorer, users can use the "text zoom" feature to enlarge or shrink just the text. (See the examples in Figures 2.13 and 2.14.)

Figure 2.13

This is a Web page from Tallahassee.com through Internet Explorer with text sized at 100%.

Figure 2.14

In Internet Explorer, when the text is zoomed in, the text enlarges, but the images stay the same.

In contrast to IE, Opera increases or decreases the size of both the text and graphics, creating a truer "zoom" effect, as shown in Figures 2.15 and 2.16.

Figure 2.15

This is how Tallahassee.com looks under Opera's browser under "normal" viewing conditions.

Figure 2.16

When the page is zoomed using Opera's browser, everything is enlarged, not just the text. This method is the ideal way to handle zooming.

This ability to let users adjust how they view your Web pages is just more incentive to shore up your designs. Design pages to grow and shrink based on the user's desires at the end of the spectrum. You do this by making sure you base your designs on relations to the different elements in the Web document and not basing them entirely on pixel measurements.

Use Percentages When Possible

When possible, use percentage units for column widths, images, and font sizes. Unfortunately, percentages are not always an option. For instance, images predominantly have set dimensions; stretching images set in formats such as GIF and JPEG distort the image. If a picture is worth a thousand words, a distorted picture is a thousand words in a foreign language.

With other embedded graphics such as SVG and Macromedia's SWF (see Figure 2.19), it's possible to stretch an image without losing too much of the image's display. This is due to the vector-based nature of the image format. Because the information is stored as vector paths, the image is drawn to whatever dimensions are set for it. Therefore, you can scale a vector-based image without losing clarity.

Figure 2.17

A raster image presented at its own width and height.

If you place a GIF, JPEG, PNG, or similar raster image in a SWF, that raster image will be distorted (see Figure 2.18), but the other elements of the SWF will be fine.

Figure 2.18

The raster image is stretched and its image is distorted.

By themselves GIFs and JPEGs, that are raster file formats in which every pixel is accounted for in its "natural" width and height, will result in stretching and scaling the image results in distortions (see Figure 2.17).

Figure 2.19

A SWF file placed in its own width and height.

If you specify the width and height values to something other than a GIF's or JPEG's native aspect ratio (see Figure 2.20), expect the distortions.

Figure 2.20

The vector's size settings have changed, but the "image integrity" is still intact, allowing a shrunken but still legible image.

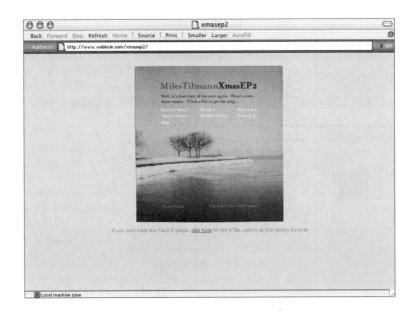

With column widths, it's best to use percentages for your columns. Designers often use pixels for the second- or third-level columns, however, which is fine if you are aware that the font sizes will vary inside the column. Each line of the text in the columns will contain a varying amount of words depending on the size of the column.

In style sheets, you can set the percentage of fonts by using percentage units, or em units. An em is equal to the height of the font size that is currently on the screen. Therefore, 1.2em units equals 120% of the font size.

Ems as an Alternative

Because em units are based on the size of the font, they are great for dealing with laying out type—when you want to work with spacing between columns, leading (spaces between lines), paragraph spacing, indents, and so on.

As a user enlarges or shrinks the text and you have used em units to mark these typographic treatments, the type on the page will grow as well in proper proportion. If you used pixels to measure your fonts and other typographic treatments, then that amount of space will remain the same as text enlarges and shrinks. Therefore, if you created an indent at 12px, but the user set his type to be three times as large as you intended, the indent would be hard to discern because the amount of the indent would still be 12 pixels.

Vertical Values, Parent's Width

If you want to set the margin or padding of an element to a percentage value, you will need to use the element's *parent* element. For example, let's say that you have an element set to 300 pixels wide and inside this element is a child element set with a width of 50px. Now, for the child element, you set a margin of 10%. The margin won't be 5 pixels (10% of 50 pixels). Instead, the margin will be 50 pixels (see Figure 2.21).

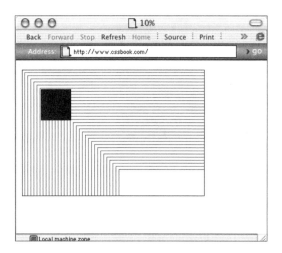

Figure 2.21

Notice that the margins are the same.

Not only will the margin width be 50 pixels, but so will the height. Even though the parent element is set for a height of 200 pixels, you would *expect* a 10% margin to be set to 30px. Yes, it's weird.

This isn't just for margins, but also for paddings. Therefore, when you begin building page layouts, keep in mind how you measure out your padding and margins.

Practice Is Much Different Than Theory

Due to poor CSS implementations in browsers, the use of percentages and em units is often cause for hair loss. If you try to be sophisticated in some older browsers with percentages and em units to specify font sizes and line heights and put in images aligned to the left or right, chances are you will get gibberish.

The workaround for this problem is to set the font size in units of pixels or not do anything with your fonts, leaving the user's browser to render the font in the way it sees fit. If you are wondering which method I recommend, I suggest that you take a look at your audience and see how to best suit them. If your Web site project is serving the latest and greatest browser, bypass the workarounds and go straight to em units. If you know that most of your audience is using one of the popular browsers on the market today, go with pixel units. If you don't know what your audience will be using, just leave well enough alone and don't specify your font sizes.

Pushpin Design

In print or other dead tree media, you get exacting control over the placement, size of type, photos, and so on. Heck, you only need one set of table of contents. You don't need to drag the navigation structure of a book through each page like you do on a Web site. On the Web, of course, things are different.

One of the key ways to design a Web page is something called *pushpin design*. The concept behind it is simply to have a point of origin and build around that point. When you build around a point of origin, you must realize that items will shift due to different browsers, but that these elements will be positioned in relation to the point of origin.

Most designs begin with a top-to-bottom approach: The important material is placed at the top and everything else is placed in a descending order. In this method, the point of origin is usually a logo or some other central image that carries that design. It's a safe approach to Web design because the upper-left corner won't change much from browser to browser (see Figures 2.22 and 2.23). In fact, more than 80% of company Web sites reviewing in *Homepage Usability: 50 Websites Deconstructed* by Jakob Nielsen and Marie Tahir (New Riders Publishing, 2001) have their logos in the upper left-hand corner.

Figure 2.22

CNET places its logo in the upper-left column and wraps its content in yellow padding.

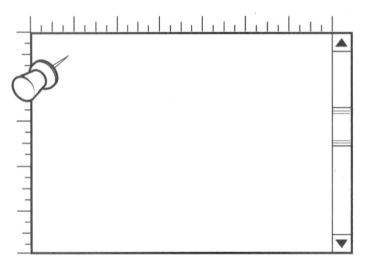

Figure 2.23

A simplified look at the pushpin technique being used at CNET.

On my site (christopher.org), the central image is that of a car exploding (see Figure 2.24). However, you will notice that the logo is not in the upper-left corner. Instead, the logo is in the right, middle area of the Web page that's called above the fold (see Figure 2.25).

Figure 2.24

The logo is placed in the middle of the viewport.

Figure 2.25

A simplified look at the pushpin technique used at `christopher.org`.

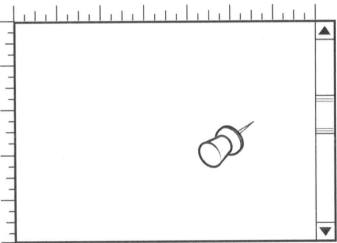

Note

Above the fold is an expression used in newspapers to talk about the elements on the front page when the paper is folded in half. It's the part of the newspaper that sells the rest of the newspaper. It's the part of the newspaper that catches the reader's eye.

In Web design, above the fold refers to the elements of the Web document that are in the viewport on the initial loading of the browser.

Taking note of the text above the `christopher.org` logo, you will notice a text blurb with the "recently" heading. Using Internet Explorer's text-zoom feature, I'll shrink the text so that you can see that the logo stays in the same place (see Figure 2.26). This was done on purpose to show that the point of origin for the "recently" blurb came from the top of the logo. The text in the blurb can grow or shrink, but it will always be displayed above the logo.

Figure 2.26

Decreasing the font size, the logo is still in the same place.

Matt Haughey's personal site (`http://a.wholelottanothing.org`) in Figure 2.27 also uses a pushpin.

Figure 2.27

A Whole Lotta
Nothing places
the pushpin at
the bottom of
the viewport.

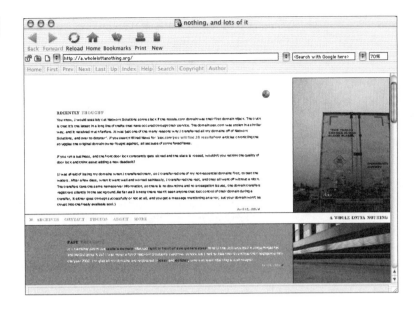

What we see is that the central focus (pushpin) is at the bottom of the
fold (see Figure 2.28). However, in Web design production, the pushpin is
actually right below the first paragraph. If you extend the viewport, the
length of the initial entry of text that Matt writes will raise or lower the
navigation bar you see in the screenshot.

Figure 2.28

The pushpin from
Matt's site is at
the bottom of
the viewport.

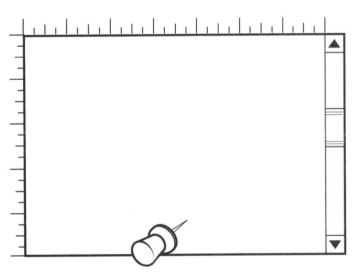

Why to Use a Pushpin

When you build a Web page without the traditional method or CSS, the page will go from top to bottom, and most of the time, the content will read from left to right.

If you are building a scientific paper, that might be fine. Designs vary in that you might want to draw the focus of a page to a different location than the upper left of a page. It really depends on what you are designing, but you can position the initial elements of a page to the different corners of a Web page.

For example, if you want to build a site about sunrises, you could build a Web site in which the pushpin is placed at the lower-left corner of the viewport so that the logo and sitewide navigation appears above the fold. The logo and navigation could incorporate sun rays blistering through little white fluffy clouds. Another example would be if you were building a site about a plumbing service company—you could place the pushpin in the center of the page and have the content come out of that point. The central image could be a drain.

No matter what you do with your pushpin, make sure it reflects the message your are trying to convey. The art of design is making sure that every element is working together for the greater good of the message. It's easy to get carried away with floating objects, shrinking fonts beyond legibility, or that crazy new Photoshop filter. If the message gets lost in your search for "cool," the design has failed. Try again.

This chapter covered issues that designers and developers need to understand and work through when they are developing Web projects. The next chapter will help you get more comfortable with using CSS. It will give you a foothold to help you reach contemporary new media design solutions.

Part II

Using CSS

Setting Up Style

The focus of this chapter is to teach you how to incorporate styles into your Web pages. We will look into common browser practices that determine how elements are stylized. We also will take a look at how to avoid some browser issues thanks in part to *how* we apply style sheets.

Getting to Know Style

CSS allows for a rule or several rules that dictate how a page's HTML elements should look. A rule in CSS is built with two parts: a declaration block and a selector.

Declaration

A declaration contains a property and the property's value.

This is an example of a CSS rule:

```
p {background-color: #CCFF00;}
```

In this example, p is the selector and the declaration block. What's between the brackets contains a single declaration: `background-color: #CCFF00;`. If applied to a Web document with multiple paragraphs of copy marked with the p tag, the color behind the paragraphs will be set to #CCFF00, a nice, bland grey color.

Selector

A selector tells the style rules you made where to apply their magic. A selector is a way of joining styles to a specific element or a group of elements. Many selectors are available. Following is a list that breaks them down:

- **Generic**—Typically an HTML or XHTML element
- **Descendent**—Applies style to elements that are a descendent of another element
- **Universal**—Applies the style rules to every element
- **Child**—Applies style to the element that is a *direct* descendent of the parent element
- **Adjacent-Sibling**—Similar to a descendent selector, but applies only to the immediate element
- **Attribute**—A type of selector that uses the values of an element's attributes to associate
- **Class**—Style that can be applied for elements that make use of the class attribute
- **ID**—Applies a style to any element that makes use of the if attribute

Table 3.1 lists the selectors and provides the general syntax.

Table 3.1   Selectors and Their General Syntax

Type of Selector	Syntax	Examples
Generic	a	P {font-color: #000;} h3 {font-weight: bold;}
Descendant	a b c	div p blockquote h3 {font-weight: bold;} p strong {font-weight: normal;}
Universal	*	* {color: #fc0;} p * li {display: none;}
Child	a > b	p > blockquote {color: #666;} div>p {font-weight: bold;}
Adjacent-Sibling	a + b	div p + blockquote {color: #666;} h1+p {font-weight: bold;}
Attribute	a[attr] a[attr="value"] a[attr~="value"] a[attr!="value"]	a[link] {color: #666;} a[link="http://www.cssbook.com/"] {font-weight: bold;} img[title-="Chabon"] {padding: 10px;} img[title!="Author"] {border: 10px solid #666;}
Class	a.class .class	p.summary {font-weight: bold;} .bammo {padding: 30px;}
ID	a#id #id	p#header {font-size: 2em;} #footer {color: #666;}

Attribute Selector in More Detail

The attribute selector has four types. Below is a listing and a description of how they are used:

- a[attr]—Matches the attribute.

- a[attr="value"]—Applies the style to the element that matches the attribute and value.

- a[attr~="value"]—Applies the style rule to the element that matches the attribute; the value is a listing separated by a space.

- a[attr!="value"]—Applies the style rule to the element that matches the attribute; the value is a listing separated by a comma.

You can set up a selector to be something more than a paragraph tag or other HTML elements, such as h1, td, and so on. You can apply a style to HTML elements that contain precise class or id attributes.

Let's change the previous CSS rule to apply only to a specific class. The selector will begin with a period.

```
.grey {background-color: #666666;}
```

Now, look at Listing 3.1, the Web document snippet.

Listing 3.1   Applying a Bit of Style

```
<p>
This text is boring since there isn't any color behind it. I sure wish I
could have some great Hostess Twinkies to pass the time. It would
be a swell ending to end a day with a treat like that.
</p>

<p class="grey">
This text is so exciting. I sure wish I could have some great Hostess
Twinkies to pass the time. It would be a swell ending to end an
awesome day with a treat like that.
</p>
```

Figure 3.1 shows what the Web document snippet looks like on your browser.

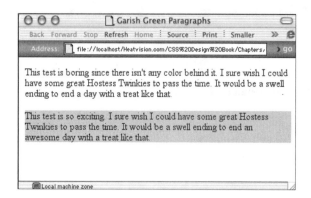

Figure 3.1

We've added color to the second paragraph without breaking a sweat or, more importantly, without using a `bgcolor` attribute through the HTML `table` and `td` elements.

The paragraph with the `class` attribute and its value set to Grey will get the grey background color. The paragraph without the `class` will be rendered to the default styling of the browser.

We can get the same effect for applying the grey background color to a paragraph of text by using the `id` class. This method changes the format of the CSS rule to let the browser know to look for a precise `id` value.

The CSS rule will be preceded with a hash mark (#) looking like this:

`#grey {background-color: #666666;}`

The HTML for the paragraph would look like this:

```
<p id="grey">
This text is so exciting. I sure wish I could have some
great Hostess Twinkies to pass the time. It would be a
swell ending to end an awesome day with a treat like that.
</p>
```

Associating Styles to a Web Page

You can apply a CSS rule or set of CSS rules to a Web page in four ways:

- **Inline**
- **Embedded**
- **Linked**
- `@import`

Inline

By directly applying a CSS rule to a HTML element, you can identify a precise CSS rule at a precise point in a Web document.

```
<p style="background-color: #666666;">The background will be
grey</p>
```

You can also set up multiple CSS rules by making sure you use a semi-colon to separate the declarations.

```
<p style="background-color: #666666; color: #00000;
font-family: Verdana, Arial, sans-serif;">The background
will be grey while the text will definitely be black. And
the paragraph will be set in Verdana, if the user's com-
puter has it installed.</p>
```

Embedded

The second method for associated styles is to place the CSS code in the head of the Web document between the <head></head> tags.

```
<style type="text/css">
  p {
    background-color: #666666;
  }
</style>
```

With this example, every paragraph will have a grey background color.

The attribute of `type` with the value of `"text/css"` is included because, in the future, other styling languages might exist besides CSS. To ensure that future browsers do not misinterpret your document or ignore apply-ing your CSS rules at all, make sure you include the `type/css`.

Linked

Instead of the internal methods of associating a style sheet to a Web doc-ument like with the inline or embed methods, you can link to a separate file that contains the CSS rules.

Let's put the CSS rule for creating grey background paragraphs into a clean document with the filename of style.css. The only thing in the style sheet is the following bit of CSS:

```
p {
background-color: #666666;
}
```

In the Web document, instead of a container of style tags (`<style></style>`), we will need only the one HTML element, `link`:

```
<link rel="stylesheet" type="text/css" href="style.css"
media="screen">
```

Now that the style sheet has been associated through a `link`, the paragraphs should be displayed with grey backgrounds.

You can place more than one linked style sheet in the head. If, for example, you want to separate the background colors from your font selections, you could set up your CSS associations like this:

```
<link rel="stylesheet" type="text/css" href="style.css"
media="screen">
  <link rel=" stylesheet" type="text/css"
href="fonts.css" media="screen">
```

The font.css file could contain the following:

```
P {
  font-family: Verdana, Arial, sans-serif;
}
```

With the `link` element, however, we introduced some new attributes. Let's look at those a little bit more closely.

The `rel` attribute tells of the relation of the file that is being called from the `link`. With style sheet linking, `rel` has two values: `stylesheet` and `alternate stylesheet`. A style sheet that is being linked and that has the `rel` attribute with the value of `stylesheet` will be rendered in the browser by default.

If you have placed an alternative style sheet, a user will be able to select the style sheet to have the document rendered differently (see Figure 3.2). You can have a style sheet for practical purposes, such as having a large, sans-serif font with high contrast colors for people with poor eyesight. Alternatively, you can have style sheets for trivial purposes, such as a design for each of the seasons or a favorite sports team. Whatever the reason, make sure you use alternative style sheets to facilitate the message you want to convey. Design for the sake of communication rather than for design's sake.

Figure 3.2

Selecting an
alternative
style sheet.

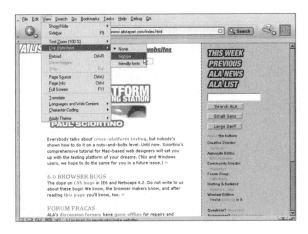

Notice the attribute of `type`. This declares the data format that will be sent for the browser to interpret. The only acceptable value for the attribute is `"text/css"`.

The value of the `href` attribute is the URL for the file location of the style sheet. The URL could either be relative or absolute.

The media attribute can be used to specify a certain style sheet to be delivered for a certain media type. The types of media that are available include these:

- **All**
- **Aural**
- **Braille**
- **Embossed**
- **Handheld**
- **Print**
- **Projection**
- **Screen**
- **Tty**
- **Tv**

The default value of media in a `link` element is All, which means that your style sheet will be used for all media devices. You can set the media to be more than one by using commas to separate the media types.

```
<link...media="screen, projection">
```

Note

As of this writing, only Mozilla handles the swapping of alternative style sheets natively. Through JavaScript and a set of cookies, you can perform the same effect inside your Web document. For more information, see `http://www.alistapart.com/stories/alternate/`.

@import

Along with linking a style sheet to a document, you can hook in an external CSS with an at-rule. At-rules are formed with an @ and then by an identifier. For including an external sheet, use the @import import identifier.

```
<style type="text/css" >@import url(style.css);</style>
```

Development Tips from Style Associations

With the external methods for associating styles to a document, we have greater flexibility not only to stylize Web sites, but also to manage the styles that our site designs and to work around certain browser-flawed implementations of CSS.

Early browsers that adopted CSS did not implement the specification correctly. Some "complex CSS" forced these browsers to jumble up the visual display, ruining the Web designs from a little bit to making them completely incoherent. This effect caused some major consternation among Web designers and developers; however, the holes in the implementation allowed Web builders to hide complex CSS rules by way of writing valid CSS.

Use External Associative Methods

The best way to deliver style sheets into a Web project is through an external solution. However, when starting out from scratch or testing a CSS implementation in browsers, having inlined or embedded style sheets is acceptable.

The big draw for CSS is the ability to store the styles in a separate file. Following the concept of "separating style from structure" to separating the two in different files, this method allows you to make global changes to a site's look and feel in file without having to touch the site's actual content.

In traditional Web design, if a client requested a font change, you would have to do a global search and replace to swap out the face attribute for the font element. Luckily, you would have remembered to list the fonts exactly; otherwise, you would spend hours if not days going through the entire Web site correcting the font tags. With CSS, however, it's simply a matter of revising the appropriate CSS rules and you're done.

Exploring the link Method

Through CSS, you can separate the font selections and backgrounds into two CSS files, but that would be like getting your food at McDonald's and your drinks at Burger King (see Listing 3.2). It's perfectly legal to do that, and both places would appreciate your money, but it involves putting too much work into the process to get a meal.

Listing 3.2   Two Style Sheets Does Not Necessarily Mean Better CSS Management

```
<link rel="stylesheet"  type="text/css"  href="tablestyle.css" media="screen">
<link rel="stylesheet"  type="text/css"  href="reportsummary.css" media="screen">
```

Multiple style sheets have some appropriate uses. For example, the ability to leverage more than one style sheet at a time becomes a great tool in the designer's toolkit if you want to manage different subsections of a Web site or different parts of a Web page, such as online polls, e-mail a friend boxes, and so on.

For example, let's say we had a fan site for a rock band and wanted to add a Community section. After installing a bulletin board system on our server, we would then create a style sheet with a series of CSS rules that would affect only the elements from the bulletin board system.

Because not every page will be in the Community section, we should not include this section in a site-wide style sheet. The solution is to remove the style from the generic menu styles and put it into its own style sheet. This special style sheet would only be used on pages in the Community section of the Web site. For example, you could save it to a file called community.css; then, in the head of every community piece, include the following:

```
<link rel="stylesheet" type="text/css" href="style/community. css">
```

If you were in the Community section, you could link to more than one style sheet.

```
<link rel="stylesheet" type="text/css" href="style/sitewide.css">
<link rel="stylesheet" type="text/css" href="style/community.css">
```

In this way, you can control the Web site style from a series of central style sheets.

Excluding Netscape Navigator with `@import`

When Navigator 4 came on the market, it could handle only a portion of the CSS specification. However, the CSS that Netscape did manage to support was in an almost reckless manner. Trying to apply some bit of CSS meant designers had to scale back their designs and strip your pages to get the CSS to work. If you didn't, the page looked like a mess; even worse, your CSS code could actually crash the browser as it attempted to render your styles (see Figure 3.3).

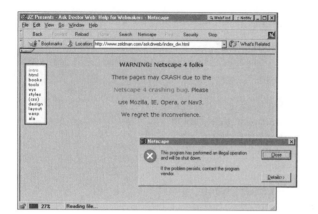

Figure 3.3

Netscape
Navigator 4
crashing.

On a good day, this crash would only slightly irritate a user. On a bad day, the irritated user would initiate the blame game by placing blame on the designer, even though designers don't typically write browser software, good or bad.

What's the best way to design for Netscape 4? Don't. Netscape 4 is a browser that is generations past its useful lifespan. Instead of bending over backward to handle Netscape 4 quirks, designers should ensure that their content is structured with quality markup and then import a style sheet with more "sophisticated" CSS rules accepted by better and more current browsers:

```
<style type="text/css" media="all">@import "/sophisticated.
css";</style>
```

If you want to, you can apply a basic style sheet consisting of fonts, background colors, and text and link colors, while also importing a sophisticated style sheet for competent browsers.

```
<link rel="stylesheet" type="text/css" media="screen" href="
/Websafe.css">
<style type="text/css" media="all">@import "/sophisticated.
css";</style>
```

If you want to lend people who are using less than appealing browsers (in terms of CSS) support, you can follow this method.

In the "sophisticated" style sheet, set up a CSS rule to hide content:

```
.no {
  display: none;
  }
```

In your document, place a message telling your user that to see the Web document as you had intended, he must download the latest browser from either Netscape or Microsoft (or, if you are reading this in the far-flung future, whichever browser has most of the browser market). After you have the message, wrap it around a div, p, or h1 element with a class attribute set to "no" like so:

```
<p class="no">This site is designed with a browser implementing
a majority of the CSS specification. You will be able to surf
the content of the site just fine without the design, but to
get the full experience, please download one of the latest browsers.</p>
```

With this technique, the modern browsers show only the desired style, but Navigator 4 shows the preceding paragraph and the rest of the structured and unstylized content.

Windows Flicker with @import

An incident is known to occur in Windows Internet Explorer 5 and higher if you use just the @import to associate a style to a Web page (see http://www.bluerobot.com/Web/css/fouc.asp). When you're loading a page in Windows IE, the Web page flickers briefly as it loads a style sheet. Before the flicker, you see the unstylized content; then the browser begins to redraw the page with the CSS rules listed in the external style sheet.

The way around this method is to add at least one link or script element in the head of the Web document. I recommend placing a Web-safe CSS in a separate style sheet and using that style sheet for the link element:

```
<link rel="stylesheet" type="text/css" href="/style/Websafe.css">
<style type="text/css" media="all">@import "/sophisticated.css";</style>
```

If you are already planning to include some JavaScript or another scripting language in your document, then you can just apply <script> element in the head of your document.

This problem is not a bug or any other apparent problem with the browser. Rather, it's a matter of how the browser executes rendering of the page per the specification of CSS, and it's perfectly valid.

CSS Aids: The Way Things Are

The following are aids in helping mark up content in HTML. These HTML elements and attributes allow you to create "hooks" in your content to bring about better design control through CSS rules.

Learn to Love the Box Model

The box model is a description for how elements are rendered via CSS through many properties (see Figure 3.4).

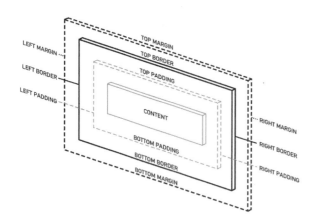

Box models are created with `div` tags. An element such as `div` can have several properties related to the box model.

```
div {
  padding: 25px;
  margin: 55px;
  border: 1px solid #000000;
}
```

Padding deals with the inside of the element—inside the border. The margin specifies the area around the border—the outside of the border. In Part IV, "Launching Progressive Design with CSS: Deconstructions," we will be getting into some serious and not-so-serious implementations with the box model and the properties that affect it.

Color Your CSS

CSS allows you to specify colors a number of ways besides the hexadecimal scheme that's in typical HTML markup. So far, my examples have included the typical six-digit hex value.

```
background-color: #CCFF00;
```

However, I can call out the same color with a shorthand version:

```
background-color: #CF0;
```

In the preceding example, each digit is doubled automagically by the browser to create #CCFF00.

Another way to specify color is through RGB in integer values from 0 to 255.

```
background-color: rgb(204, 255, 0);
```

Alternatively, you can do it in RGB through percentages.

```
background-color: rgb(80%, 100%, 0%);
```

Besides using numerals to specify colors, you can still use the set of 16 color names, as follows:

- **Aqua**
- **Black**
- **Blue**
- **Fuchsia**
- **Grey**
- **Green**
- **Lime**
- **Maroon**
- **Navy**
- **Olive**
- **Purple**
- **Red**
- **Silver**
- **Teal**
- **White**
- **Yellow**

Although browsers are required to handle 16 color names, in practice, browsers recognize a much larger list of keywords (see `http://www.w3.org/TR/SVG/types.html#ColorKeywords`), ranging from aliceblue to yellowgreen. You could use these names, but I suggest sticking with hexadecimal values.

Distance Units

You can use several units in CSS to dictate distance and sizes:

- **Pixels (px)**
- **Points (pt)**
- **Picas (pc)**
- **Em-height (em)**
- **Ex-height (ex)**
- **Inches (in)**
- **Millimeters (mm)**
- **Centimeters (cm)**

Centimeters, millimeters, inches, picas, and points are great for physical measurements, such as printouts. However, on the Web when people have different monitors set to different resolutions, measurement units that are used in the physical world tend to mess up Web page designs.

Units that should be used for screen media are pixels, em-height (the width of the letter *M* in the default font for the user), and ex-height (the width of the letter *x* from top to bottom).

For more information about how CSS and measurement units can be fatal to your Web design, check out the "Fear of Style Sheets" at *A List Apart* (see http://www.alistapart.com/fear/) and Todd Farhner's essays, such as "Why Points Suck" (see http://style.cleverchimp.com/).

class **Versus** id

What's the difference between id and class? Besides the syntax difference of the hash mark and the period, you can use id only once in a Web document, whereas class is used on repeating elements, such as numerous paragraphs or table cells.

Note

Because name is deprecated every-where except for form elements, this listing *will not* vali-date in strict XHTML, but it *will* validate in transitional XHTML.

An id is used to mark a single instance in a document, much like the name attribute. In fact, the name attribute is being deprecated in favor of the id except in form elements, where the name is still used to build name-value pairs for passing data to the server.

If you used name and are planning to use XHTML, you need to include the identical value for the name and id attributes in your markup. For example:

```
<a href="somewhere.html" name="same" id="same">Take me away </a>
```

div **Versus** span

HTML has two main types of structural elements: block and inline. An example of a block element is the <p> tag as a structure element because it defines a certain portion of a Web document as a paragraph of text.

An example of an inline element is an img, which doesn't define a portion of text, but inserts graphical content into the Web page. Content wraps around inline elements rather than setting off portions of the document as its own space.

When structuring a document, you frequently need to be able to mark up content as either block-level or inline-level elements. When none of the standard HTML tags help, div and span elements come into use.

div and span are generic elements that do nothing but mark content as either a block-level (div) or inline-level (span) element and allow you to then apply styles as necessary. The div tag represents a division in a document's structure and is a block-level element. A span does not create a division in the document's structure; rather, it sets its contents out as an inline-level element.

The power of the div is that you can stylize major chunks of your Web document—chunks that could include numerous HTML elements that imply document structure.

For instance, let's say you want to group an image and its caption together to have a grey background with a thin border around it (see Listing 3.3). In traditional Web design, one solution would be to include the image and caption text in an HTML table and then nest that table into another HTML table with a darker background color with a 1-pixel padding to achieve the effect.

Listing 3.3   HTML Table Example

```
<table border="0" cellspacing="0" cellpadding="1">
  <tr>
    <td bgcolor="#333333">
      <table border="0" width="250" cellspacing="0" cellpadding="7">
        <tr>
          <td bgcolor="#CCCCCC">
            <img src="dancing.jpg">
            <br>
            <p>
              The glorious caption would be placed here. Without regard to
              what was going on inside the picture.
            </p>
          </td>
        </tr>
      </table>
    </td>
  </tr>
</table>
```

In this example, we see that a lot of markup goes a little distance (see Figure 3.5). We employ two tables, one nested in the other. Along with tables come the requisite <tr> and <td> elements.

Figure 3.5

Traditional Web
design approach.

Now we can achieve a similar, almost identical
effect by using one CSS rule and one `div` tag
instead of two HTML tables.

Listing 3.4 is the CSS that will power the
presentation.

Listing 3.4   A Quick CSS Rule

```
<style type="text/css">
  .photo    {
    border: 1px solid #333333;
    padding: 7px;
    width: 250px;
    background-color: #CCCCCC;
    }
</style>
```

Listing 3.5 is the HTML from inside the `body` tags.

Listing 3.5   Markup Using `divs`

```
<div class="photo">
  <img src="dancing.jpg">
  <p>
    The glorious caption would be placed here. Without regard to what was going
    on inside the picture.
  </p>
<div>
```

With CSS rules and a change in the approach to how we use markup, we have a leaner presentation of our pages that's amazingly similar to the HTML table method (see Figure 3.6).

Figure 3.6

`divs` example shows that CSS does the presentation, leaving your markup for structure.

As you can see, we placed an image and <p> tag inside a `div` tag. Viewing the page without styles, we can see that the Web page that is presented does not include remnants from the `div` (see Figure 3.7). The structured content of the `img` and the `p` tags is presented only to those people who have browsers that do not understand CSS.

Figure 3.7

Just the markup, ma'am, in this "unstylized" `divs` example.

For the `span` tag, we can achieve a similar feat, but only with elements that are inlined—not block level, such as `images`, `p`, `tables`, and so on. Instead, we can change the effect of words in a sentence. For example, we can change the type size of a company's product in the first sentence of a company's home page.

By using font tags in the traditional method of Web design, we would use two sets of font tags, as in Listing 3.6.

Listing 3.6   Use of font **Tags**

```
<p>
   The glorious <font size="+7">WhizBang <font color="#666666">Battle
Bat</font></font> allows kids to play baseball with an edge not seen since the
1940s when everything was in black and white. You couldn't see the color of blood
in those days. It was all just chocolate milk; the kind of chocolate milk that
tastes good after a day on the baseball diamond slugging home runs after home run
with your lucky WhizBang Battle Bat.
</p>
```

Figure 3.8 shows the result of Listing 3.6.

Figure 3.8

Font tags at work.

To get the same effect through span tags, these are the CSS rules we should use:

```
.grey      {
    color: #666666;
}

.bigfont      {
    font-size: 45px;
    line-height: 0.8em;
}
```

The HTML markup would look like Listing 3.7.

Listing 3.7   Cleaner Markup with the span **Element**

```
<p>
   The glorious <span class="bigfont">WhizBang <span class="#666666"><span
class="grey">Battle Bat</span></span> allows kids to play baseball with an edge
not seen since the 1940s when everything was in black and white. You couldn't see
the color of blood in those days. It was all just chocolate milk. The kind of
chocolate milk that tastes good after a day on the baseball diamond slugging
homer runs after home runs with your lucky WhizBang Battle Bat.
</p>
```

Figure 3.9 shows the result of Listing 3.7.
Notice that thanks to CSS, we can affect the
leading of the large text. This was utterly impos-
sible to do with the `font` tag.

Figure 3.9

span **tag example**
shines.

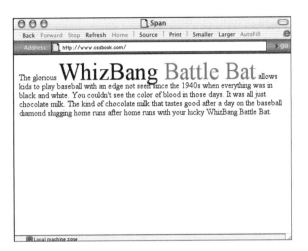

Notice that through the use of CSS selector
line-height, designers are now able to
achieve leading—the distance between two
lines—between the first sentence and the
second. With the `font` tag, that type of
control just isn't possible. Therefore, not
only is using `font` tags bad because they
permit presentational issues to the content
in a Web document, but they also simply
don't allow the control that designers need.

To ensure that you understand the difference between `divs` and span, Listing 3.8
presents the code of the paragraph when
the span tags are switched to `divs`.

Listing 3.8   Spans as `divs`

```
<p>
   The glorious <div class="bigfont">WhizBang <div class="#666666"><div
class="grey">Battle Bat</div></div> allows kids to play baseball with an edge not
seen since the 1940s when everything was in black and white. You couldn't see
the color of blood in those days. It was all just chocolate milk. The kind of
chocolate milk that tastes good after a day on the baseball diamond slugging
homer runs after home runs with your lucky WhizBang Battle Bat.
</p>
```

Figure 3.10 shows the result of Listing 3.8.
Notice the automatic breaks that are put in
after the large text.

Figure 3.10

From inline to block,
`divs` convert spans
into block-level
elements.

Notice the automatic break after the end of each `div`. That break is a characteristic of block-level elements, such as `p` and `tables`. If you want to apply a style inside a block-level element, like the words in a sentence, you reach for the `span` tag in your developer's toolbox.

Pseudo-Classes and Pseudo-Elements

Special classes and elements allow you to stylize sections of markup without placing a `class` or `id` in the markup. For instance, let's say that you want to stylize the first line of a paragraph to be bold, but not the entire paragraph. The CSS rule would be something like this:

```
p:first-line {
   font-weight: bold;
}
```

If you try to accomplish the same effect with "typical" CSS, the markup would look something like this:

```
.bold     {
   font-weight: bold;
}

<p>
   <span class="bold">The glorious WhizBang Battle Bat
allows kids to</span> play baseball with an edge not seen
since the 1940s when everything was in black and white.
You couldn't see the color of blood in those days. It was
all just chocolate milk. The kind of chocolate milk that
tastes good after a day on the baseball diamond slugging
home runs after home runs with your lucky WhizBang Battle
Bat.
</p>
```

However, this example gives you only a section of the first sentence in bold from "The glorious" to "to." If the user's monitor is larger than yours, then the user will see only those eight words as bold—not the entire first line of the paragraph. A first line could include anywhere from two words to 22 and up, for example. With the pseudo-element and classes, though, we are able to ensure that the first line of the paragraph, no matter how many words, will always be bold.

The tricky part about pseudo-classes and pseudo-elements is that browser support for them is limited at best. Don't count on these pseudo-elements to work in browsers that claim to be 100% CSS compliant.

A pseudo-class acts as a selector methodology. For example, you can "grab" text that is in a link and apply a style to it when a user has "hovered" over it like it's a rollover as well as applying a style to it after it's been visited. In essence, you can apply text that's a link with four CSS rules by having the text marked up once (see Listing 3.9).

Listing 3.9   Pseudo-Classes in Action

```
a:link {color: #600; background-color: transparent;}
a:visited {color: #000; background-color: transparent;}}

a:hover {color: #fff; background-color: #600;}
a:active {color: #f00; background-color: transparent;}
```

Table 3.2 is a listing of pseudo-classes.

Table 3.2   Pseudo-Classes

Pseudo-Class	Description
:first-child	Applies style to the first element and first child of another element
:link	Applies style for unvisited elements; commonly used for styling links
:visit	Applies style to elements that have been visited; commonly used for styling links
:hover	Applies style for the "mouseover" effect; commonly used for styling links
:active	Applies style to elements when you activate them; commonly used for styling links
:focus	Applies style to elements that have focus.
:lang()	Applies style to an element that is written in a certain language code
:left	Used for printing
:right	Used for printing
:first	Used for printing

Pseudo-elements are elements that insert elements where there were none before. You can actually generate text after a normal element using the pseudo-element `:after`. However, as of this writing, the only browser that can handle that affect is Mozilla. Pseudo-elements contain the following: first-letter, first-line, before, and after. The rest are pseudo-classes. Table 3.3 is a listing of pseudo-elements.

Table 3.3   Pseudo-Elements

Pseudo-Element	Description
:first-letter	Applies style to the first letter of an element
:first-line	Applies style to the first line
:before	Generates content before an element
:after	Generates content after an element

Incorporating CSS Ideally

Where does that leave us? We have various associative methods—both external and internal—and now we've thrown in `class`, `id`, `div`, and spans. That's just enough to make a good Web page go bad quickly if the designer doesn't know the basic techniques of applying CSS.

Listings 3.10 and 3.11 show two ways of applying CSS to a Web page. Both are perfectly valid ways of marking up content for the Web; however, they both hinder you in the long run.

Listing 3.10   Too Many Breaks

```
<div class="bodycopy">
  The glorious WhizBang Battle Bat allows kids to play baseball with an edge not
seen since the 1940s when everything was in black and white. You couldn't see
the color of blood in those days. It was all just chocolate milk. The kind of
chocolate milk that tastes good after a day on the baseball diamond, slugging
home runs after home runs with your lucky WhizBang Battle Bat.
  <br>
  <br>
  <br>
  "Without this Battle Bat, I wouldn't have had the amazing pleasure of being
picked first," said high school nerd, Brian Smith. "You have no idea how much
therapy I've needed to get past the fact that I'm unpopular in a lot of areas of
school interaction. The kids say it's mostly hygiene, but I think it's that I'm
a rebel in that I write everything in lowercase letters—even the note I forged
from 'my mom' to get out of gym class."
  <br>
  <br>
  <br>
```

```
    However, all that changed with the birthday gift of Battle Bat. Now, Young Mr.
Smith is being picked first for sports with his peers and appreciating life on a
whole new level. You can, too, for the low, low price of one cent.
</div>
```

Listing 3.11 Too Many Non-Breaking Spaces ( )

```
<div class="bodycopy">
       The glorious WhizBang Battle Bat allows kids to
play baseball with an edge not seen since the 1940s when everything was in black
and white. You couldn't see the color of blood in those days. It was all just
chocolate milk. The kind of chocolate milk that tastes good after a day on the
baseball diamond, slugging home runs after home runs with your lucky WhizBang
Battle Bat.
</div>

<div class="bodycopy">
        "Without this Battle Bat I wouldn't have the
amazing pleasure of being picked first," said high school nerd, Brian Smith. "You
have no idea how much therapy I've needed to get past the fact that I'm unpopu-
lar in a lot of areas of school interaction. The kids say it's mostly hygiene,
but I think it's that I'm a rebel in that I write everything in lowercase let-
ters—even the note I forged from 'my mom' to get out of gym class."
</div>

<div class="bodycopy">
       However, that all changed with the birthday gift
of Battle Bat. Now, Young Mr. Smith is being picked first for sports with his
peers and appreciating life on a whole new level. You can, too, for the low, low
price of one cent.
</div>
```

In Listing 3.10, a class called "bodycopy" was applied to a DIV element
that encased three paragraphs' worth of content. The paragraphs were
then broken apart by a few br tags.

In Listing 3.11, several divs were wrapped around the paragraphs. Also,
there were several non-breaking space entities;   was used to cause
an indent in each of the paragraphs.

These approaches are both valid technically; however, the Web developer
who created the markup has placed restrictions on the content to be
reformatted and how it can be presented to other media.

The ideal approach when marking up content is to use markup that carries with it inherent presentational meaning and then apply CSS rules to
those HTML tags. In doing this, you redefine the presentation of the CSS,

unleashing the power of the technology, but ensuring that your content will be able to be revisited, redesigned, and redelivered with minimal or no effort.

This is the ideal method for approaching markup and then applying CSS rules. First take a look at the markup (see Listing 3.12).

Listing 3.12   An Ideal Version of Approaching Content Markup

```
<p>
The glorious WhizBang Battle Bat allows kids to play baseball with an edge not
seen since the 1940s when everything was in black and white. You couldn't see
the color of blood in those days. It was all just chocolate milk. The kind of
chocolate milk that tastes good after a day on the baseball diamond, slugging
home runs after home runs with your lucky WhizBang Battle Bat.
</p>

<p>
"Without this Battle Bat, I wouldn't have had the amazing pleasure of being
picked first," said high school nerd, Brian Smith. "You have no idea how much
therapy I've needed to get past the fact that I'm unpopular in a lot of areas of
school interaction. The kids say it's mostly hygiene, but I think it's that I'm
a rebel in that I write everything in lowercase letters—even the note I forged
from 'my mom' to get out of gym class."
</p>

<p>
However, all that changed with the birthday gift of Battle Bat. Now, Young Mr.
Smith is being picked first for sports with his peers and appreciating life on a
whole new level. You can, too, for the low, low price of one cent.
</p>
```

Now take a look at the CSS rules. In Listing 3.10, several brs were used to create padding between the paragraph chunks. This CSS rule would achieve the same or a similar result:

```
p {
   margin-bottom: 3em;
}
```

In Listing 3.11, several non-breaking spaces were used to create indents in the first line of each paragraph. We can achieve that effect with the following bit of CSS:

```
p {
   text-indent: 5em;
}
```

However, let's say that we have coded our content as in Listing 3.10, but we want to put an indent in the first line in each of our paragraph chunks. Looking at how the markup is produced, the easiest method is to do what the Listing 3.11 did and insert several non-breaking spaces in front of the first sentence of the paragraph chunk.

That's acceptable if we have only one page of content to work on. However, imagine a client Web site with several pages. Now think of sites with hundreds or thousands of pages. The task of making all those updates by hand suddenly becomes less appealing.

However, if we mark up the content with inherent-presentational markup, such as the p tag, we can readily go into a style sheet that is associated through an external method and add the new CSS rule. Instead of modifying the Web site at several points in a multitude of Web pages, we update one file only once.

Making changes to a style sheet and having the design changes applied instantly across a Web site is one benefit of marking up your content in this ideal method. Another benefit is making different style sheets for delivery to other media.

For instance, you can create a different style sheet to handle how your Web pages look when they are sent to a printer. With the traditional method of marking up your content, your pages will display exactly like you have them marked up for display in the browser. Sure, the colors might be translated to greyscale because you have a black-ink only printer, but the br won't go away and the indents will always be there on the paper. In essence, you won't take full advantage of the other media because your content is trapped in markup destined for a Web browser that is geared toward visual presentation.

The Cascade

We have gone over CSS rules that dictate the design transformation of normal, everyday HTML elements. However, these CSS rules have rules of their own. The CSS rules fall into certain guidelines when you're determining how to style a document. This guideline, or process, if you will, is called the *cascade*. The following list is a "cascade" overview describing the rules that are used to interpret styles and quell potential conflicts between CSS rules:

- **Cascade Guideline #1**—In the media type (screen, printer, and so on), look for all the declarations for an element *and* property. The style is rendered if the selector and the element match.

- **Cascade Guideline #2**—The second guideline deals with where the style sheet came from. If a designer created a style sheet, those declarations in the style sheet override the default style sheet set in the browser. However, if you, the user, have a style sheet set up for ensuring that text sizes are large enough to read, for example, your style sheet overrules the designer's.

You don't want the user's settings to override your carefully crafted design? As a designer, you can specify your declarations as being more important than the user's because that #CCFF00 color is important to carrying out your branding message. Maybe everything you write needs to be lowercase, for example. In that case, you could write a CSS rule like the following to achieve that effect:

```
body {
    background-color: #CCFF00 !important;
    font-family: Verdana, Arial, sans-serif;
    text-transform: lowercase !important;
}
```

Note

Eric Meyer has a great article about using the !important declaration to create mischief with other people's Web pages. The article is titled "The CSS Anarchist's Cookbook" (July 2000), and it's available online at http://www.oreillynet.com/pub/a/network/2000/07/21/magazine/css_anarchist.html.

However, a user's own style sheet might include !important rules, which beat out any CSS rules you use. The order of importance (from the least to greatest) follows this pattern:

1. Browser default rules
2. User-defined rules
3. Author-defined rules
4. Author-defined !important rules
5. User-defined !important rules

- **Cascade Guideline #3**—The third guideline states that specific selectors will be given more weight than general selectors. For more information on specific selectors, check out the discussion about specificity in "Links, Specificity, and Math" later in this chapter.
- **Cascade Guideline #4**—If two selectors have the same weight and the same origin, as detailed in guidelines #2 and #3, then the selector that is written last in the style sheet will be used to style the element. What if a style sheet is associated externally? Well, those CSS rules are thought of as becoming before the CSS rules that are in the actual Web document, either inline or embedded.

Inheritance

Unlike in real life, inheritance is something to take for granted in CSS—for the most part. If you declare an element, such as the body, to have the background color set to #CCFF00, then the HTML elements p in the document also have the same background color (see Figure 3.11).

```
body {
    background-color: #7F7F7F !important;
}
```

Figure 3.11

Inheritance in action.

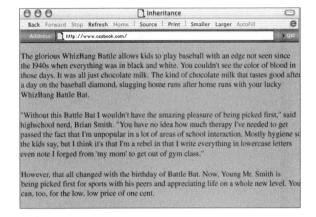

However, if we set up a CSS rule for the p tag to be a different color, then the CSS rule stops the background color from being inherited (see Figure 3.12).

```
body {
    background-color: #7F7F7F;
}

p {
    background-color:#FFFFFF;
}
```

Figure 3.12

Inheritance being stopped.

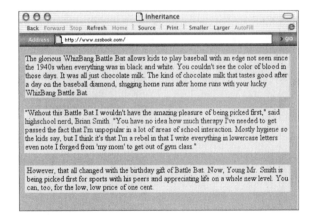

Links, Specificity, and Math

Each selector in a CSS rule has a level of specificity, which is used in Cascade Guideline #4. The value of a selector's specificity is based on the selector.

Let's go through the method of determining a selector's specificity:

1. **Total the number of ID selectors in the selectors. Store that as the "ID value."**

2. **Total the number of other attributes and pseudo-class attributes in the selector. Store that as the "Selector value."**

3. **Total the number of other element names in the selector. Store that as the "Element value."**

4. **Forget about pseudo-elements altogether. Their value is worthless here, for the most part. In practice, this guideline has some flexibility unless you have a pseudo-element setting, a style that overrides a generic element. For example, a CSS rule like this one,** `p:first-line {font-weight: bold;}`**, makes the first line of text appear bold over a rule for just the p element. This is because the** `p:first-line` **is more specific.**

Now you need to arrange the values of a selector's specificity like so:

ID Value – Selector Value – Element Value

The ID value has more weight than the Selector Value. And the Element Value has less weight than ID and Selector. Let's look at some examples of selectors and determine their specificity:

- `p { color: #000033; }`—**This selector has a specificity of 0-0-1 because it uses only one element:** p.
- `body p {color: blue;}`—**This selector has a specificity of 0-0-2 because it has two element names:** body **and** p.
- `div.green {color: green;}`—**This selector has a specificity of 0-1-1 because it uses the element** div **and the class** green.
- `#topnav {background-color: blue;}`—**This selector has a specificity of 1-0-0 because it uses the ID of** topnav.

Now that we have determined the specificity values, when do they come into some sort of importance? When a selector has more than one CSS rule applied to itself, knowing which selector will win out and stylize your page is an important bit of knowledge for making sure your designs appear like you want them to appear.

In an example, let's say we have a div element wrapped around a paragraph and we have these two CSS rules:

```
div {
  background-color: #CCFF00;
}

#black {
  background-color: #000000;
}
```

The HTML code that we have is this:

```
<div id="black">
   The glorious WhizBang Battle Bat allows kids to play
baseball with an edge not seen since the 1940s when every-
thing was in black and white. You couldn't see the color of
blood in those days. It was all just chocolate milk. The
kind of chocolate milk that tastes good after a day on the
baseball diamond, slugging homer runs after home runs with
your lucky WhizBang Battle Bat.
</div>
```

The div element matches both selectors because it follows both the div and the id rule. However, the background color will be black, even though we stated in the style sheet that we wanted the div to be grey. This discrepancy is because the specificity of the latter CSS rule has a specificity of 1-0-0, and the former has a specificity of 0-0-1. The value on the left side, the "IDValue," has more weight than its counterparts of "Selector Value" and "Element Value" that property value of black wins out.

Chapter 4

Laying Out Pages

In this chapter, we will involve ourselves with the importance of building Web standards-compliant sites with an interview with Jeffrey Zeldman.

First, we will interview Zeldman about how to build Web pages correctly through valid CSS and HTML and how that affects Web builders. After that discussion, we will look at some examples of standards-compliant Web pages that you can use in your Web sites: splash page, two-column, and three-column layouts.

Jeffrey Zeldman on Web Standards and Development

Part of designing pages for new media is to understand how to *best build* for the medium as well. For any great designer, there is knowledge of the process of how their designs are manufactured albeit a print designer, furniture designer, or typographer.

You can still design without knowing how best to build your pages, but that disconnect from production to aesthetic will hurt your pages and your designs more than you care to believe. If you don't know what happens to your pages after you turn your digital comps over to a production artist or just let a WYSIWYG tool do the job for you, you will end up with bloated code and designs that fail to achieve their intended "look" in a Web browser.

Part of that understanding is knowing how browsers handle (some would say "manhandle") HTML and CSS. As a beginning Web builder, no doubt you came across the phenomenon known as *cross-browser hell*—where the design looks different in the different browsers that are available.

One organization is hoping to help Web designers dig out of that hell by promoting Web standards. *Web standards* is a collective term for recommendations that the World Wide Web Consortium (W3C) makes. To learn more about Web standards, I talked with Jeffrey Zeldman.

Interview with Jeffrey Zeldman

Jeffrey Zeldman

Jeffrey Zeldman is the publisher and creative director for *A List Apart* (see http://www.alistapart.com/) and group leader of the Web Standards Project (WaSP) (see http://www.Webstandards.org). He's also the author of *Taking Your Talent to the Web* (New Riders, 2001) and founder of Happy Cog, a Web agency whose clients include Warner Bros., The New York Public Library, and Clear Channel Entertainment.

Christopher Schmitt: What are Web standards? Where did they come from?

Jeffrey Zeldman: Technically speaking, "Web standards" refers to ratified protocols like HTTP, without which the Web would not exist. But most of us currently use "Web standards" to mean the technologies recommended by the World Wide Web Consortium (W3C) for interpreting Web-based content. The details can be found in The Web Standards Project's original (1998) mission statement, archived at http://archive.Webstandards.org/mission.html. To quote from that document:

When we speak about "standards" for the Web, we mean:

> Structural Languages
> HTML 4.0 (and now XHTML 1.0)
> XML 1.0
>
> Presentation Languages
> Cascading Style Sheets 1
> Cascading Style Sheets 2
> XSL
>
> Object Models
> Document Object Model 1 Core HTML/XML
>
> Scripting
> ECMAScript (the "official" version of JavaScript)

...as well as emerging standards, such as those for television-based and PDA-based browsers.

These standards were created by W3C (with the exception of ECMAScript) with the intention of balancing the needs of designers for a sophisticated set of presentation and interactive features against the desire to make the Web accessible to the largest possible number of browsers (and other client devices) and environments.

CS: What tools do you use to build your clients' sites?

JZ: I author my (X)HTML, CSS, and JavaScript in Optima System's PageSpinner (see `http://www.optima-system.com/pagespinner/`), a professional HTML editor for [the] Mac OS. I've "hand-coded" my work in this application since 1995, and it just keeps getting better.

For complex search and replace, I use Bare Bones Software's BBEdit (see `http://www.barebones.com/products/bbedit.html`). To quickly convert outdated documents to standards compliance, I use Tidy (see `http://www.w3.org/People/Raggett/tidy/`), which is free from [the] W3C.

For images and comp layouts, I choose Adobe Photoshop 5.5; for logos and vector art, Illustrator 8. I use Macromedia Flash for the occasional .swf, QuickTime 5 Pro for video clips, and that's about it.

CS: What is the importance of coding sites to be "standards compliant" for designers? For developers?

JZ: How much time have you got?

For one thing, coding to "standards" ensures what I call *forward compatibility* and what librarians and others interested in the preservation of our intellectual heritage refer to as *durability*. In the world of print, if you print on acid-free paper and follow certain other procedures, there's a good chance that your book will last a while. With other procedures, the book falls apart after a few years of use.

Likewise, the kind of coding most developers still use ensures that the sites they design and build will become obsolete within a few years. Let me repeat: The kind of coding that is the industry norm absolutely guarantees obsolescence. Build it today; throw it in the trash tomorrow. By contrast, authoring in valid XHTML and CSS ensures that, at the very least, your site will work in today's browsers and will keep working for years and years, because even as they advance, browsers will continue to support old, existing standards.

For another thing, coding to standards helps make your site accessible to all—to the blind person using an audio browser, and to the executive using a wireless device. By contrast, the current method of designing to the quirks of a few popular browsers ensures that millions of users (including many with disabilities) will be locked out of your site and forces you to add costly development if you wish to support wireless and other non-traditional devices. Accessibility is now part of U.S. law, which means that if your site is inaccessible, you're not only cruelly alienating millions of people (who could be potential customers), [but] you're also in jeopardy of lawsuits and legal penalties.

By contrast, my magazine, *A List Apart*, is authored in structural XHTML and designed entirely with CSS. The site is accessible to any browser or device—even if the design doesn't show up in older browsers or non-graphical Internet devices—and we create a wireless version on-the-fly via a simple CGI script instead of spending hundreds of hours creating separate wireless versions using proprietary wireless markup languages that won't be around much longer.

Finally, if you're a control freak—and what designer isn't?—standards like CSS when backed by the appropriate DOCTYPE ensure that your design will look the same in all compliant graphical browsers.

CS:　**What are the drawbacks of writing standards compliant code?**

JZ:　If done right, there are no drawbacks.

For instance, some say you can't create standards-compliant sites if you have to support non-compliant browsers like Netscape Navigator 4. But that's rubbish. The New York Public Library has thousands of Netscape 4 installations across its many branches, yet the new sites of the branch libraries are all created in valid XHTML and CSS. (See the NYPL Online Style Guide at `http://www.nypl.org/styleguide/` to see how they do that. It also makes a dandy tutorial for those converting legacy sites to valid XHTML.)

Admittedly, with the approach just mentioned, sites won't look exactly the same in a non-compliant browser as they do in, say, IE5+, Netscape 6, Mozilla, or Opera 6. But that's perfectly okay: In lousy browsers, the sites look close enough to what the designer intended. The desire to create an identical user experience in Netscape 2, WebTV, and IE 6 is the primary cause of expensively produced multi-version sites filled with non-valid markup and obsolete scripting, and these are the sites that become obsolete almost the moment they launch. Designing with standards avoids all those problems, yet need not alienate anyone.

In addition to all the above, once the 4.0 browsers go away and we can really harness the power of standards, site design and development will become faster and more streamlined as we will have full separation of style from structure, meaning that one source fits all (see http://www.alistapart.com/stories/netscape/).

Some sites, like *A List Apart*, are already separating their structure/content from their design. Others that can help you do the same include Owen Briggs's *Little Boxes* (see http://www.thenoodleincident.com/tutorials/box_lesson/ boxes.html) and Eric Costello's *CSS Layout Techniques* (see http://glish.com/css/). We run numerous tutorials on this subject in *A List Apart* as well, and phase two of *The Web Standards Project* will list the best of these resources.

One difficulty you might encounter in designing and building with Web standards is that scripts—sophisticated site functions—based on the W3C standard DOM will not work in non-compliant browsers and might not even work in otherwise excellent browsers, such as Opera 6. That's a real issue for those developing sophisticated presentations, and the situation will only improve when all browsers fully support DOM Level One.

CS: What is the mission of the Web Standards Project?

JZ: From 1998 through 2001, our mission was to persuade browser makers to fully support the W3C recommendations—Web standards—listed in our original mission statement (see http://archive. Webstandards.org/mission.html).

To a great extent, what we asked for has come true. IE 5/Mac, IE 6/Windows, Mozilla, Netscape 6, and Opera 6 do a superb job of supporting all or most of HTML, XHTML 1.0 compatible, and CSS Level One, and all but Opera do a great job of supporting the DOM—and Opera is getting there.

So to our original mission, we've added the goals of increasing developer/designer awareness of and use of Web standards (because good browsers don't mean much if site builders still generate rotten code) and improved compliance in the visual tools many designers and developers use to create their sites—tools such as Adobe's GoLive and Macromedia's Dreamweaver.

Now that we've covered some background on Web standards and how important it is to our development of Web pages, we will move on to the building of Web pages. First up is the splash page. Then we will cover two and three-column Web pages.

Splash Pages

Splash pages are pages that are (often) quick-loading introductions to a Web site. They allow people to get prepared for the type of design that is used in the real site.

The use of a splash page on the Web is similar to an exercise that the theme parks do for crowd management for popular shows. Some theme park shows use pre-show entertainment for the people in line. While the previous crowd exits the show area and they are getting the stage reset for the new crowd, the people waiting in line are entertained. This concept is similar to using splash pages on the Web. On the Web, however, these splash pages act as a distraction for their site guests as the real page is loading. If splash pages are not properly executed, they can be a nuisance. Some sites don't need them and sites might throw in a splash page that sticks out like a sore thumb from the rest of the site.

For information designers who are concerned that each page a user pulls off the Internet and into his browser is filled with just information and links and maybe a graphic here or there, splash pages aren't an appropriate design solution. And often, the sites they built wouldn't be conducive to the use of a welcome page. The information on the site is all the welcome they require.

What about the designers who make extensive use of Flash? Some would say that these Flash designers are the exact opposite of the information designers. Do these Flash designers make splash sites? Yes, in a way they do. The sites like Barney's seen in Chapter 1, "Planning and Structuring Content," often use *preloader* pages that allow the user to see some eye candy while waiting for the rest of the Flash presentation to load in the background. I consider these preloaders as splash pages.

If a Flash preloader (or splash page) is done correctly, it will look consistent with the rest of the site. The preshow sets up how the show's message will be delivered through a similar mood, tone, and style. Although the pre-show isn't the main experience, it allows the audience to be prepared for what's to be expected.

Web site designers can use the splash pages as a way to set the guide for information types of sites. If their pages are lean and their servers are fast, designers can set up a splash page as an expectation of what's to come—speedy Web experience.

Traditional Splashes: A Practical Example

With traditional Web design, splash pages need to rely primarily on the image to provide the visual impact needed for a successful design. However, through CSS, we can now apply presentation to standard markup. A splash page's content, usually a tagline, would download quickly, and the only limiting factor would be the ability for the browser to read and render the style sheet. If you want to throw in the logo of the company or the Web site, you'll be charged extra in terms of download time for the user.

For an example of a splash page set with CSS and XHTML, let's look at the content you'll need:

- **Company/Web site name**
- **Slogan**
- **Description of Web site**
- **Enter message**

Let's create a Web document with content that meets the splash page requirement list for a make-believe dance club Web site, Club Altruism (see Listing 4.1 and Figure 4.2).

Listing 4.1   Club Altruism Splash Page

```
<?xml version="1.0" encoding="iso-8859-1"?>
<!DOCTYPE html PUBLIC "-//W3C//DTD XHTML 1.0 Strict//EN"
        "http://www.w3.org/TR/xhtml1/DTD/xhtml1-strict.dtd">
<html xmlns="http://www.w3.org/1999/xhtml"
 xml:lang="en" lang="en">
  <head>
    <meta http-equiv="content-type"
content="text/html; charset=iso-8859-1" />
    <title>Club Altruism - ClubAltruism.com</title>
  </head>
  <body>

    <a href="/main/"><img src="bkgd.jpg"
title="People dancing at Club Altruism" alt="Club
Altruism" border="0" /></a>

  <h1><a href="/main/" title="Enter the club's
Web site">Club Altruism</a></h1>

    <h2>Serving today's ultra cool till the break
of dawn.</h2>

    <p>Located at First St. and Electric Avenue,
we feature:</p>
```

continues

Listing 4.1   Club Altruism Splash Page   (Continued)

```
  <ul>
    <li>Four dance floors
    <li>In-house Djs
    <li>Our own record label
    <li>No cover charge Mondays
    <li>All you can drink Tuesdays
    <li>Wednesday's Women's Night
    <li>80s Cosby Thursdays
  </ul>

  <p><a href="/main/" title="Enter the club's
Web site">Go to the main page.</a><p>

  </body>
</html>
```

Now that we have the content in place, let's start applying design through CSS rules to give the page a heightened visual impact.

The first step is to remove portions of the text that won't help in creating a visual impact. By adding the CSS rule in Listing 4.2, we eliminate text within p elements.

Listing 4.2   CSS Rule

```
p {
  display: none;
}
```

The next portion is to set up the layout properties for the entire viewport of the browser. I want the margins to be set to zero to create a "full bleed" effect. Also, I want to set the background color to black while the text is a light shade of grey (see Listing 4.3).

Listing 4.3   Setting Up the Layout Properties

```
body {
  margin: 0;
  color: #ccc;
  background-color: #000;
}
```

Now I get to play with the main image of the splash page (see Listing 4.4). With a couple of simple declarations, I've made a bold visual.

Listing 4.4   Sizing the Main Image

```
img {
  width: 100%;
  height: 100%;
}
```

The image is now flush with the left, top, and right part of the browser. Depending on how well your browser renders the height declaration, it will also be flush with the bottom (see Figure 4.1). If the image doesn't stretch to become flush at the bottom, the black color declared in the body selector will smooth the visual transition from image to background.

Figure 4.1

Results of applying the first layer of style.

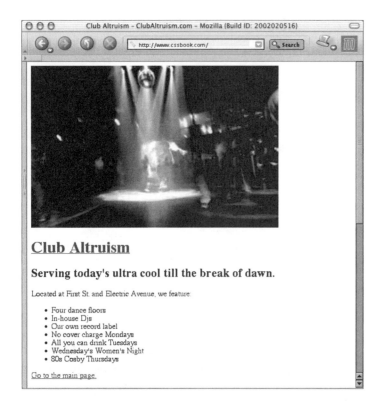

Figure 4.2

The splash page without CSS.

Note

If you want, you can swap out the name of the club with a logo of the club. Be sure to save the file in the GIF format with transparency matted to black so that the image will fit smoothly with the background color.

Next, I'm going to work on the name of the club. Wrapped up in an h1, the name is identified as the first-level heading, giving the highest weight in terms of document structure. Visually, however, it's not sending the right message. Listing 4.5 shows a CSS rule set that we can use to solve that problem.

Listing 4.5   The Name of the Club

```
h1 {
  z-index: 5;
  position: absolute;
  top: 100px;
  left: 300px;
  font-size: 2em;
  font-family: Impact, sans-serif;
  font-style: italic;
  color: #fff;
  padding: 1em;
  margin: 0;
  border: 1em dashed #fff;
  background-color: transparent;
}
```

For the title, I positioned the contents to absolute, and the declarations top and left to 100 and 300 pixels, respectively. Then I set the font styles and a border for a dashed border.

I put in the Z-index and set it to a value of 5 to make the title rest higher on the page. The title is now in its own layer, above the bottom Viewport layer of the browser. In Listing 4.5, h1 is five steps away from the bottom, which the image is occupying. I often use multiples of five when assigning the Z-index just in case I need to bring in another layer between two other layers later on in the development process.

Too Much Thinking About Stacking

That's a simplification of the stacking process with the Z-index. To get more detailed, the Z-index values always give the stack order relative to the canvas, but whatever the stacking context is. For example, let's say there are two `div` elements with different Z-indexes of 5 and 10. A nested element in the `div` with the Z-index of 10 could have two children elements with Z-index levels of 1 and 2. Those children wouldn't be below both the `div`s with 5 and 10 Z-indexes; rather, they would be in relation to the 10 index. It would be like 10.1 and 10.2 for the children of the Z-index parent element.

Now that the title of the club has been taken care of, I focus my attention on the tagline of the club set in the h2 element (see Listing 4.6). Because we have an image size based on percentages, I can use that to my advantage with the placement. I see that the ceiling lights hit the dance floor around four-fifths from the top of the image. I want to place the tagline text using that approximation (see Figure 4.3).

Listing 4.6   The Tagline of the Club

```
h2 {
  z-index: 10;
  position: absolute;
  top: 78%;
  width: 95%;
  color: #ccc;
  margin: 0;
  padding: 0;
  text-align: center;
  font-size: 1.5em;
}
```

Figure 4.3

Setting up the tagline.

Setting to the next multiplier of five (10), I position the layer "absolutely" with a top declaration of four-fifths, or 80%, but tweak it to go to 78%.

Because the width of the element is going to be centered (as seen in the
text-align: center declaration), the width should occupy the width of
the viewport. However, having a width of 100% causes a bottom scrollbar to appear in Mac IE. Dropping the width from 100% to 95% eliminates the extra scrollbar.

Because we are dealing with the h2 element, it carries over some default
padding and margins just like the h1 element. To get rid of those, I set
the margin and padding to 0.

Dealing with Unordered Lists

After that, we focus our attention on the list of services. The header for
the list is in a p and is, therefore, hidden by our previous CSS rule, which
hides contents of p elements.

To get rid of the native HTML ul margin and padding settings, I set them
to 0 right off the bat. Apply the Z-index to the next multiplier of 5.

I want to put the list items between the left of the viewport and the title
of the club. I set the width to be 275 pixels and put the distance from the
top of the viewport to be equal with the club name (see Listing 4.7).

Listing 4.7   Detailing the Unordered List

```
ul {
  margin: 0;
  padding: 0;
  z-index: 15;
  position: absolute;
  top: 100px;
  left: 25px;
  color: #fff;
  background-color: transparent;
  width: 275px;
  margin: 0;
}
```

The next step is to style the items in the list (see Listing 4.8).

Listing 4.8   Styling the Items

```css
li {
  list-style: none;
  font-family: Georgia, Times, serif;
  font-size: 1em;
  display: inline;
  text-align: center;
  font-weight: bold;
}
```

I convert the list items from block elements to inline elements by using `display: inline`, which creates a run-on sentence effect. Next, I set up the font styles to a serif font that contrasts with the text in the club's name.

As for the links, I set them to white and keep the underline link. Also, I add a `META` `refresh` tag in the header that will jump to the main page after a period of seven seconds (see Listing 4.9).

Listing 4.9   The Tag for the Header

```html
<meta http-equiv="refresh" content="14; url=/main/" />
```

Although we are designing for visual impact and setting the visual tone for the rest of the site for the visitor, we don't want to forget that the information for our Web site is still a page away. Including several redundant links to the main page in the HTML links and a META refresh ensures an easy path to the content. Figure 4.4 shows the result.

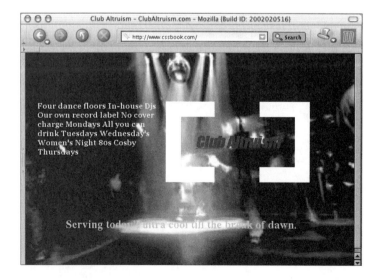

Figure 4.4

Club Altruim's splash page is up to get down.

Column Layouts

Now that we have covered the entrance to your Web site, let's talk about the pages that will captivate your audience with content: column layouts. Web pages have been designed into columns for as long as HTML tables have allowed Web designers to do so. It's the effect of print design of newspapers and magazines being brought over to a new media. We carry over visual techniques to carry multiple design and informational elements into a limited amount of space.

In traditional Web design, HTML tables are used for column layouts. In the following examples, the two- and three-column layouts are accomplished through the power of CSS.

Two-Column Layout

As always, let's start with the content. For this case, we will use a Web document that describes the Web development mailing list, Babble. Listing 4.10 is the content structured with HTML markup. Figure 4.5 shows the unstyled content as a browser might render it.

> **Note**
>
> The W3C has a multi-column layout in their CSS3 working draft (see `http://www.w3.org/1999/06/WD-css3-multicol-19990623`). If it were to be finalized and then properly implemented in the major browsers, then this new method would be the "correct" way to do these types of layouts. Until then, we are stuck with other ways to pull off multi-column layouts.

Listing 4.10   Structured Markup for Babble

```
<!DOCTYPE html PUBLIC "-//W3C//DTD XHTML 1.0 Transitional//EN"
"http://www.w3.org/TR/xhtml1/DTD/xhtml1-transitional.dtd">
<html xmlns="http://www.w3.org/1999/xhtml"
xml:lang="en" lang="en">
  <head>
    <title>
      Welcome to Babble List
    </title>
    <meta http-equiv="Content-Type" content="text/html;
charset=iso-8859-1" />
  </head>
  <body>
    <h3>
      Babble List
    </h3>
    <p>
      Navigation
    </p>
    <ul>
      <li>
        <a href="#maincontent">
          Main Content
        </a>
```

continues

Listing 4.10   Structured Markup for Babble   (Continued)

```
      </li>
      <li>
        <a href="#search">
          Search Archives
        </a>
      </li>
      <li>
        <a href="#bob">
          Best of Babble
        </a>
      </li>
      <li>
        <a href="#standards">
          Standards
        </a>
      </li>
      <li>
        <a href="#signup">
          Sign-up
        </a>
      </li>
      <li>
        <a href="#copyright">
          Copyright
        </a>
      </li>
    </ul>
    <h4>
      <a name="maincontent">
        Welcome
      </a>
    </h4>
    <p>
        This is the Web site for the mailing list, Babble. Geared to advanced Web
design issues, the site includes a lively exchange of information, resources,
theories, and practices of designers and developers. Our overall goal is to hone
our skills and share our visions of where this new medium is going.
    </p>
    <p>
        Although many try to define it, Web design has no universally fixed defi-
nition; therefore, the subjects we cover here can range from usability, new tech-
niques, copy writing, project/client management, back-end, programming, and, of
course, design. I guess you could say the definition is as diverse as we are.
    </p>
    <h4>
```

```
      Keeping Quality
   </h4>
   <p>
      The discussions on Babble, contrary to our name, are about quality over
quantity. Most of us are busy working in the field of Web design, so we don't
have much time to pontificate obscure ideas or read treatises on the latest new
browser. Please take into account our guidelines before adding your thoughts to
the discussion. Being well-versed in our guidelines ensures that we continue the
conversation and exploration of our field rather than another email we delete
from our Inbox.
   </p>
   <ul>
     <li>
        Use viable and succinct subject lines that reflect the content of your
posting.
     </li>
     <li>
        Please do your best to post only in reference to Web design issues.
     </li>
     <li>
        Do not make extraneous posts, such as copying and pasting articles from
Web pages, sending repetitive posts, HTML code, and/or other long messages. If
need be, please create a Web page on which to place this information and then
post the URL to the list.
     </li>
     <li>
        Please limit e-mail "signatures" or "sig files" to 4 lines or less.
     </li>
     <li>
        If you are sending HTML e-mail to this list, please discontinue to do
so. If you don't know whether you are or not, check your e-mail client's manual
or help documents to become aware. This precaution will help get your messages
read by the Babble community.
     </li>
   </ul>
   <p>
      By following these guidelines, you will be ensuring that your messages
will create dialog and will be enjoyed by the Babble community as a whole.
   </p>
   <h4>
      How to Join
   </h4>
   <form method="get" action="/subscribe/highfivebabble">
     <p>
You can start the subscription process by typing in your e-mail address in the
form below. You will be asked to confirm the subscription request by entering
        <input type="text" name="user" value="your email address here" />
```

continues

Listing 4.10   Structured Markup for Babble   (Continued)

```
          and then pressing the
          <input type="submit" name="Click here to join highfivebabble" />
          button.
      </p>
      <p>
          Don't be confused if you get an e-mail from Yahoo! Groups regarding the
list. The Babble List is powered by
          <a href="http://www.babblelist.com/">
            Yahoo! Groups
          </a>
          which makes my life administrating the list so much easier while also
providing a slew of cool features for its members.
      </p>
    </form>
    <h4>
        Privacy
    </h4>
    <p>
        The list is powered by Yahoo! Groups, which maintains the privacy policy
used for the list. Below are the list of questions answered on their privacy
policy page.
    </p>
    <ul>
      <li>
        <a href="info/privacy.html#1" target="_new">
          What personally identifiable information is collected from you?
        </a>
      </li>
      <li>
        <a href="info/privacy.html#2" target="_new">
          What cookies are and how they are used?
</a>
      </li>
      <li>
        <a href="info/privacy.html#3" target="_new">
          Who is collecting the information?
        </a>
      </li>
      <li>
        <a href="info/privacy.html#4" target="_new">
          How the information is used?
        </a>
      </li>
      <li>
        <a href="info/privacy.html#5" target="_new">
```

```
          With whom the information may be shared?
        </a>
      </li>
      <li>
        <a href="info/privacy.html#6" target="_new">
          What choices are available to you regarding collection, use, and dis-
tribution of your information?
        </a>
      </li>
      <li>
        <a href="info/privacy.html#7" target="_new">
          How you can access, update, or delete your information?
        </a>
      </li>
      <li>
        <a href="info/privacy.html#8" target="_new">
          What security procedures are in place to protect the loss, misuse, or
alteration of the information?
        </a>
      </li>
      <li>
        <a href="info/privacy.html#9" target="_new">
          How eGroups protects children's privacy?
        </a>
      </li>
      <li>
        <a href="info/privacy.html#10" target="_new">
          What else you should know about your online privacy?
        </a>
      </li>
    </ul>
    <h4>
      Thanks
    </h4>
    <p>
      The Babble List would be nothing without its sense of community. A very
special thanks to all the members both present and gone.
    </p>
    <h5>
      <a name="search">
        Search Archives
      </a>
    </h5>
    <form name="searchform" action="research" method="get" target="_new"
style="margin: 0;">
      <input type="hidden" name="type" value="query" />
```

continues

Listing 4.10   Structured Markup for Babble   (Continued)

```
        <input type="hidden" name="where" value="/group/highfivebabble/
messagesearch" />
        <input type="text" name="query" value="" size="20" />
        <input type="submit" value="go" />
    </form>
    <p style="padding-top: 0; margin-top: 0;">
      Look for past posts about
      <a href="http://groups.yahoo.com/group/highfivebabble/messagesearch?query=
      css"target="_new">
        CSS</a>,
      <a href="http://groups.yahoo.com/group/highfivebabble/messagesearch?query=
      Flash" target="_new">
        Flash</a>,
      <a href="http://groups.yahoo.com/group/highfivebabble/messagesearch?query=
      browser+bugs" target="_new">
        browser bugs</a>,
      <a href="http://groups.yahoo.com/group/highfivebabble/messagesearch?query=
      Mac+resolution"target="_new">
        Mac resolution</a>, and more.
    </p>
    <h5>
      <a name="bob">
        Best of Babble
      </a>
    </h5>
    <ul>
      <li>
        <a href="http://groups.yahoo.com/group/highfivebabble/message/5106"
title="Finding better ways of doing the same old, same old" target="_new">
          Mother's Tools
        </a>
      </li>
      <li>
        <a href="http://groups.yahoo.com/group/highfivebabble/message/5134"
title="Best uses for Flash" target="_new">
          Site Navigation in Flash
        </a>
      </li>
      <li>
        <a href="http://groups.yahoo.com/group/highfivebabble/message/3503"
title="Don't look at me. I just work here" target="_new">
          Someone here hates the Web?
        </a>
      </li>
      <li>
```

```
            <a href="http://groups.yahoo.com/group/highfivebabble/message/2120"
title="Should one do speculative work to land the client?" target="_new">
            Request for Proposal Deliverables
        </a>
      </li>
    </ul>
    <h5>
      <a name="standards">
        Meeting Standards
      </a>
    </h5>
    <p>
      Psst! Bet you didn't you know this page contains valid
      <a
href="http://validator.w3.org/check?uri=http://babblelist.com/index.html" tar-
get="_new">
        XHTML
      </a>
      and
      <a href="http://jigsaw.w3.org/css-validator/validator?uri=http://www.bab-
blelist.com/babblelist.css" target="_new">
        CSS</a>?
      <a href="http://www.Webstandards.org/upgrade/" target="_new">
        Eh?</a>
    </p>


    <h5>
      <a name="signup">
        You're Invited
      </a>
    </h5>
    <p>
      To join the Babble List, type your e-mail address in the form below and
submit it.
    </p>
    <p>
      That's all you have to do to subscribe. Hope to hear from you on the list!
    </p>
    <form method="get" action="subscribe/highfivebabble" target="_new">
      <input type="text" name="user" value="e-mail
address" size="20" />
      <input type="submit" name="Click here to join
highfivebabble" value="Subscribe" />
    </form>
```

continues

Listing 4.10   Structured Markup for Babble   (Continued)

```
    <h5>
      <a name="copyright">
        The Usual Notice
      </a>
    </h5>
    <p>
      All contents of this Web site are copyright &copy; 2000-2002
      <a href="http://www.christopher.org/">
        Christopher Schmitt</a>.
    </p>

  </body>
</html>
```

Figure 4.5

Before the two-column layout, there was one column.

The first step in our two-column layout is to remove the page navigation, but we also will be applying a logo. We will need to remove the headline "Babble List."

To remove the page navigation, I wrapped a `div` element with a class attribute of `"nav"` around the table of contents and its header (see Listing 4.11).

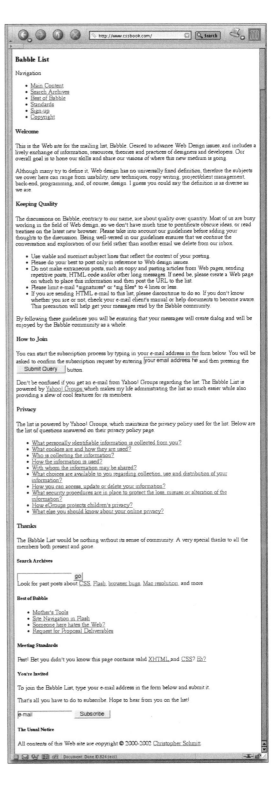

Listing 4.11   Removing the Page Navigation

```
<div class="nav">
  <p>
    Navigation
  </p>
  <ul>
    <li>
      <a href="#maincontent">
        Main Content
      </a>
    </li>
    <li>
      <a href="#search">
        Search Archives
      </a>
    </li>
    <li>
      <a href="#bob">
        Best of Babble
      </a>
    </li>
    <li>
      <a href="#standards">
        Standards
      </a>
    </li>
    <li>
      <a href="#signup">
        Sign-up
      </a>
    </li>
    <li>
      <a href="#copyright">
        Copyright
      </a>
    </li>
  </ul>
</div>
```

Then I applied the following CSS rule (see Listing 4.12) in a separate CSS, which is linked from the head of the Web document.

Listing 4.12   CSS Rule

```
h1, .nav {
  display: none;
}
```

The secret to the two-column layout is to manipulate the padding of the page to create a gutter of white space on the left side and then position the second column.

To achieve this effect, let's refine the margin and padding of the body (see Listing 4.13).

Listing 4.13   Refining the Margin and Padding

```
Body {
  margin: 200px 0 0 0;
  padding: 0 7% 0 235px;
}
```

For the margins in the body, we have the top coming down by 200 pixels. This will make enough room for the logo graphic to be shown through. The padding is set for the right side to have a width of 7% of the `html` element's width; the width of the left side is set to 235 pixels. The space provided by setting the left padding length of 235 pixels allows us to slide a second column into its place.

With the margin and padding set, we can add in the logo for the site, color, and font styles to flesh out the CSS rule for the body (see Listing 4.14 and Figure 4.6).

Listing 4.14   Adding the Logo

```
Body {
  margin: 200px 0 0 0;
  padding: 0 7% 0 235px;
  background-image: url("hed.gif");
  background-repeat: no-repeat;
  color: #030;
  background-color: #fff;
  font-family: Georgia, Times, serif;
  font-size: 1em;
}
```

Now the main column is set. Let's work on making the second column a reality.

Starting the Second Column Process

The first step in the second column process is to mark off the content in the main column that will be placed in the second column. We do this with the `div` element, with a `"sidecol"` for the value of a class attribute (see Listing 4.15).

Figure 4.6

The first of two columns takes shape.

Listing 4.15   Marking the Second Column Content

```html
<div class="sidecol">
  <h5>
    Search Archives
  </h5>
  <form name="searchform" action="research" method="get">
    <input type="hidden" name="type" value="query" />
    <input type="hidden" name="where" value="/group/highfivebabble/messagesearch" />
    <input type="text" name="query" value="" size="20" />
    <input type="submit" value="go" />
  </form>
  <p>
    Look for past posts about
    <a
href="http://groups.yahoo.com/group/highfivebabble/messagesearch?query=css">
      CSS
    </a>
    ,
    <a
href="http://groups.yahoo.com/group/highfivebabble/messagesearch?query=Flash">
      Flash
    </a>
    ,
    <a
```

```
href="http://groups.yahoo.com/group/highfivebabble/messagesearch?query=browser+bug
s">
        browser bugs
      </a>
      ,
      <a
href="http://groups.yahoo.com/group/highfivebabble/messagesearch?query=Mac+
resolution">
        Mac resolution
      </a>
      , and more.
    </p>
  <h5>
    Best of Babble
  </h5>
  <ul>
    <li>
      <a href="http://groups.yahoo.com/group/highfivebabble/message/5106"
title="Finding better ways of doing the same old, same old">
        Mother's Tools
      </a>
    </li>
    <li>
      <a href="http://groups.yahoo.com/group/highfivebabble/message/5134"
title="Best uses for Flash">
        Site Navigation in Flash
      </a>
    </li>
    <li>
      <a href="http://groups.yahoo.com/group/highfivebabble/message/3503"
title="Don't look at me. I just work here">
        Someone here hates the Web?
      </a>
    </li>
    <li>
      <a href="http://groups.yahoo.com/group/highfivebabble/message/2120"
title="Should one do speculative work to land the client?">
        Request for Proposal Deliverables
      </a>
    </li>
  </ul>
  <h5>
    Meeting Standards
  </h5>
  <p>
    Psst! Bet you didn't you know this page contains valid
  <a href="http://validator.w3.org/check?uri=http://babblelist.com/index.html">
```

continues

Listing 4.15   Marking the Second Column Content   (Continued)

```
    XHTML
  </a>
  and
  <a href="http://jigsaw.w3.org/css-validator/validator?uri=http://www.
babblelist.com/babblelist.css">
    CSS
  </a>
  ?
  <a href="http://www.Webstandards.org/upgrade/">
    Eh?
  </a>
</p>

<h5>
  You're Invited
</h5>
<p>
  To join the Babble List, type your e-mail address in the form below and
submit it.
  </p>
  <p>
  That's all you have to do to subscribe. Hope to hear from you on the list!
  </p>

  <form method="get" action="subscribe/highfivebabble">
    <input type="text" name="user" value="e-mail
address" size="20" />
    <input type="submit" name="Click here to join
highfivebabble" value="Subscribe" />
  </form>

  <h5>
    The Usual Notice
  </h5>
  <p>
    All contents of this Web site are copyright &copy; 2000-2002
    <a href="http://www.christopher.org/">
      Christopher Schmitt
    </a>
    .
  </p>
</div>
```

Now we apply a CSS rule that will raise the content higher on the z-index and position it on the left-hand side of the main column (see Listing 4.16).

Listing 4.16   Appling a CSS Rule

```
.sidecol {
  position: absolute;
  z-index: 5;
  width: 191px;
  top: 200px;
  left: 0;
  margin: 0 22px 0 22px;
  padding:  0 22px 0 22px3%;
}
```

We set the width of the second column to 191 pixels and use the padding sides to make small gutters. Now we can add some font styles to finish (see Listing 4.17). Because this is going to be a second column, I want to distinguish it by setting the column's type to a sans-serif font.

Listing 4.17   Adding Style to the Text

```
.sidecol {
  position: absolute;
  z-index: 5;
  width: 191px;
  top: 0;
  left: 0;
  margin: 0;
  padding:  0 22px 0 22px;
  font-family: Verdana, Helvetica, Arial, sans-serif;
  font-size: .9em;
}
```

With the left column in place, the overall two-column layout is now in place (see Figure 4.7). Let's tidy up the design a bit by polishing some of the details.

Figure 4.7

The second column appears.

We can get rid of the invisible padding that comes with the `form` tag by setting the padding and margin to 0. Then we can get the headers of our copy to rest upon the paragraphs that they correspond to by setting the bottom padding and margins to 0. For paragraphs, we will eliminate the padding and margins on the top by zeroing them out as well (see Listing 4.18 and Figure 4.8). We need to manually zero these properties because horizontal padding and margins do not shrink like padding and margins on the vertical sides of block elements (see `http://www.w3.org/TR/REC-CSS2/box.html#collapsing-margins`).

In testing, I found out that Netscape's Navigator 6+ has padding to the first header in the left column correctly. I can set that padding and margin to 0 by adding the `".sidecol h5"` selector as an additional selector for the rule set used for p.

Listing 4.18   Zeroing Padding and Margins for Various Block-Level Elements

```
form {
  padding: 0;
  margin: 0;
}

h1, h2, h3, h4, h5, h6 {
  padding-bottom: 0;
  margin-bottom: 0;
}

.sidecol h5, p {
  padding-top: 0;
  margin-top: 0;
}
```

Figure 4.8

Finessing the leading through padding and margins.

Instead of having the two columns be level, it's possible to raise the left column a bit to give the layout a more dynamic presence. With a few keystrokes in a CSS rule, I change the margin on the left-hand column from 200 pixels to 120 pixels (see Listing 4.19).

Listing 4.19   Raising the Left Column a Bit

```
.sidecol {
  position: absolute;
  z-index: 5;
  width: 190px;
  top: 0;
  left: 0;
  margin: 120px 0 0 0;
  padding:  0 3% 0 3%;
  font-family: Verdana, Helvetica, Arial, sans-serif;
  font-size: .9em;
}
```

Figure 4.9 shows our two-column masterpiece.

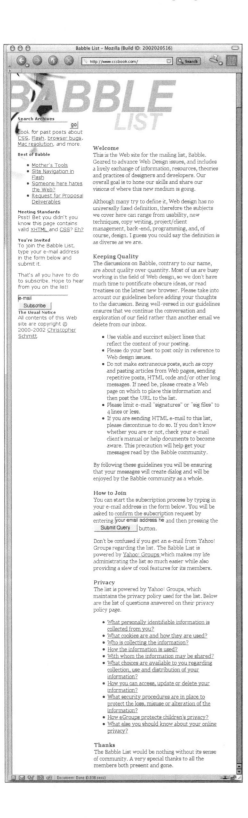

Figure 4.9

Final two-column
layout.

Using the Float Property

Another way to tackle a two-column layout is to use the float property in CSS. This method is demonstrated in the *A List Apart* article, "From Web Hacks to Web Standards: A Designer's Journey." The article showcases an elegant two-column execution in its own right (see `http://www.alistapart.com/stories/journey/`).

Three-Column Layout

For this example, we will deconstruct Mark Newhouse's three-column layout, which works in Netscape 4—no small accomplishment. It contains the typical page elements, such as a page header and footer (`http://realworldstyle.com/`). Listing 4.20 shows the initial code, and Figure 4.10 shows the code rendered in a Web browser.

Listing 4.20 The Markup for the Three-Column Layout

```
<!DOCTYPE HTML PUBLIC "-//W3C//DTD HTML 4.0 Transitional//EN"
      "http://www.w3.org/TR/REC-html40/loose.dtd">
<html>
  <head>
    <title>
      Three column layout
    </title>
  </head>
  <body>

    <h1>
      Main Header
    </h1>
    <p>
      A witty tagline goes here
    </p>

    <h3>
      Left Column
    </h3>
    <p>
      Navigation:
    </p>
```

continues

Listing 4.20   The Markup for the Three-Column Layout   (Continued)

```
<ul>
  <li>
    First page
  </li>
  <li>
    Second page
  </li>
  <li>
    Third page
  </li>
  <li>
    Fourth page
  </li>
  <li>
    Fifth page
  </li>
</ul>

<h4>
  Right Column
</h4>
<p>
  Lorem ipsum dolor sit amet, comsect quis nostrud exercitation ullam corp
consquet, vel illum dolore eu fugat execeptur sisint occaecat cupiri tat non. Nam
liber tempor cum soluta nobis. Temporibud autem quinsud et aur delectus ut ayt
prefer endis dolorib. At ille pellit sensar luptae epicur semp in indutial
genelation.
  </p>

<h2>
  Center column
</h2>
<p>
  Sed ut perspiciatis, unde omnis iste natus error sit voluptatem
accusantium doloremque laudantium, totam rem aperiam eaque ipsa, quae ab illo
inventore veritatis et quasi architecto beatae vitae dicta sunt, explicabo. nemo
enim ipsam voluptatem, quia voluptas sit, aspernatur aut odit aut fugit, sed quia
consequuntur magni dolores eos, qui ratione voluptatem sequi nesciunt, neque
porro quisquam est, qui dolorem ipsum, quia dolor sit, amet, consectetur, adip-
isci velit, sed quia non numquam eius modi tempora incidunt, ut labore et dolore
magnam aliquam quaerat voluptatem. ut enim ad minima veniam, quis nostrum
exercitationem ullam corporis suscipit laboriosam, nisi ut aliquid ex ea commodi
consequatur? quis autem vel eum iure reprehenderit, qui in ea voluptate velit
esse, quam nihil molestiae consequatur, vel illum, qui dolorem eum fugiat, quo
voluptas nulla pariatur?
```

```
    </p>

    Copyright notice could go here
    <a href="mailto:iblog@mac.com">
      Email Us
    </a>

  </body>
</html>
```

Figure 4.10

Before there was a three-column layout there was content, and it was good.

The first part is to wrap the sections of the Web document with `divs`: the header, the footer, the left column, the center column, and the right column (see Listing 4.21).

Listing 4.21   Wrapping with `divs`

```
<div id="header">
  <h1>
    Main Header
  </h1>
  <p>
    A witty tagline goes here
  </p>
</div>
<div id="leftcol">
  <h3>
    Left Column
  </h3>
  <p>
    Navigation:
  </p>
  <ul>
    <li>
      First page
    </li>
    <li>
      Second page
    </li>
    <li>
      Third page
    </li>
    <li>
      Fourth page
    </li>
    <li>
      Fifth page
    </li>
  </ul>
</div>
<div id="rightcol">
  <h4>
    Right Column
  </h4>
  <p>
    Lorem ipsum dolor sit amet, comsect quis nostrud exercitation ullam corp
consquet, vel illum dolore eu fugat execeptur sisint occaecat cupiri tat non. Nam
liber tempor cum soluta nobis. Temporibud autem quinsud et aur delectus ut ayt
prefer endis dolorib. At ille pellit sensar luptae epicur semp in indutial
genelation.
  </p>
</div>
```

```
<div id="content">
  <h2>
    Center column
  </h2>
  <p>
    Sed ut perspiciatis, unde omnis iste natus error sit voluptatem accusantium
doloremque laudantium, totam rem aperiam eaque ipsa, quae ab illo inventore
veritatis et quasi architecto beatae vitae dicta sunt, explicabo. nemo enim
ipsam voluptatem, quia voluptas sit, aspernatur aut odit aut fugit, sed quia
consequuntur magni dolores eos, qui ratione voluptatem sequi nesciunt, neque
porro quisquam est, qui dolorem ipsum, quia dolor sit, amet, consectetur,
adipisci velit, sed quia non numquam eius modi tempora incidunt, ut labore et
dolore magnam aliquam quaerat voluptatem. ut enim ad minima veniam, quis nostrum
exercitationem ullam corporis suscipit laboriosam, nisi ut aliquid ex ea commodi
consequatur? quis autem vel eum iure reprehenderit, qui in ea voluptate velit
esse, quam nihil molestiae consequatur, vel illum, qui dolorem eum fugiat, quo
voluptas nulla pariatur?
  </p>
</div>
<div id="footer">
  Copyright notice could go here
  <a href="mailto:mail@csscook.com">
    Email Us
  </a>
</div>
```

Next, we set up the header CSS rules. We just add a one-pixel line to separate it from the columns (see Listing 4.22).

Listing 4.22   Setting Up the Header Rules

```
#header {
  margin-left: 10px;
  color: #000;
  border-bottom: 1px solid #333;
}
```

Next, we work on the columns. To achieve the three-column effect, we work on compartmentalizing the page into three areas.

The left column is set with a width of 150 pixels (see Listing 4.23). It's positioned flush to the left, but padded 10 pixels on the left to achieve a gutter.

Listing 4.23   Working on the Left Column

```
#leftcol {
  position: absolute;
  left: 0;
  width: 150px;
  margin-left: 10px;
  margin-top: 0px;
  color: #000;
  padding: 3px;
}
```

The center column doesn't specify a width. It does have a right margin of 25% and a left margin of 165 pixels. The content in the left and right columns is fixed to a specific width, but the main content can still expand to the size of the viewport (see Listing 4.24).

Listing 4.24   Working on the Center Column

```
#content {
  margin: 0px 25% 0 165px;
  padding: 3px;
  color: #000;
}
```

The right column slides into the right. The width is 140 pixels, which is 25 pixels less than what is left over by the right margin of the content (see Listing 4.25). In addition, there's the left margin, which increases the space between the columns. (There's also a margin of three pixels to all sides of column.)

Listing 4.25   Working on the Right Column

```
#rightcol {
  position: absolute;
  left: 80%;
  width: 140px;
  padding-left: 10px;
  z-index: 3;
  color: #000;
  padding: 3px;
}
```

Figure 4.11 shows the three columns that we just created.

Figure 4.11

Three-column
layout in all
its glory.

The Footer

The next step is the footer. In his example, Newhouse put elements
aligned to the left and to the right. This effect can be achieved by using
two span elements and a couple of CSS rules. First, let's set up the
structured markup (see Listing 4.26).

Listing 4.26   Setting Up the Markup

```
<div id="footer">
  <span class="date">
    Copyright notice could go here
  </span>
  <span class="contact">
    <a href="mailto:emailaddress">
      Email Us
    </a>
  </span>
</div>
```

Listing 4.27 shows the CSS rules for the footer.

Listing 4.27   CSS Footer Rules

```
#footer {
  clear: both;
  width: 95%;
  margin: 10px;
  text-align: center;
```

continues

Listing 4.27   CSS Footer Rules   (Continued)

```
    padding: 3px;
    border-top: 1px solid #333;
    color: #000;
}
```

To achieve the effect of the date on the left and the contact on the right, Newhouse used the `float` property (see Listing 4.28). The `float` property is similar to the `align` attribute often used in `table` and `img` tags. The rules that govern the rendering of content that will be floated state to move the element as high and as far as possible to the specified direction (left or right).

For More Information

For a more detailed explanation of the `float` property rules, check out *Eric Meyer's Cascading Style Sheets 2.0 Programmer's Reference* (McGraw-Hill Professional Publishing, 2001).

Listing 4.28   Using the `float` Property

```
#footer .date {
  float: left;
  text-align: left;
}

#footer .contact {
  float: right;
  text-align: right;
}
```

Figure 4.12 shows the result.

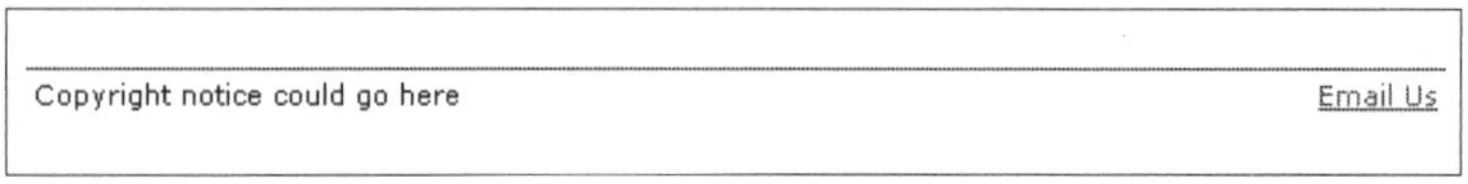

Copyright notice could go here   Email Us

Figure 4.12

Aligning left and right items inside the footer.

While we are floating the elements, Newhouse uses the `text-align` attribute to ensure that the text inside the `span` elements aligns properly.

The Final Touches

After setting up the page layout, Newhouse sets the design to his taste
(Listing 4.29).

Listing 4.29   Adjusting the Design

```
html, body {
  margin: 0;
  padding: 0;
  background-color: #fff;
  color: #000;
}

p, a {
  font-family: Verdana;
}

h1, h2, h3, h4, h5, h6 {
  font-family: Georgia;
  margin-top: 0px;
}

#leftcol p, #rightcol p {
  font-size: 11px;
}
```

Now that the page is set up, there are some minor tweaks to make the
page ready for delivery for a couple of browsers.

To make sure the bottom scrollbar in Macintosh Internet Explorer does not
show up, the `html` element has the width set to 97% (see Listing 4.30).

Listing 4.30   Setting the Width

```
html {
  width: 97%;
}
```

Netscape Navigator 4 has an infamous bug. When a user resizes a
browser, the CSS rules appear to lose their hold on elements in the Web
document. The only solution is to reload the page. Setting up a notice in
the Web site asking users to reload their pages if they use Navigator 4 and
resize their Web browser is not a viable solution.

The solution is to use a bit of JavaScript that will automatically refresh the page if the user resizes the browser window (see Listing 4.31).

The great part about this solution is that Navigator 4's CSS engine uses JavaScript to render the styles. So, if the user disables JavaScript, there's no reason to worry about the style taking affect after the user resizes the window; the design from the CSS won't show.

Listing 4.31   The JavaScript Solution

```
<script type="text/javascript" language="Javascript">
<!--

//reloads the window if Nav4 resized
function MM_reloadPage(init) {
  if (init==true) with (navigator) {
    if ((appName=="Netscape") &&
(parseInt(appVersion)==4)) {
      document.MM_pgW=innerWidth;
      document.MM_pgH=innerHeight;
      onresize=MM_reloadPage;
    }
  }
  else if (innerWidth!=document.MM_pgW ||
innerHeight!=document.MM_pgH) history.go(0);
}

MM_reloadPage(true);

//-->
</script>
```

With that, we wrap up a three-column layout. While we used absolute positioning to primarily achieve our multicolumn effects, here are some resources that take the float property and create multicolumn layouts. These sites are excellent learning examples if you take the time to deconstruct the CSS on your own:

- **The Noodle Incident's Little Boxes** —http://www. thenoodleincident.com/tutorials/box_lesson/boxes.html
- **Glish.com's CSS Layout Techniques**—http://www. glish.com/css/

For More Information

Here are some reading recommendations on how to write or improve your writing for the Web delivery:

- "Be Succinct! (Writing for the Web)" by Jakob Nielsen (useit.com, March 15, 1997). Available from the Internet at http://www.useit.com/alertbox/9703b.html.

- *Hot Text: Web Writing That Works by* Jonathan Price and Lisa Price (New Riders, 2002).

- "Language: The Ultimate User Interface" by Julia Hayden (*A List Apart*, 2000). Available from the Internet at http://www.alistapart.com/stories/ultimate/.

- *Net Words: Creating High-Impact Online Copy* by Nick Usborne (McGraw-Hill Professional Publishing, 2001).

CSS for Dynamic HTML

When CSS, JavaScript, and the Document Object Model (DOM) are used together, they are known as Dynamic HTML, or DHTML for short. In this chapter, we will talk with Steven Champeon, an expert on the subject of DHTML. Then we will move onto examples of incorporating DHTML elements into your Web pages.

Steven Champeon on Dynamic HTML

Steven Champeon is the Chief Technical Officer at hesketh.com/inc., a Web design and development shop in Raleigh, North Carolina. He co-wrote *Building Dynamic HTML GUIs* (Hungry Minds, 1999), which was an attempt to show the way toward a cross-browser and cross-platform approach to building Web applications. Champeon has also contributed to or edited a dozen other books mostly related to XML, Web design, and theory. He runs Webdesign-L (see `http://www.Webdesign-l.com`), a mailing list community for Web designers and developers.

Steven
Champeon

Christopher Schmitt: What is DHTML?

Steven Champeon: DHTML is an acronym for Dynamic HTML, as well as a catchall term for the interaction between HTML (or XHTML, or custom XML), Cascading Style Sheets, scripting languages, and the Document Object Model.

In less acronymic terms, DHTML is the combination of technologies that enables the dynamic construction and manipulation of Web documents, and, depending on how you look at it, of client-side Web applications.

Part of the problem with DHTML as a name is that it got a very bad rap during the heyday of the browser wars between Netscape and Microsoft—where each vendor had its own object model, and building cross–browser-compatible applications was a nightmare of compromises, workarounds, and lowest common denominator solutions.

However, due to the ongoing efforts of groups like the Web Standards Project, among others, modern browsers now have excellent support for the DOM recommendations published by the W3C. This support makes it possible, perhaps for the first time, to build powerful and dynamic client-side Web applications as well as to augment more traditional sites with dynamic components—such as the ubiquitous DHTML pop-up navigation menus or image-swapping routines, for example. DHTML has a bit of a split personality as a result: Some people think of the old nightmare days, while others take advantage of the new stability and features of the current implementations.

CS: What are some of the things you like about DHTML?

SC: I personally like JavaScript and find it a clean and powerful language that's getting better all the time. To get anything done in a client-side Web application, you need some sort of logic, and that's what JavaScript provides. The DOM provides the programmatic interface between JavaScript and the HTML document and style sheets so that you can create and manipulate documents on the fly, handle interaction with the user, and generally provide a far richer experience than static documents alone can provide.

There's a clean separation between a document's structure and meaning (as reflected in its markup), its presentation (as defined in style sheets), and its behavior (as defined in its scripting logic).

However, there is a great degree of integration to it as well. For the most part, things are pretty tightly bound to each other—styles can be defined using an element's ID, which might also be used by scripts to determine other characteristics on-the-fly.

CS: What are some of the challenges with authoring DHTML?

SC: Well, the down side is that you do have to become familiar with all three—or four, if you count the DOM and JavaScript as separate—technologies and their unique syntax and approach to their function.

For the novice, this can be a bit much at times. It's tough enough to know HTML and CSS—adding scripting into the mix can be too much. But fortunately, not everyone needs to provide dynamic logic on their Web sites, and many who do have programmers around who can do custom work when necessary.

The flip side of this is that many so-called WYSIWYG editors feature commonly used DHTML routines that can be associated with your pages or sites, such as *mouseover* graphic swaps and dynamic navigation. But for the most part, if you're building custom applications, you need to understand the fundamentals behind scripting and how to structure your documents to work best with CSS and the behavioral logic you're developing.

CS: What would you recommend for a person wanting to learn JavaScript who hasn't had any programming experience?

SC: I'd recommend that person learn a simpler programming language first. Though JavaScript is actually very powerful and full-featured, its nature as a primarily browser-interpreted language makes for some complex environmental issues that you don't see running something from a UNIX command line. But then, few people nowadays have a UNIX command line if they don't have programming experience, so maybe JavaScript in the browser isn't *that* bad of a place to learn. The trick is understanding that JavaScript executing in the browser is only part of the picture—the rest includes HTML, CSS, the DOM. And JavaScript itself is just the programming core language; it's the DOM (or DOMs) that make it such a powerful environment for dynamic content.

CS: **Where can a person learn more about the DOM?**

SC: The Mozilla project has some great reference/tutorial material (see `http://www.mozilla.org/docs/dom/`). That's a great place to start.

CS: **What would you recommend for people wanting to learn how to program in general and/or learn more about DHTML?**

SC: Just dive right in! If you have a text editor and a browser, you have all you need. You don't need a compiler, an IDE (integrated development environment), or any fancy, expensive tools—you just need a browser and a text editor. It doesn't hurt to have a friend on tap when you need help, either. There are many books available that introduce you to the basics of programming: loops, variables, arrays, conditionals, and so forth.

Just pick one you like, based on the tone and depth of the writing and geared toward the speed at which you intend to proceed, and dive in.

There are many mailing lists and forums full of people who can help you, too, though they all vary widely in terms of how willing their members are to help neophytes. So be sure to read up on the guidelines for each before you join, and then lurk (read without posting) for a while to get a sense of the tone of the place so that you can find out how much work you'll need to do beforehand to avoid getting flamed.

Most folks online are friendly and willing to help, provided you've shown that you've tried a few different things and failed and aren't just looking for a handout. There's a deeper reason for this reluctance to help people who haven't done their homework, though, and that is that people recognize the value of actually doing something as an important part of any learning experience. If you haven't tried something yourself, any advice they might give is less likely to take hold in your head. Remember: Their time is worth just as much as your time, so respect that when asking for their assistance.

CS: **What does the future hold for DHTML?**

SC: The future of DHTML—or whatever you want to call it in order to avoid the taint that comes from the early days—is very bright. The support for standard DOM interfaces, XHTML, and CSS has never been better, the popularity of JavaScript is unquestionable, and the demands of modern Web applications are well handled by dynamic, client-side technologies like those we've been discussing. We'll see a shift toward more and more powerful, complex, and semantically meaning-ful markup, presentation, and behavior, as more and more Web devel-opers realize the power of the DOM and related technologies.

CS: **What do you mean by semantically meaningful markup, presentation, and behavior?**

SC: Well, *semantic markup* is markup that gives an indication of the meaning—as opposed to the intended display—of the content it contains. For example, the address element in HTML is supposed to contain an address, the title element contains the document title, and so on. With XML, you can create your own markup languages for whatever purpose you have in mind.

By *presentation*, I mean the logic (style sheet rules, for example) used by the browser when rendering the document. It can also mean the output of a transformation from one document format to another, such as XML into XHTML using XSLT or some other transformation language—such as those used in content management systems and database-driven sites poured into templates. However, I prefer to think of it in the pure, end user sense of that which may be cleanly separated from a document's structure and content.

Behavior is simply how the document behaves—whether by way of functionality hard-wired into browsers (such as the way that clicking on a link takes you to another page) or scripting logic that handles user input and interactivity.

CS: **What name would you give to DHTML if you couldn't use the "DHTML," "Dynamic," or "HTML"?**

SC: We've come a long way since the days when DHTML was just another advanced technology apart from basic HTML. Now, it's the whole platform—you can either use it to its fullest, or not, depending on your needs. But it should no longer be considered apart from the rest of Web design. In my mind, DHTML *is* the Web—a dynamic, powerful platform for enabling document delivery, presentation, and interactivity. To distinguish between the older, more proprietary, and non-standard DHTML implementations from the new world of stan-dard W3C DOM and CSS implementations, I've begun to refer to the latter as Dynamic XHTML.

Now that we know about DHTML and about where it's going, we are going to follow Champeon's advice and dive on in. The following examples will show you how to use CSS, HTML, and the DOM to create more robust Web pages.

Slight of Hand: Dynamic HTML in Action

One of the basic tricks with JavaScript, CSS, and HTML is hiding and showing portions of a Web document at the click of the mouse. Here is a little demonstration of how it works.

First, Listing 5.1 sets up the content.

Listing 5.1   Setting up the Content

```
<p>We worked all week on the proposal. We even included a discount on the
ceramic coffee mugs with a picture of the company mascot. If you want to know
more about the proposal, please follow <a href="#hiddenagenda">this link</a>.
Thank you for your time.</p>
<p id="hiddenagenda" >Hello, I'm glad you are taking the time to read this pro-
posal of amazing consequences. Our company is looking to gain ground with our
various lines of pie crusts. Now with the marketing idea to give away ceramic
coffee mugs with a picture of the company mascot, we will surely get the brand
name recognition we've always wanted.</p>
```

Currently, the Web document will display both paragraphs (see Figure 5.1), and the link in the first paragraph will jump the user to the second paragraph by way of targeting to the anchor.

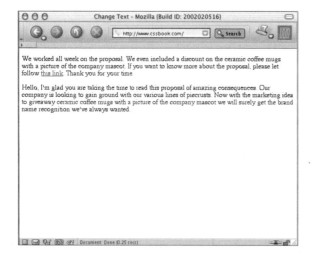

Figure 5.1

Two paragraphs of text.

Now let's add a bit of CSS that will go, of course, between the head element tags of our Web document (see Listing 5.2).

Listing 5.2   Adding a Bit of CSS

```
<style type="text/css">
#hiddenagenda {
  display: none;
}
</style>
```

Now when we view this Web page with a browser that can handle the
CSS, the second paragraph won't be visible (see Figure 5.2).

Figure 5.2

We can see only one
paragraph now.

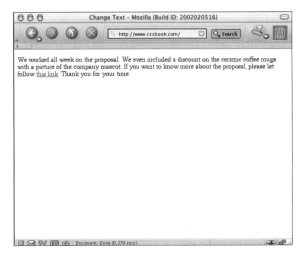

Now let's use JavaScript to make the paragraph appear with the click of
the mouse (see Listing 5.3).

Listing 5.3   Using JavaScript

```
<script type="text/javascript" language="Javascript">
function mirage() {
  if (!document.getElementById) return false;

  var secretObj = document.getElementById("hiddenagenda");

  if (secretObj.style.display == "block") {
    secretObj.style.display = "none";
  } else {
    secretObj.style.display = "block";
  }
}
</script>
```

By using the JavaScript code, we can click on the link (see Figure 5.3). As you can see in Figure 5.4, the paragraph returns! Click it again, and it disappears.

Figure 5.3

Clicking on
the link.

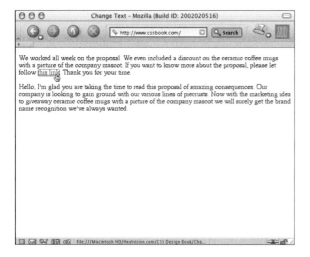

Figure 5.4

The paragraph
returns!

Listing 5.4 uses the `getelementid`, which is a JavaScript method for grabbing an element from the document if we know its `id` value. After we've retrieved an element, we can do all sorts of things with it by manipulating its properties. Changing the value of the `display` property is just one example. We can also change the font family, the size of the fonts, the colors, and many other properties available through CSS.

Listing 5.4   Complete Web Page Showing CSS, JavaScript, and HTML Working Together

```
<!DOCTYPE HTML PUBLIC "-//W3C//DTD HTML 4.01 Transitional//EN"
  "http://www.w3.org/TR/html4/loose.dtd">
<html lang="en">
  <head>
    <meta http-equiv="content-type" content="text/html; charset=iso-8859-1">
    <title>
      Change Text
    </title>
<style type="text/css">
#hiddenagenda {
  display: none;
}
</style>
<script type="text/javascript" language="Javascript">
function mirage() {
  if (!document.getElementById) return false;

  var secretObj = document.getElementById("hiddenagenda");

  if (secretObj.style.display == "block") {
    secretObj.style.display = "none";
  } else {
    secretObj.style.display = "block";
  }
}
</script>
  </head>
  <body>
    <p>
      We worked all week on the proposal. We even included a discount on the
ceramic coffee mugs with a picture of the company mascot. If you want to know
more about the proposal, please follow
      <a href="#hiddenagenda" onclick="mirage();">
        this link</a>. Thank you for your time.
    </p>
    <p id="hiddenagenda" name="hiddenagenda">
      Hello, I'm glad you are taking the time to read this proposal of amazing
consequences. Our company is looking to gain ground with our various lines of
pie crusts. Now with the marketing idea to give away ceramic coffee mugs with a
picture of the company mascot, we will surely get the brand name recognition
we've always wanted.
    </p>
  </body>
</html>
```

Changing More Styles on-the-Fly

From our previous example, let's say we wanted to change the color of
the first paragraph to grey to add emphasis to the second paragraph.
And while we are at it, we also will change the font size and family of
both paragraphs (see Listing 5.5). It's a little overkill in terms of aesthetics
for a usable DHTML page, but that reason never stopped me before in
trying to get a point across.

Listing 5.5   Changing More Than One Style

```html
<!DOCTYPE HTML PUBLIC "-//W3C//DTD HTML 4.01 Transitional//EN"
  "http://www.w3.org/TR/html4/loose.dtd">
<html lang="en">
  <head>
    <meta http-equiv="content-type" content="text/html; charset=iso-8859-1">
    <title>
      Change Text
    </title>
<style type="text/css">
#hiddenagenda {
  display: none;
}
</style>
<script type="text/javascript" language="Javascript">
function mirage() {
  if (!document.getElementById) return false;

  var openObj = document.getElementById("intheopen");
  var secretObj = document.getElementById("hiddenagenda");

  if (secretObj.style.display == "block") {
    secretObj.style.display = "none";
    openObj.style.color = "#000";
    openObj.style.fontFamily = "Verdana, Arial, Helvetica, sans-serif";
  } else {
    secretObj.style.display = "block";
    secretObj.style.fontSize = "1.5em";
    openObj.style.color = "#999";
    openObj.style.fontFamily = "Georgia, Times, serif";
    secretObj.style.fontFamily = "Verdana, Arial, Helvetica, sans-serif";
  }
}
</script>
  </head>
  <body>
    <p id="intheopen">
```

```
       We worked all week on the proposal. We even included a discount on the
ceramic coffee mugs with a picture of the company mascot. If you want to know
more about the proposal, please follow
          <a href="#hiddenagenda" onclick="mirage();">
            this link</a>. Thank you for your time.
       </p>
       <p id="hiddenagenda">
          Hello, I'm glad you are taking the time to read this proposal of amazing
consequences. Our company is looking to gain ground with our various lines of pie
crusts. Now with the marketing idea to give away ceramic coffee mugs with a pic-
ture of the company mascot, we will surely get the brand name recognition we've
always wanted.
       </p>
    </body>
</html>
```

For Listing 5.5 to work, it was necessary to make some changes to the code. To access the first paragraph, I assigned it the ID of "intheopen". Otherwise, the markup is just the same, leaving the initial view of the page similar to the previous example (see Figure 5.5).

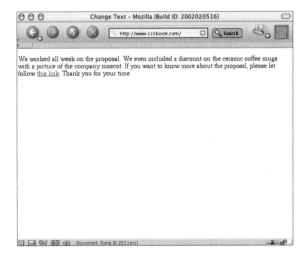

Figure 5.5

Default view, before more styles are applied.

In the `if-else` conditional shown in Listing 5.6, I've added some items to be changed when a user clicks on the link.

Listing 5.6   The `if-else` Conditional

```
if (secretObj.style.display == "block") {
    secretObj.style.display = "none";
    openObj.style.color = "#000";
```

continues

Listing 5.6   The `if-else` Conditional

```
        openObj.style.fontFamily = "Verdana, Arial, Helvetica, sans-serif";
    } else {
        secretObj.style.display = "block";
        secretObj.style.fontSize = "1.5em";
        openObj.style.color = "#999";
        openObj.style.fontFamily = "Georgia, Times, serif";
        secretObj.style.fontFamily = "Verdana, Arial, Helvetica, sans-serif";
    }
```

When a user clicks on the link for the first time, the second paragraph text will grow to 1.5 em units, switch to a sans serif font family (Verdana as the first choice, then Arial, then Helvetica, and then the browser's default sans-serif font). The first paragraph, on the other hand, will turn grey and into a different font family (Georgia, Times, or the browser's default serif font, as available). Figure 5.6 shows what happens.

Figure 5.6

The stylistic changes made after the first click.

After the second click, the second paragraph disappears altogether (see Figure 5.7). The font for the first paragraph changes from a serif-based font in grey to a sans-serif-based font in dark grey.

Figure 5.7

The stylistic changes made after the second click.

Manipulating Images Using DHTML

One of the most popular things to do with images in Web design is the rollover effect. Because the rollover effect has been documented many times in other books and materials, I'm not going to cover it in this book. For more information on rollovers, check out these articles:

- **"The Definitive Rollover Script" by Nick Heinle (WebReview. com, 1997). Available from the Internet at** `http://www.Webreview.com/1997/06_13/Webauthors/06_13_97_4.shtml.`
- **"Back to JavaScript and (DOM) Basics: <IMG> Revisited" by Makiko Itoh (WebReview.com, 2001). Available from the Internet at** `http://www.Webreview.com/2001/04_27/Webauthors/index01.shtml.`

Instead of a conventional rollover, I want to showcase how you can change a style and swap out an image using DHTML (see Listing 5.7). The code in Listing 5.7 is for a basic layout.

> **Note**
>
> When you're working in JavaScript with CSS selectors that use a hyphen, you will need to change the format slightly. You will need to remove the hyphen and capitalize the first letter after the hyphen. For example, to manipulate the CSS `font-size` property, you would access it as `fontSize` in JavaScript.

Listing 5.7   Code for a DHTML Image and Style Swap

```
<!DOCTYPE HTML PUBLIC "-//W3C//DTD HTML 4.01 Transitional//EN"
"http://www.w3.org/TR/html4/loose.dtd">
<html lang="en">
  <head>
    <meta http-equiv="content-type" content="text/html; charset=iso-8859-1">
    <title>
      Designing CSS Web Pages : cssbook.com
    </title>
<style type="text/css">
```

continues

Listing 5.7   Code for a DHTML Image and Style Swap   (Continued)

```css
body {
    margin: 5em 10% 3em 25%;
    font-family: Verdana, Arial, Helvetica, sans-serif;
    font-size: 0.9em;
    color: #030;
    background-color: #fff;
    }

h1 {
    margin: 0 0 0.3em 0;
    padding: 0 0 0 0.4em;
    font-family: "Book Antiqua", Georgia, "Times New Roman", Times, serif;
    font-size: 2em;
    font-weight: normal;
    white-space: nowrap;
    }

h2 {
    margin: 0 0 1.5em 0;
    padding: 0 1em 0 0.8em;
    font-family: "Book Antiqua", Georgia, "Times New Roman", Times, serif;
    font-size: 1.2em;
    font-weight: normal;
    font-style: italic;
    }

img {
    margin: 0 1em 0 1em;
    border-top: 1px solid #999;
    border-right: 1px solid #666;
    border-bottom: 1px solid #666;
    border-left: 1px solid #999;
    background-color: #6c3;
    }

b {
    font-weight: bold;
    }

a {
    color: #090;
    background-color: transparent;
    }

a:hover {
```

```
      color: #0c0;
      background-color: #fff;
      text-decoration: none;
      }

   p.first  {
      margin: 1em 0 0 0;
      padding: 1em;
      background-color: #9f6;
      }

   p  {
      margin: 0;
      padding: 1em;
      background-color: transparent;
      }

   #inset {
      float: right;
      width: 125px;
      margin: 0 0 1em 1em;
      }

   </style>


   </head>
   <body>
      <h1>
         Designing
         <b>
            CSS
         </b>

         Web Pages
      </h1>
      <div id="inset">
         <a href="http://www.amazon.com/exec/obidos/ASIN/0735712638/" title="Pre-
order book" onmouseover="embiggen('yes');" onmouseout="embiggen('no');">
            <img src="css.jpg" name="covertn" alt="A thumbnail image of the book
cover">
         </a>
      </div>
      <h2>
         A new book by
         <a href="http://www.christopher.org/" target="_new" title="There's no place
like a homepage">
```

continues

Listing 5.7   Code for a DHTML Image and Style Swap   (Continued)

```
        Christopher Schmitt
    </a>
    about contemporary new media design through Cascading Style Sheets,
Dynamic HTML, PNG &amp; SVG
    </h2>
    <p class="first">
 .    To be notified about this book's availability or when the book site
(you're soaking it in right now) goes live, send a blank email to
    <a href="mailto:cssbookupdate@christopher.org" title="Sign-up for infre-
quent updates">
        cssbookupdate@christopher.org</a>.
    </p>
    <p>
    For anxious readers, you may
    <a href="http://www.amazon.com/exec/obidos/ASIN/0735712638/" title="_new">
        <strong>
          pre-order the book
        </strong>
        at Amazon.com.
    </a>
    </p>
  </body>
</html>
```

The page is set up so that the cover thumbnail floats to the right of the content thanks to a `div` element with an ID of `"inset"` (see Figure 5.8).

Figure 5.8

The initial view
of the page.

The b Tag

You might have wondered why I put the b element in the style sheet and applied a bold font weight to it. The rationale is that the b tag is deprecated in future versions of HTML. In theory, browsers won't have to render the content in bold if the browser follows the specification correctly.

The reality is that browsers will probably never get rid of the b tag. It is an easy way to make something bold, after all. Therefore, you probably don't need to be seriously concerned about the b tag not rendering correctly in future browsers, but don't hold me to it.

When someone moves his mouse over the thumbnail, I'd like to see a larger image shown allowing for more detail of the artwork. This will require us to use getElementByID and swap out the image source file at the same time. We will need to change the size of the div "inset" element because the width is set to 125 pixels.

If we put a larger image in a small width, the browser will more than likely display some weird behavior to facilitate the change. In this scenario, you are essentially saying you want to put a stretch limousine in a garage that's only big enough for a compact-sized car; the part of the limousine that will crash through the walls depends on how well the garage was built. If the large car were to somehow fit into a small garage it would break all known rules of physics. More realistically, the limousine would crash through one or more of the garage walls.

To avoid breaking the garage or laws of physics, we need to accommodate the change in size. We do this by changing the div "inset" width from 125 pixels to 300 pixels, which is the width of the new, larger book cover image. While we are accommodating the new size of the element, we will also need to facilitate the new image to "rollover" the previous image. The function in Listing 5.8 handles both requirements.

Listing 5.8   Making Accommodations for the New Size of the Element

```
function embiggen(x) {
  // if getElementByID does not work,
  // then don't run the rest
  // of the function
  if (!document.getElementById) return false;
```

continues

Listing 5.8   Making Accommodations for the New Size of the Element (Continued)

```
var insetObj = document.getElementById("inset");

if (x == "yes") {
  // change the width and the source of the image
  insetObj.style.width = "300px";
  document['covertn'].src = "css_big.jpg";
} else {
    // change the width and the source of the image
    // back to default values
  insetObj.style.width = "125px";
  document['covertn'].src = "css.jpg";
  }
}
```

For our function (called `"embiggen"`) to execute the change when we roll over the image, we need to provide hooks into the content. These hooks allow us to trigger what are called *events*. Let's look at the snippet in Listing 5.9.

Listing 5.9   The Snippet

```
<a href="http://www.amazon.com/exec/obidos/ASIN/0735712638/" title="Buy the book"
onmouseover="embiggen('yes');" onmouseout="embiggen('no');">
  <img src="css.jpg" name="covertn" alt="A thumbnail image of the book cover">
</a>
```

For the anchor tag, we've added the proper handlers to call the function: `onmouseover="embiggen('yes');"` and `onmouseout="embiggen('no');"`. Both `onmouseover` and `onmouseout` are events used in JavaScript that allow you to trigger JavaScript functions when a user moves his mouse (or other input device) over or off a selected area respectively. For a list of event handlers, see Table 5.1.

Table 5.1   Common Event Handlers Used in JavaScript

Event Handler	What It Does
onabort	Used to trigger a function when a user stops an image from loading
onblur	Used to trigger a function when an element loses focus
onchange	Used to trigger a function when a change occurs in the value of a `select`, `text`, or `textarea` form field

Event Handler	What It Does
onclick	Used to trigger a function when a user clicks the mouse on a link or form element
onerror	Used to trigger a function when a window or an image fails to load
onfocus	Used to trigger a function when a user tabs to or clicks on a frame, window (Web document), or the form fields select, text, or textarea
onload	Used to trigger a function when a Web document has fully loaded or when all the frames of a frame-set have fully loaded
onmouseout	Used to trigger a function when a user moves his pointer off a link or an area
onmouseover	Used to trigger a function when a user moves his pointer over a link or an area
onreset	Used to trigger a function when a user resets a form using a Reset button
onselect	Used to trigger a function when a user highlights some part of a text in a Web document or in a text or textarea form field
onsubmit	Used to trigger a function when a user hits a sub-mit object associated with a form
onunload	Used to trigger a function when a window has been left (you've surfed to a new page), or when all frames in a frameset have been exited

Now that we have our JavaScript function with the hooks for the event handlers in place, take a look at the before screenshot, which is shown in Figure 5.9, and the after screenshot, which looks exactly like Figure 5.8.

Figure 5.9

The book cover image seems to enlarge, but it's just being swapped out for a larger image.

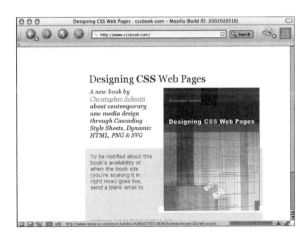

Another use for this script includes enhancing your photo galleries, allowing users to see an enlarged version of a thumbnail before they decide to take the risk to download a larger version.

Hiding and Showing Page Elements

For an expanded version of the `display` toggle technique, you can take whole portions of text and slide them in as completely new pages. In the example shown in Listings 5.10 and 5.11, I wanted to take the book site and expand on it, allowing visitors to sign up for notices about the book and site itself, as well as offering free desktop backgrounds based on an early version of the book cover.

Listing 5.10   The JavaScript That Handles Two Pages in One

```
function turn(x) {
  if (!document.getElementById) return false;

  var introObj = document.getElementById("intro");
  var desktopObj = document.getElementById("desktop");
  var contentObj = document.getElementById("content");

  if (x == "bottom") {
    introObj.style.display = "none";
    desktopObj.style.display = "block";
    contentObj.style.backgroundColor="#666666";
    document.bgColor="#333333";
    } else {
    introObj.style.display = "block";
    desktopObj.style.display = "none";
    contentObj.style.backgroundColor="#cccccc";
    document.bgColor="#ffffff";
    }
}
```

Listing 5.11   The HTML Between the Body Element

```
    <div id="header">
      <h2>
        Christopher Schmitt
      </h2>
      <h1>
        <a href="#content" onclick="turn('bye'); return true" name="top">
          Designing CSS Web Pages</a>
      </h1>
    </div>
    <div id="content" name="content">
      <div id="intro">
        <h3>
          Contemporary new media design through
          <br>
```

```
      Cascading Style Sheets, Dynamic HTML, PNG &amp SVG
   </h3>
   <p>
      The Web building book will be out later this year.
      <br>
      However, the following are currently being offered for your pleasure:
   </p>
   <form>
      <p>
         Free
         <a href="#desktop" title="free eye candy" onclick="turn('bottom');">
            Desktop wallpaper
         </a>
         or
         <input type="button" value="subscribe" class="submit">
         to announcement list,
         <input type="text" value="email address" name="email" class="email"
         size="13">
         required
      </p>
   </form>
</div>
<div id="desktop">
   <h4>
      <a name="desktop">
         Desktop Wallpaper</a>
   </h4>
   <div class="detail">
      <img src="desktop01_tn.gif">
   </div>
   <h5>
      Download:
   </h5>
   <table>
      <tr>
         <td class="cell">
            <a href="desktop01_1280x960.jpg">
               1280 x 960
            </a>
         </td>
         <td>
            228K, jpg
         </td>
      </tr>
      <tr>
         <td class="cell">
            <a href="desktop01_1024x768.jpg">
```

Listing 5.11   The HTML Between the Body Element   (Continued)

```
                1024 x 768
          </a>
        </td>
        <td>
          160K, jpg
        </td>
      </tr>
      <tr>
        <td class="cell">
          <a href="desktop01_800x600.jpg">
            800 x 600
          </a>
        </td>
        <td>
          108K, jpg
        </td>
      </tr>
    </table>
    <h5>
      Instructions:
    </h5>
    <table>
      <tr>
        <td class="cell">
          PC
        </td>
        <td>
          Select the appropriate size, right-click on the image, and choose
          "Set As Wallpaper".
        </td>
      </tr>
      <tr>
        <td class="cell">
          OS 9
        </td>
        <td>
          Save image to your hard drive, and open the Appearance control
          panel. Then select the Desktop folder tab and place the picture.
        </td>
      </tr>
      <tr>
        <td class="cell">
          OS X
        </td>
        <td>
```

```
              Open System Preferences, and click on Desktop settings. Drag the
              image from the desktop to the preview box in the Desktop
              Preferences window.
            </td>
          </tr>
        </table>
        <div class="bottomnav">
          <p>
            <a href="#top" onclick="turn('bye');">
              Back</a>
          </p>
        </div>
      </div>
    </div>
    <div id="footer">
      <p>
        Copyright 2002 Christopher Schmitt. All rights reserved.
      </p>
    </div>
  </body>
</html>
```

Instead of localizing the display property to only a paragraph of text
or a div around an image like in the previous examples, I made a whole
section of a Web page disappear and reappear (see Figures 5.10,
Figure 5.11, and Figure 5.12).

Figure 5.10

Expanded mini
book site with-
out CSS.

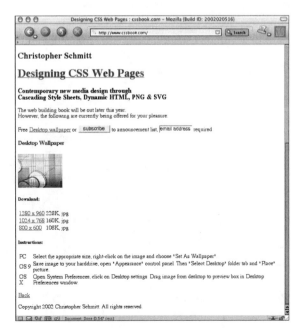

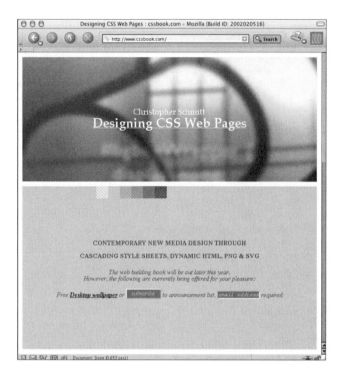

Figure 5.11

The mini book site's "main" page.

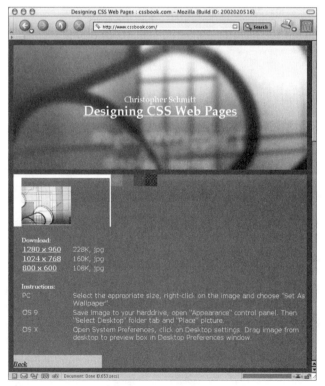

Figure 5.12

On the "download" page, which is technically the same Web document.

Since the content for the site was shallow, I didn't need (or want) to make several Web pages. Instead, I hid the portions of the content regarding the desktop download links and instructions on how to install them through CSS. This allowed me to focus on creating a strong visual impact with the main message of the site

Then I put in a link that would make the main portion of the content disappear, while sliding in the desktop wallpaper content. In the desktop wallpaper, I put in a link to force the user back to the top of the page while switching back to the main message of the site.

Resizing Form Fields

The Web form is a common enough phenomenon. People fill them out when registering for a site, searching for shareware, or just trying to log on to their Yahoo! account to play a game of Literati. Usually these forms tend to flow from top to bottom all the way to the Submit button. There are some good reasons to keep a form aligned top to bottom rather than horizontal.

One reason is that if you combined the form field labels and the form fields, the width would often be greater than the available real estate on the page. A horizontal scrollbar would no doubt appear. Who wants to scroll sideways?

Another reason that forms are often top to bottom is that everyone else does it that way. If you are building a Web form for a business or a halfway respectable organization, use the top to bottom method. However, if you are building for your own expression, you have a little more leeway in how you present your material.

Do Something Different

One of the activities I try to do with Web design is to take known or accepted Web design practices and try to put them on their ear or sideways, as the case might be.

I wanted to create a Web form in which the filling out of the form went from left to right instead of top to bottom. To get around the problem of the width of form field elements being larger than the available width in most viewports, I resorted to resizing the form fields with JavaScript and CSS.

Look at the typical Web mail form in Figure 5.13. It includes form fields for entering a message, a name, an email address, an optional home page address, and a Submit button.

Figure 5.13

The Web form without CSS applied to it.

In Figure 5.14, you can see how the form looks by default. The initial form field for your message is larger than the others (see Figure 5.15). As you fill out the form and go to the next form field, the previous form field shrinks to 20 pixels—much shorter than the 250 pixels of the form field that you are filling in as it is in focus.

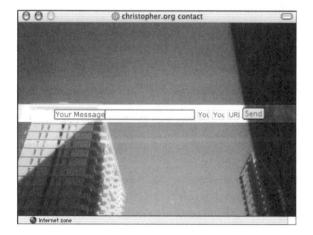

Figure 5.14

Form with CSS applied.

Figure 5.15

Form being
filled out.

Listing 5.12 contains the code for the horizontal form.

Listing 5.12   Code for a Horizontal Form

```
<!DOCTYPE html PUBLIC "-//W3C//DTD XHTML 1.0 Strict//EN"
"http://www.w3.org/TR/xhtml1/DTD/xhtml1-strict.dtd">
<html xmlns="http://www.w3.org/1999/xhtml" xml:lang="en" lang="en">
  <head>
    <meta http-equiv="content-type" content="text/html; charset=iso-8859-1" />
    <title>
      christopher.org contact
    </title>
<script type="text/javascript" language="Javascript">
  var fields = new Array("message", "name", "email", "url");
  var fieldObjects = new Array();

  function Init() {

    for(var i = 0; i < fields.length; i++) {
      fieldObjects[i] = document.getElementById(fields[i]);
    }
    fieldObjects[0].focus();
  }

  function GetJiggy(hotfield) {

    for(var i = 0; i < fieldObjects.length; i++) {
      (i == hotfield) ? Glow(i, fieldObjects[i]) : Fade(hotfield, i,
fieldObjects[i]);
    }
  }
```

continues

Listing 5.12   Code for a Horizontal Form   (Continued)

```
  function Glow(curIdx, nodeObj) {

    with (nodeObj.style) {
      color          = "#936";
      width          = "250px";
      border         = "1px solid #9f6";
    }

  }

  function Fade(hotIdx, curIdx, nodeObj) {

    var newwidth = 20;

    with (nodeObj.style) {
      color          = "#936";
      width          = newwidth + "px";
      border         = "1px solid #9f6";
    }

  }

  </script>
<style type="text/css">

  body  {
    background-image: url(bkgd.jpg);
    background-repeat: no-repeat;
    margin: 0;
    padding: 0;
    background-color: transparent;
    }

  form  {
    background-color: transparent;
    background-image: url(bkgd_hilite.jpg);
    background-repeat: no-repeat;
    background-position: 0 0;
    background-attachment: fixed;
    position: fixed;
    left: 0;
    width: 500px;
    top: 125px;
    text-align: center;
    padding: 5px;
```

```
      font-size: .9em;
      font-family: Verdana, Arial, sans-serif;
      color: #993366;
      }

  .input  {
      border: 1px solid #9f6;
      color: #993366;
      background-image: url(bkgd_hilite.jpg);
      background-repeat: no-repeat;
      background-position: 0 0;
      background-attachment: fixed;
      font-size: .9em;
      font-family: Verdana, Arial, sans-serif;
      }

  .submit  {
      color: #993366;
      background-color: #9f6;
      }

  h1, b  {
      display: none;
      }

  p  {
      display: inline;
      }


  </style>
  </head>
  <body>
<script type="text/javascript" language="Javascript">
  onload = Init;
</script>

    <h1>
      Contact form
    </h1>
    <form method="post" action="/contact/index.html">
      <p>
        <b>
          Your Message:
        </b>
        <input type="text" id="message" name="message" class="input" value="Your
        Message" onfocus="GetJiggy(0);" />
```

continues

Listing 5.12   Code for a Horizontal Form   (Continued)

```html
      </p>
      <p>
        <b>
          Your Name:
        </b>
        <input type="text" id="name" name="name" class="input" value="Your Name"
        onfocus="GetJiggy(1);" />
      </p>
      <p>
        <b>
          Your Email:
        </b>
        <input type="text" id="email" name="email" class="input" value="Your
        Email" onfocus="GetJiggy(2);" />
      </p>
      <p>
        <b>
          URL (optional):
        </b>
        <input type="text" id="url" name="url" class="input" value="URL" onfo-
        cus="GetJiggy(3);" />
      </p>
      <input type="submit" value="Send" class="submit" />
    </form>
  </body>
</html>
```

Although this design solution won't work for every audience, it does show you how you can approach a Web page design differently on the Web while staying true to Web standards. It's my hope that you take Web standards and see a possibility of Web page designs that are different from the almost cliché two- and three-column layouts and push the boundaries and find something different and maybe even unique.

JavaScript: Great Power, Great Responsibility

With the power of scripting languages, Web builders have the ability to go beyond static presentation with their Web pages. This has good possibilities as well as bad.

The potential of enhancing a visitor's experience with a Web site is exciting; however, there can be a downside. Working against the grain, visitors to sites sometimes run afoul of Web designers and developers who either don't use the technology correctly (causing syntax or other programming errors) or do know what they are doing but still insist on creating wonderfully awful Web experiences. For example, the JavaScript Source from `internet.com` offers its readers a script on how to pop a window when you leave a site. When you leave a site, you leave a site. You don't want to be reminded about the site you're leaving.

When you're adding JavaScript and manipulating the elements on your Web pages, make sure your message can still get across. You do this through testing your Web page in various browsers—and hopefully, testing with select portions of your target audience as well.

Recommended Reading

To help you on your way to complementing Web page designs with smart usage of JavaScript, I recommend the following books:

- *JavaScript Design* by William B. Sanders (New Riders Publishing, 2001).
- *Designing with JavaScript* by Nick Heinle and Bill Pena (O'Reilly & Associates, 2001).
- *Practical JavaScript for the Usable Web* by Paul Wilton, Stephen Williams, and Sing Li (glasshaus, 2002).

Reading these books, not only will you learn about JavaScript without getting a sterile taste of a programming book, but you will learn how to apply scripts to a Web page with delicious results.

> **Note**
>
> *Building Really Annoying Web Sites* by Michael Miller (Hungry Minds, 2001) has an interesting perspective on learning how to build Web pages. Instead of building upon positive aspects of Web publishing, he looks at certain Web pages that absolutely infuriate a visitor's experience and then shows you how to build them! The thought is that if you can learn what practices introduce problems, you can learn to avoid them.

Part III

Advanced CSS

Creating CSS for Beyond the Screen

Up to this point, we have concerned ourselves with how to move our Web sites into more contemporary techniques to reach a visual design, but the power of CSS is not limited merely to screen media (which is hinted at in the media attribute as you learned in Chapter 3, "Setting Up Style"). In this chapter, we look at how CSS can be used today for stylizing pages that are printed and, in the future, how they can be heard.

Designing CSS for Print

Either your company's Web page looks awful after you click the Print button and your boss wants you to "pretty up" the page, or your latest e-zine totals chapters in the teens and people are more likely to print it out than read it online. Either way, one day you might need to present a printable version of a Web page. To print out a page's contents, some sites offer a link to a different Web page. Often, the link is wrapped around text that reads *Printer-friendly format* (see the example shown in Figure 6.1) or just simply *Print*. What often happens in this case is that a script is written to generate a new page that's a combination of the content being poured into a different template with bare bones, printer-friendly markup. Some designers go so far as to manually copy the content into a new page and maintain the same content on two different files.

Teen attacked by shark off St. George Island

The Associated Press
Posted June 2, 2002, 1:23 PM EDT

TALLAHASSEE -- A shark bit the foot of a teen-age swimmer off St. George Island, the first known shark attack on the north Florida island.

☑ Email this story to a friend
🖶 Printer friendly version 👆

The 16-year-old boy underwent three hours of surgery after the attack Friday afternoon and is recovering well, said Jay Abbott, chief of St. George Island Fire and Rescue.

Figure 6.1

A Web page using the printer-friendly feature.

With the magic of CSS, you don't need to go to the extra hassle of providing an alternative page from which your visitors can print. Printing should be as easy as pressing a button, instead of a couple clicks and pressing a button.

To use the easy CSS method, we create a new CSS file called `print.css` and earmark it for print media. In the code sample that follows, we slide in the second linked style sheet that has the media attribute set to `print`.

```
<link href="screen.css" rel="stylesheet"
type="text/css" media="screen">
<link href="print.css" rel="stylesheet"
type="text/css" media="print">
```

To get started, look at the example in Figure 6.2, which shows a CSS styled page for the screen. However, as you can see in Figure 6.3, it really needs help when it's time to print.

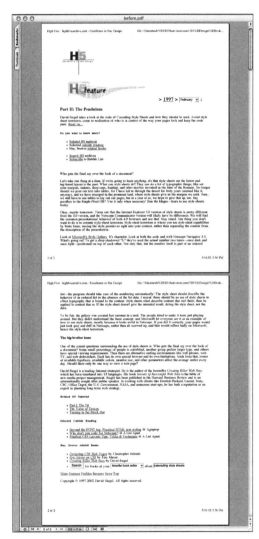

Figure 6.2

The Web page with CSS screen styling.

Figure 6.3

The Web page without CSS print styling.

Remove the Clutter

The first thing that you want to do is get rid of page elements that don't translate onto a piece of paper. That way you can work on designing the elements that are left over without working with extraneous material. Items to get rid of for printing include site navigation, page navigation, and any multimedia advertisements.

If you do use graphic ads and want them to appear as-is, make sure not to use animation. You'll never know for sure what frame of the animation will be displayed when the viewer chooses Print. If you're concerned with making sure an advertisement gets on the print page, you might want to use text ads, if possible. Or, if you want to have print-only advertising, you could try using display:none to hide text ads from screen displays, but make them visible when users print them.

For this example, get rid of the main logo, which is wrapped between the h1 element. It gets duplicated in the feature header. That way, you allow more text to be on the printed page and conserve paper doing it.

```
#footer a, .infotease, h1, .breadcrumbs, .prompt {
    display: none;
}
```

So, with this simple rule, you've gotten rid of the footer navigation, the links that rest in the middle of the page that go related content at the bottom, and, yes, the logo. If we had animated GIFs, PNGs, SVGs, or SWFs, I would have blocked those as well. However, if having an iron-handed control over the graphical elements isn't a big deal for you in your Web page, you can just leave the element.

Designing the Heart of Printed Content

Now let's work on formatting what is left after we have removed the clutter to create attractive printed pages.

Background Color and Point Size of Body Text

The first step is to style the body element. You want to make sure the background is white so that any other background colors or images won't come through. This saves on ink for the user, but it also helps to ensure there aren't competing elements that would make the page illegible.

Then transform the base font for the page from sans serif to serif. Serif fonts are easier to read on paper than on screen. Next, change the size of the font to be 12pt. Because you are dealing with material destined for *print* and not the screen, a larger point size is more suitable to the task.

This example shows how this is accomplished:

```
body {
    font-family: Georgia, "Times New Roman", Times, serif;
    font-size: 12pt;
    background-color: #fff;
}
```

Points Versus Pixels

Why do we use points for type? Well, remember that we are designing a page for print, and using points for print is what graphic designers have been doing for years. It's only when you start using points for screen delivery that things get nasty; points are rendered inconsistently across Macintosh and PCs. Pixels, on the other hand, are better.

Alignment of Footer and Paragraphs

Next, move on to the layout of the rest of the page: Move in the content and footer from the left by 45px. This is an effort to align the body copy with the letter *h* in the H5 Features header.

```
#content, #footer  {
   margin-left: 45px;
}
```

After that, work on formatting the type and space between the headlines and the paragraphs. To offset the headlines from the body copy, change the typeface to a sans serif font.

Next, I set the margin-bottom for the headlines to 0, except for the h3, which is set to 10pt. This gives the bottom margin distance from the abstract of the article. Then, to make the page similar in some regard to the onscreen version, put a border around the title.

For the paragraphs, give a margin-bottom spacing of 0.75em to put some space between paragraphs and headlines:

```
h3, h4, h5    {
   font-family: Verdana, Arial, Helvetica, sans-serif;
   margin-bottom: 0;
}

h3 {
   font-family: Georgia, Times, "Times New Roman", serif;
   border: 1px solid #000;
   font-size: 15pt;
   padding: 6pt;
   margin-bottom: 10pt;
}

p  {
   margin: 0 0 0.75em 0;
   padding: 0;
}
```

This opens up the text and makes it more legible.

Note

Yes, sometimes, like now, pixels are important units of measurement when you're writing your print style sheet. Because I want to align the body copy with a certain distance in from the left with an image, pixels is the way to go. Just because you are making a style sheet for print delivery doesn't mean you should convert everything to points.

Indenting the Paragraphs

Instead of spacing out the paragraphs and headlines to make it easier for the reader to get through the article, you can indent the paragraphs. (I decided against it in this example.) If you want to, you can modify the p tag properties like this:

```
p   {
  text-indent: 50pt;
  margin: 0;
  padding: 0;
}

.abstract, .pullquote {
  text-indent: none;
}
```

Formatting the Web Page Abstract

As for the abstract, you will want to distinguish it from the rest of the body copy. You do this by setting the margins on the left and right side to a width of 10%. Also, change the font from a set of serif fonts (as specified in a typical p element) to a set of sans-serif fonts:

```
.abstract     {
  padding: 0 10% 0 10%;
  font-family: Verdana, Arial, Helvetica, sans-serif;
}
```

Distinguishing the Author's Bio Section

For the author's bio section, it is best to work in a similar vein of trying to distinguish it from the article's body content. To do this, you need to keep the theme of changing the font from serif to sans-serif, but also shrink the size to 11pt. Then put some space between the last paragraph of the article and the related material at the bottom of the page.

```
.byline    {
  margin: 22pt 0 22pt 0;
  font-size: 11pt;
  font-family: Verdana, Arial, Helvetica, sans-serif;
}
```

The Pull Quote

For the pull quote, transfer it from the screen style sheet into the new print style sheet:

```
.pullquote    {
  float: left;
  width: 100pt;
```

```
    font-size: 0.8em;
    font-weight: bold;
    text-align: justify;
    line-height: 0.9em;
    position: relative;
    padding: 0.5em 2em 0 0;
  }
```

The Article Links

Now turn your attention to the links in the article. Because this is going to be printed, you can't have rollovers or expect the user to have a color printer. So, make the link's font color black, turn off default underlining, and make the font-weight bold.

```
a {
  color: #000;
  font-weight: bold;
  text-decoration: none;
}
```

A great example of how CSS can make a printed copy of a page more useful is by manipulating the information contained in the links. With a typical page printout, the URL information in the links is lost. Often, text used as links is just underlined. However, in browsers like Netscape 6.2 and Mozilla 1.0 (browsers that support the adding of content with the :before and :after pseudo-elements and the content property), you can automagically insert the URLs of links next to the links in the articles. Thereby, readers who have just the printout won't need to look up your Web page to get to the referenced material. Sure, you won't get return visits, but you get a more satisfied user. Here's the rule to make it happen:

```
#content p a:after, .info ul li a:after      {
  content: " <" attr(href) "> ";
}
```

The Ready-to-Be-Printed Version

That wraps up a print style sheet. We've primed a document for print and the Web with some simple CSS rules. Listing 6.1 is the final version of the print style sheet. You can compare it to the screen style sheet (see Listing 6.2) as well as to the printout of the page (see Figure 6.4).

Listing 6.1   Complete CSS for Print Linked in the Head of the Web Page

```
/* Remove */
#footer a, .infotease, h1, .breadcrumbs, .prompt  {
  display: none;
```

continues

Listing 6.1   Complete CSS for Print Linked in the Head of the Web Page (Continued)

```css
}


/* Format */
body  {
  font-family: Georgia, Times, "Times New Roman", serif;
  font-size: 12pt;
  background-color: #fff;
}

#content, #footer  {
  margin-left: 45px;
}


h3, h4, h5  {
  font-family: Verdana, Arial, Helvetica, sans-serif;
  margin-bottom: 0;
}

h3  {
  font-family: Georgia, Times, "Times New Roman", serif;
  border: 1px solid #000;
  font-size: 15px;
  padding: 6px;
  margin-bottom: 10pt;
}

p  {
  margin: 0 0 0.75em 0;
  padding: 0;
}

a  {
  color: #000;
  font-weight: bold;
  text-decoration: none;
}

/* Display URL */ #content p a:after, .info ul li a:after   {
  content: " <" attr(href) "> ";
}

.abstract  {
```

```
    padding: 0 10% 0 10%;
    font-family: Verdana, Arial, Helvetica, sans-serif;
}


.byline  {
    margin: 22pt 0 22pt 0;
    font-size: 11pt;
    font-family: Verdana, Arial, Helvetica, sans-serif;
}


.pullquote  {
    float: left;
    width: 100px;
    font-size: 0.8em;
    font-weight: bold;
    text-align: justify;
    line-height: 0.9em;
    position: relative;
    padding: 0.5em 2em 0 0;
}
```

Listing 6.2 Complete CSS for Screen Delivery Linked in the Head of the Web Page

```
body {
    font-family: Verdana, Arial, Helvetica, sans-serif;
    font-size: 1em;
    margin: 0 0 5em 0;
    color: #666;
    background-color: #fff;
}

form, select {
    display: inline;
}

#content, #footer {
    margin: 0 100px 0 150px;
}

#footer {
    margin-top: 4em;
    font-size: 0.8em;
}

#footer a {
    margin-right: 1.5em;
```

continues

Listing 6.2   Complete CSS for Screen Delivery Linked in the Head of the Web Page (Continued)

```
}

.abstract {
  font-family: Georgia, Melior, Times,
"Times New Roman", serif;
  padding: 1em 50px 2.5em 50px;
  margin: 0;
  font-size: 0.8em;
  line-height: 1.25em;
}

.pullquote  {
  float: left;
width: 100px;
  font-size: 0.8em;
  font-weight: bold;
  text-align: justify;
  line-height: 0.9em;
  position: relative;
  padding: 0.5em 2em 0 0;
}

h1, h2, h3, h4, h5, h6  {
  font-family: Georgia, Melior, Times,
"Times New Roman", serif;
  padding: 0;
  margin-bottom: 0;
}

h1  {
  margin: 0;
}

h2  {
  margin-top: 0;
  font-family: Verdana, Arial, Helvetica, sans-serif;
  font-size: 0.8em;
}

h3  {
  font-family: Georgia, Melior, Times,
"Times New Roman", serif;
  font-size: 1.25em;
  border: 1px solid #999;
```

```
  padding: 0.25em
}

.breadcrumbs  {
  display: block;
  margin: 0 0 0 150px;
}

p  {
  margin: 0 0 0.75em 0;
  padding: 0;
  font-size: 0.9em;
  line-height: 1.8em;
}

.infotease  {
  color: #999;
}

.infotease h5 {
  margin: 0 0 0 0;
}

.infotease li  {
  font-size: 0.8em;
  font-weight: normal;
  font-family: Verdana, Arial, Helvetica, sans-serif;
}

.byline  {
  font-size: 0.8em;
  font-weight: normal;
  font-family: Georgia, Melior, Times,
"Times New Roman", serif;
  padding: 1em 0 2em 0;
  margin: 2.5em 0 1em 0;
  line-height: 1.25em;
  color: #999;
  border-bottom: 1px dotted #999;
}

img  {
  display: block;
}

ul  {
list-style-type: square;
```

continues

Listing 6.2   Complete CSS for Screen Delivery Linked in the Head of the Web Page (Continued)

```
    }

.right  {
   float: left;
   width: 35%;
   margin-bottom: 2em;
}

.left  {
   float: right;
   width: 35%;
}


ul li  {
   margin: 0 0 0 1em;
}

.info ul  {
   margin: 0 0 0 1em;
}

.info ul li  {
   font-size: 0.8em;
   margin: 0;
   padding: 0;
}

a {
   color: #000;
   background-color: transparent;
}

a:hover {
   color: #000;
   background-color: transparent;
   text-decoration: none;
}

br {
   clear: both;
}
```

Figure 6.4

Here's how the page looks now with the print style sheet.

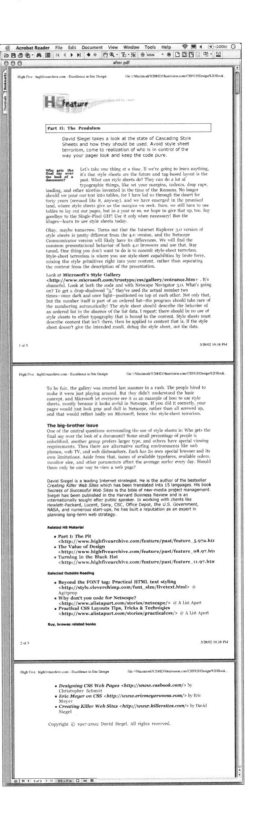

CSS for Audio Presentation

A screen reader can examine a document and read it aloud using speech synthesis. Although it's most often used by people with poor vision, this type of aural presentation can also be used in other situations. For instance, imagine using a screen reader to get directions from a Web page while driving, having your computer assist in teaching a user how to read, or using this feature to support in the visual presentation of a Web experience—just to name a few.

Right now, the major browser vendors like Netscape and Microsoft (and even the popular screen readers on the market today) don't handle aural CSS. This section of the chapter is included primarily just to let you know that it exists, to get you used to the technology, and to have you start thinking about how to present your Web site by letting people hear it, instead of reading it.

Note

For the sections of
the CSS2 Recom-
mendation that
describe the aural
style properties, see
`http://www.w3.org/`
`TR/REC-CSS2/`
`aural.html`.

The Aural CSS Properties

Aural CSS properties can be divided into four different categories:

- **Volume**
- **Spatial**
- **Voice characteristics**
- **Timing properties**

Volume

The Volume aural category includes two different properties: `volume` and `speak`.

The `volume` property, as you might have guessed, deals with how loud something is. Volume range is expressed in these values: numerals (no units) from 0–100, or percentages. There are also keyword values that correspond to specific numerical values:

- **Silent (0—no sound is produced)**
- **X-soft (0)**
- **Soft (25)**
- **Medium (50)**
- **Loud (75)**
- **X-loud (100)**

Following are examples of these properties:

```
body     {
  volume: 45;
}


.ad      {
  // volume will be a third times the inherited value,
  // which--if inherited from the body--would be about 15.
  volume: 33%;
}
```

The `speak` property is used to tell the screen reader how the text will be read:

- **None**
- **Normal**
- **Spelled out**

Next are examples of these properties:

```
body {
  speak: normal;
}
.phone {
```

```
  speak: spell-out;
}
.notanicethingtosay {
  speak: none;
}
```

Spatial

The set of spatial properties allows users to differentiate sounds in a three-dimensional sound space. This is done through the use of two properties:

- **azimuth—Deals with the space—360 degrees—around the user. It can be described in degrees or keyword values:** left-side, far-left, left, center-left, center, center-right, right, far-right, right-side, leftwards, rightwards, **and** behind.
- **elevation—Talks about how high or low the sound is. It is also described in degrees as well as keyword values:** below **(–90deg),** level **(0deg),** above **(90),** higher **(+10 degrees to current value), and** lower **(–10 degrees to current value).**

Following are examples of these properties:

```
.nav {
  elevation: 45deg;
  azimuth: center;
}

#content {
  elevation: level;
  azimuth: center;
}

.ads {
  elevation: behind;
  azimuth: -90deg;
}
```

Voice Characteristics

Voice characteristics of aural CSS deal with how the speech will sound through the speech-rate, voice-family, pitch, pitch-range, stress, and richness properties.

speech-rate determines how fast the voice speaks. It's specified in words per minute (wpm) and the following keyword values:

- **X-slow (80wpm)**
- **Slow (120wpm)**
- **Medium (180–200wpm)**
- **Fast (300wpm)**

- **X-fast (500wpm)**
- **Faster (+40wpm)**
- **Slower (–40wpm)**

voice-family is a lot like font-family, where you pick a set of fonts (usually grouped in sans-serif, serif, monotype, and so on). Just like in font-family, you pick a collection of voices with the first one having higher priority than the next one in line. For example:

```
body {
    Voice-family: Paul, David, Christopher, Tiffany, kid;
}


b {
    voice-family: Richard, Meg, authority;
}
```

pitch refers to the frequency of the speaking voice. A higher than normal pitch—an average male's pitch is around 120 hertz (Hz) and an average female's pitch is about 210Hz—could annoy your visitors instead of providing a stylistic quality to your content. pitch has keyword values of x-low, low, medium, high, and x-high. These keyword values do not correspond with set values because the pitch varies with respect to the unique nature of the voice.

Following is an example of this property:

```
b {
    pitch: high;
}
```

pitch-range sets the variation of the average pitch. A number between 0 and 100, with a pitch greater than 50, produces animated voices and sets the value of pitch-range.

stress concerns the inflection that happens on the stressed parts of a word. The value of stress is expressed in a value between 0 to 100.

richness concerns the "brightness" of a voice and is set with a value of 0 to 100. The higher the value, the richer the voice.

Also in this category, I've put speech properties. Speech properties refer to how the punctuation (speak-punctuation) and numerals (speak-numeral) are spoken. For numerals, you can have digits said individually or continuously. For example, 25 would be said either as *two five* using the value of digits, or as *twenty-five* if you use the value of continuous.

Following is an example of this property:

```
.phonenumber {
    speak-numeral: digits;
}
```

For punctuation, you can set the value of speak-punctuation to code or none. The code value would, of course, be used to speak every punctuation mark, whereas the none value would allow the text to be presented naturally.

Following is an example of this property:

```
code {
    speak-punctuation: code;
}
```

Timing Properties

The pause property can dictate how much time should pass before or after an element in a Web document is read. The timing of the pauses is measured in milliseconds and seconds or percentage.

By itself, the pause property is used as a shorthand element for pause-before and pause-after. pause-before defines the amount of silent time before the content of the next element is read, and pause-after defines the amount of silence after the content of an element. However, when you're just using pause, the two values correspond to the amount of time to be silent before and after an element, respectively.

An example of this property follows:

```
h2 {
    pause: 45ms 23ms;
}
```

The cue property allows you to insert a sound before or after a point in a Web document. For instance, if you want to say *Headline Level 1* before reading a first-level heading in a Web page, it would go something like this:

```
h1 {
    cue-before: url("Heading1.wav");
}
```

You can also put in play a sound element after a point in a Web document. That, of course, would be through the property of cue-after. You can use the shorthand property of cue to place a sound event before and after an element. For example:

```
h6 {
    cue: url("notimportant.au") url("reallyitwasnt.au");
}
```

If you want to have a sound run on in the background, you would use the play-during property. Using the mix keyword, you can have the sound from the parent element play through. With repeat, you can have a sound repeat in the background until the element has been spoken. If you use `auto`, then the parent element will continue to play instead of starting at the beginning. If you set it to `none`, the parent element sound (if there is one) won't play.

Following is an example of this property in action:

```
.bio {
  play-during: url("hithere.wav") mix;
}
```

Potential Strategies for Coding Aural CSS

Although aural CSS properties haven't been implemented in major browsers yet, that doesn't mean we can't think about how best to use them just for the fun of it.

For Novice Web Users

If you know your audience is new to interacting with the Web, you might consider being explicit in how the information is conveyed.

For example, if a user encounters the form, put in cues before each `form` element explaining what type of information he should enter. Also, you might want to add a cue that will tell the user what level headline (H1, H2, H3) he is getting, as well as emphasize the logo or slogan.

Of course, if a user becomes a repeat visitor, this type of setup would be overkill. A good solution would be to allow visitors to select an advanced aural style sheet for their surfing. Also, you can have a cookie that counts the number of times a visitor sees your site. After a number of visits, you can change the aural CSS from being explicit to one more suited for advanced or regular visitors.

Hypothetical Example

When incorporating a sound element into your Web pages, think about how people will learn to move around. In physical spaces, like driving on the road, road signs are grouped by color and style. In America, road signs convey a message in clear terms, command attention, and fulfill a need. Elements of sound should be used in a similar way.

Figure 6.5

Streets signs used by the U.S Department of Transportation.

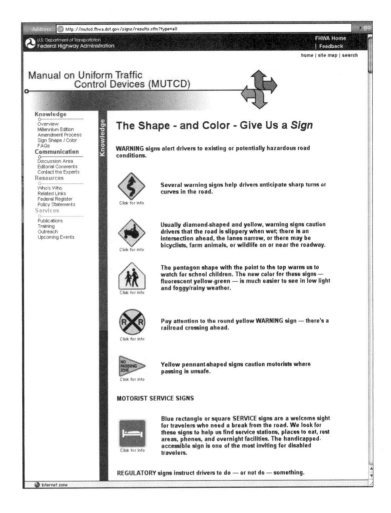

You could give different portions of your Web page a particular voice. The navigation, the legal or small print, the content, and the advertisements should have their own voice. This allows the users to identify by a vocal quality what they are listening to as well as hearing what's being said.

From our example with the print example, I'm going to add the aural style sheet (see Listing 6.3) like so:

```
<link href="screen.css" rel="stylesheet"
type="text/css" media="screen">
<link href="print.css" rel="stylesheet"
type="text/css" media="print">
<link href="aural.css" rel="stylesheet"
type="text/css" media="aural">
```

Listing 6.3   A Sample Aural Style Sheet

```
body {
  voice-family: female;
  azimuth: center;
  elevation: level;
}

/* branding */
#header  {
  voice-family: female;
  elevation: 90deg;
  richness: 60;
  }

/* navigation */
.breadcrumbs {
  voice-family: male;
  elevation: 10deg;
}

#footer a {
  voice-family: male;
  elevation: 10deg;
}


/* content voice */
#content {
  voice-family: female;
  elevation: level;
}

.pullquote {
  voice-family: male;
  elevation: 10deg;
  richness: 55;
  speech-rate: fast;
 }

i, em  {
  speech-rate: fast;
}

b, strong {
  richness: 60;
}
```

```
/* advertisement, related info */
.infotease, .info {
  voice-family: male;
  elevation: 30deg;
}


/* small print */
#footer {
  voice-family: male;
  elevation: -10deg;
}
```

Now we just have to wait and see if this aural style sheet will work in the major browsers.

Note

Keep from rotating voices in your documents. Just like the use of fonts, keep the voices to a maximum of three, which could even be stretching it a bit. You should be able to use just two voices, perhaps one male voice and one female voice. If you have any more than that, you will probably create an annoying experience.

Utilizing PNG and SVG with CSS

This chapter introduces you to Portable Network Graphics (PNG) and Scalable Vector Graphics (SVG) image formats. These image types radically change or enhance the capabilities of designers for the Web. Each section starts out with an interview with an expert in their respective technologies. Then it looks at ways of incorporating these technologies in interesting ways through CSS-based Web page designs.

PNG

In this section, we will talk with Greg Roelofs. Roelofs has been working with the PNG specification since 1995 and maintains the official Web site presence regarding the file format. In the interview, we will talk about some of the history—present and future—of this image format. Afterward, we will look at some uses and advantages of PNG.

Interview with Greg Roelofs

Greg Roelofs not only maintains the PNG Home Site (http://www.libpng.org/pub/png/), but he also wrote the book on the subject, titled *PNG: The Definitive Guide* (O'Reilly, 1999). Roelofs offers some interesting insights into the PNG image format.

Figure 7.1 shows Greg's PNG Web site.

Greg Roelofs

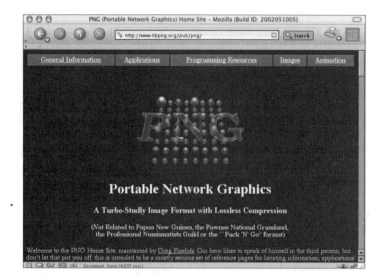

Figure 7.1

The PNG
home page.

Christopher Schmitt: What is PNG, and how did this technology come about?

Greg Roelofs: PNG is an open file format for storing digital images with reasonably good compression, no data loss (unlike standard JPEG, which is lossy), and no patent issues. It stands for Portable Network Graphics and was created in January and February of 1995 in response to the CompuServe announcement that software supporting the popular GIF format, already in wide use on the Web, was infringing a Unisys patent on the Lempel-Ziv-Welch (LZW) compression method and would henceforth be subject to license fees. This seemed like an excellent opportunity to replace GIF with something that was not only patent-free, but also technically superior— in compression, interlacing support, transparency support, and color depth. Thus, PNG was born.

CS: How are you involved in the development of the PNG format?

GR: I originally entered the fray from the compression side of things. I'd been involved with the Info-ZIP archiver project for five years before then and was familiar with the relative efficiencies of the LZW method and the main compression scheme used in Zip and UnZip "deflate," which is roughly 30% better than LZW. I also was aware of how carefully the Info-ZIP authors, particularly Jean-loup Gailly, had researched compression-related patents and had studiously avoided infringing any of them. So deflate seemed like an obvious candidate to replace LZW, and indeed, one of the first things I did was hack together a quick test program to create "ZIF" images, which were nothing more than GIFs with the LZW compression replaced by deflate.

I contributed a few small ideas to the spec and have written or improved on various PNG-supporting programs, but my main contribution has probably been the PNG Web site, which has grown into a fairly comprehensive resource for PNG programming info and sample code, test images, and information about third-party application support.

CS: What do you think is the most interesting feature of the PNG format?

GR: I personally find the transparency features the most useful, and I've done my best to encourage developers both of browsers and of other applications—such as image editors—to fully support it. The partial-transparency capability that PNG supports can be used to do anti-aliasing (smoothing) of curved and diagonal lines (such as those fund in logos and text) so that a single image can be used against *any* background, not just one. The upcoming POV-Ray 3.5 will let you ray-trace glass objects directly to PNG images that have appropriate transparency—though not refraction, of course. (For an example, see Figure 7.2.)

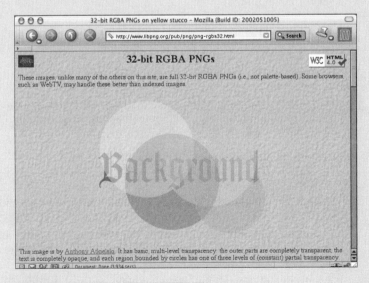

Figure 7.2

Example of a 32-bit RGBA PNG that doesn't use a color palette.

In combination with DHTML features, PNG transparency also can be used to show off some fantastic demos and user interfaces, such as the draggable "faces" (skins) for the Audion MP3 player. (For an example, see Figure 7.3.)

Figure 7.3

Example of using PNGs with Dynamic HTML.

CS: What's the status of PNG implementation in browsers?

GR: Almost every graphical browser in use today has basic PNG support; that is, they can display opaque PNGs just as well as they do opaque GIFs or JPEGs, and in the case of interlaced PNGs, they can display them progressively. Netscape and Internet Explorer have had native PNG support since 1997.

Quite a few browsers also support gamma correction, which allows a given image to look the same on very different systems—instead of too bright on Macs and/or too dark on Windows and Linux PCs, for example.

But PNG's most useful feature, from a Web-design standpoint, is its transparency capability, and that's not as evenly supported. The good news is that the latest versions of virtually every browser, with the sole exception of Microsoft's Internet Explorer for Windows, now have full transparency support.

I listed several of the more popular ones above. The PNG browsers page is the complete reference—look for entries with the notation *full alpha support* (see http://www.libpng.org/pub/png/pngapbr.html).

The bad news is that, since MSIE/Win32 accounts for something like 90% or more of the market, the fact that it has poor support for palette-based PNG transparency and no support at all for transparency in true color images is a serious roadblock for universal adoption of PNG on the Web. And Netscape 4.x had no transparency support of any kind, so it wasn't exactly helping matters.

There is an online petition to get Microsoft to fix their Windows browser (see http://www.petitiononline.com/msiepng/petition.html), and competition from other browsers might conceivably have some effect. But until they get around to it, PNG's best feature will only be used on small sites and special-purpose pages.

Now let's take a look at some of the uses that PNG offers. Roelofs mentioned that one of the important benefits for Web designers will be the alpha transparency. In the next section, we will take a look at one approach that utilizes the transparency; then we will talk about the practical nature of PNGs.

Alpha Transparency

Alpha transparency is one of the major reasons that developers and designers like the PNG image format (see Figure 7.4).

Figure 7.4

Example of an image with alpha transparency against a textured background.

It allows for greater flexibility in designs instead of the 1-bit transparency that Web builders are used to with the GIF format (see Figure 7.5).

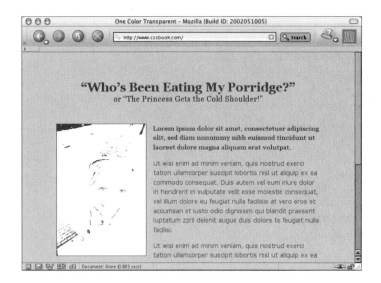

Figure 7.5

A GIF with one color being transparent.

An interesting use of PNG, in my mind, is its ability to place a partially transparent inline image over a textured background. If you want to have a nice halo glow over such a background, you would get some unwanted visual defects using a GIF or JPEG. But with PNG's alpha transparency, which allows for 256 levels of opacity instead of just one as in the GIF format, the transition between backgrounds to the image is almost non-existent, making it pleasing to the eye.

Now that you have this tool at your disposal, you can go the next step. Instead of applying an inline image essentially "over" a textured background; you can apply a PNG or several PNGs in stacked layers through CSS without fear of creating a jumbled mess.

Another interesting effect with alpha transparency is what can be done when creating monotone images. I desaturated the image in the photo that you see in Figures 7.6–7.8; in other words, I took out the color, essentially making it a black-and-white monotone. The code that I used to do this is shown in Listings 7.1–7.3. Then I saved the black as the alpha transparency in the image. Through CSS, I can give the image any color I want to create numerous types of duotone.

Figure 7.6

A PNG with a back-ground color of #333 applied via CSS.

Figure 7.7

The same PNG with a background color of #ccc—almost white—applied via CSS.

Figure 7.8

The same PNG with a background color of #666 applied via CSS.

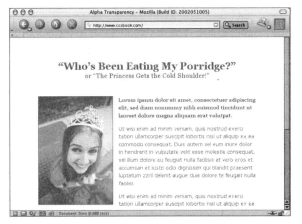

Note

In Figures 7.6–7.8, I use black, white, and grey colors due to the limitations of this publication. How-ever, if you download the image and code from this book's companion Web site (`http://www.cssbook.com`), you can experiment with blues, greens, reds, and so on to get a more dynamic change.

Listing 7.1   Color Scheme for Figure 7.6

```
body     {
   color: #fff;
   background-color: #666;
}

img     {
   background-color: #333;
   border: 1px solid #fff;
}
```

Listing 7.2   Color Scheme for Figure 7.7

```
body {
   color: #ccc;
   background-color: 333;
}

img {
   background-color: #ccc;
   border: 1px solid #ccc;
}
```

Listing 7.3   Color Scheme for Figure 7.8

```
body     {
   color: #666;
   background-color: #fff;
}

img {
   background-color: #666;
   border: 1px solid #666;
}
```

This is helpful if I want to make multiple style sheets for my different audiences. I can build my default style sheet with more of an experimental color scheme, and then I can put in an alternative style sheet that has just the black and white duotone for people with colorblindness or poor visibility.

Built-In Gamma Correction

When you do a cross-platform check of your Web pages, you might notice that on a Windows platform, images tend to be viewed darker than they do on the Apple platform (see Figure 7.9). That's because the default gamma value on an Apple is different than it is for PCs.

Figure 7.9

The same image in JPEG and PNG format with the JPEG darker than the PNG. (Notice the tone of the face.)

Support for gamma correction is built in to the PNG format. When you save an image file in your image editor, the image editing software you're using stores your monitor's gamma setting in the image file.

For example, if you create an image for Web delivery, the gamma value is stored in the file. Browsers, image editing tools, and image viewers know where to look for the gamma correction information and adjust their display automagically.

For more information about gamma, check out `http://www.inforamp. net/~poynton/notes/colour_and_gamma/GammaFAQ.html`, and for information about gamma correction, see `http://graphics.stanford. edu/gamma.html`.

The Bad News About PNGs

As Roelof stated in his interview, a major hurdle with the use of PNGs is the lack of full support in the current Windows version of Internet Explorer 5x. Although this is a concern, it's not the only problem facing developers.

The other problem is that the file sizes for PNGs are usually substantially higher if you save the alpha transparency with your images. In the gamma correction example, the JPEG was 28K, whereas the PNG with full alpha transparency was 172K—that is more than six times as big!

For the PNG without the saved alpha transparency, the file size comes out to 41K. That's a huge drop from 172K. With the same photo in a GIF file format, the image comes out to a little more than 38K, but with a noticeable drop in quality.

The lesson here is that if you want to use photographic images in your Web pages, you still need to go with the JPEG file format for most instances. You might not get the benefits from the PNG file format (like alpha transparency), but chances are you will save more in the file size.

It is my hope that in the future, everyone will have faster Internet connections and this won't be a problem. Right now, however, broadband Internet access is slowly gaining ground. The dominant usage of online users comes from people surfing on their dial-up modems. Depending on your audience, you should still keep watching the file sizes of your images. Try to squeeze the maximum impact with the smallest file size.

SVG

In this section, we will take a look at the background of SVG through the words of J. David Eisenberg. Afterward, we will examine an application with SVG and look at its current place in the world of Web designs.

Interview with J. David Eisenberg

Based in San Jose, California, J. David Eisenberg is a programmer and instructor. He wrote *SVG Essentials* (O'Reilly, 2002), which covered the details of the W3C's XML-based graphics standard. In the following interview, Eisenberg goes over the history of the SVG file format.

J. David
Eisenberg

Christopher Schmitt: What is SVG and what is its history?

J. David Eisenberg: As the spec so neatly puts it, SVG stands for
Scalable Vector Graphics, and it is a language for describing two-
dimensional graphics in XML with three types of graphic objects:
vector graphic shapes, images, and text.

According to Vincent Hardy's white paper (see `http://wwws.sun.
com/software/xml/developers/svg/`), "SVG was created by the
World Wide Web Consortium (W3C)... Over 20 organizations,
including Sun Microsystems, Adobe, Apple, IBM, and Kodak, have
been involved in defining SVG."

CS: How did you get involved with SVG?

JDE: I truly do not remember. I suspect I saw a reference to it some-
where, investigated it, and thought it was a clever technology. I
wrote an introductory article about SVG in January of 2001, and
actually put SVG to use in conjunction with XSL Formatting Objects
to do the output of the bracket sheets for a sports event.

CS: **What are the similarities between SVG and Macromedia's Flash?**

JDE: They're both based on vectors, and they both are capable of animation. Both can be deployed on the Web, though Flash is intended primarily for the Web; SVG is useful anywhere you need scalable graphics.

That's about all—other than that, the differences are far greater.

CS: **What are the benefits of using the technology?**

JDE: Because SVG is XML, it's easy to process and create with the existing base of XML tools. For example, I can use XSLT to process an XML-based aviation weather report and create a graphic of a thermometer and wind direction indicator. SVG can be embedded in other XML markups; the Apache Formatting Objects Processor (FOP) project (see `http://xml.apache.org/fop/`) lets you put SVG drawings into XSL Formatting Object text documents. Most important, it's an open and published standard.

You won't get trapped into a closed or published-but-proprietary standard if you use SVG. The technology itself scales nicely; there are viewer programs that display a subset of SVG on PDAs and handheld computers.

SVG is also useful across a wide range of applications, from print illustration to mapmaking to interactive display of hydrological data.

CS: **What are some of the drawbacks with the technology?**

JDE: The fact that it is generically useful means that it can't do as well as specialized tools. For example, Flash is designed to do Web-based animation superbly well, and it can probably do some extremely subtle Web-oriented things better than can the SMIL-based animation built into SVG. Similarly, SVG isn't focused on CAD, so if you need to create precision mechanical drawings, a dedicated CAD notation and system might be better—although you'd certainly want that system to export drawings in SVG format for portability and repurposing.

SVG is an XML file format (very much different from HTML or XHTML) that uses CSS syntax to stylize components of the image. In the next couple of examples, we will look at how this connection between CSS and SVG works and then look at the state of SVG.

Graphics from Text

The most amazing thing about SVG is the ability to create and manipulate an image by manipulating the file format in a simple text editor. Here's a simple SVG image (see Figure 7.10) that I created in my text editor (see Listing 7.4).

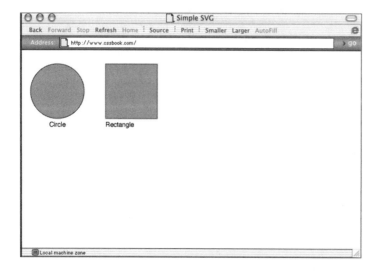

Figure 7.10

A few lines of code and an image is born.

Listing 7.4   Code for the Simple SVG

```
<?xml version="1.0"?>
<!DOCTYPE svg PUBLIC "-//W3C//DTD SVG 1.0//EN"
"http://www.w3.org/TR/2001/REC-SVG-20010904/DTD/svg10.dtd">
<svg width="400" height="200">
  <title>Simple Shapes</title>
  <g id="mycircle">
    <circle  cx="60" cy="60" r="50"
style="stroke: #000; fill: #999;" />
    <text x="45" y="125">Circle</text>
  </g>
  <g id="mysquare">
    <rect x="150" y="10" r="50" width="100" height="100"
style="stroke: #000; fill: #999;" />
    <text x="150" y="125">Rectangle</text>
  </g>
</svg>
```

With a few keystrokes (see Listing 7.5), I've changed the inside fill color
and the design of the strokes (see Figure 7.11).

Listing 7.5   Code for the Simple SVG with Slight Modifications

```
<?xml version="1.0"?>
<!DOCTYPE svg PUBLIC "-//W3C//DTD SVG 1.0//EN""http://www.w3.org/TR/2001/REC-SVG-
20010904/DTD/svg10.dtd">
<svg width="400" height="200">
  <title>Simple Shapes</title>
  <g id="mycircle">
    <circle  cx="60" cy="60" r="50"
style="stroke: #999; stroke-width: 5px; fill: #333;" />
    <text x="45" y="125"
style="font-family: Georgia, Times, serif;">Circle</text>
  </g>
  <g id="mysquare">
    <rect x="150" y="10" r="50" width="100" height="100"
style="stroke: #999; stroke-width: 5px; stroke-dasharray:
3px 3px; fill: #333;" />
    <text x="150" y="125">Rectangle</text>
  </g>
</svg>
```

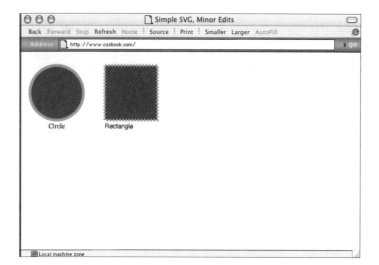

Figure 7.11

A few more lines of code, and an image is born anew.

Applying CSS to SVG

As you can see in Listing 7.4, the simple SVG example, the `style` attribute was used to define the stroke and fill of the circle and square. This is similar to the way we can associate a style to HTML elements; notice the bold code in the following code listings:

- **Listing 7.6 shows inline.**
- **Listing 7.7 shows internal.**
- **Listings 7.8 and 7.9 show external.**

Listing 7.6   SVG with Inline CSS

```
<?xml version="1.0"?>
<!DOCTYPE svg PUBLIC "-//W3C//DTD SVG 1.0//EN""http://www.w3.org/TR/2001/REC-SVG-
20010904/DTD/svg10.dtd">
<svg width="400" height="200">
  <title>Simple Shapes</title>
  <g id="mycircle">
    <circle  cx="60" cy="60" r="50"
style="stroke: #000; fill: #999;" />
    <text x="45" y="125">Circle</text>
  </g>
  <g id="mysquare">
    <rect x="150" y="10" r="50" width="100"
height="100" style="stroke: #000; fill: #999;" />
    <text x="150" y="125">Rectangle</text>
  </g>
</svg>
```

Listing 7.7   SVG with Internal CSS

```
<?xml version="1.0"?>
<!DOCTYPE svg PUBLIC "-//W3C//DTD SVG 1.0//EN""http://www.w3.org/TR/2001/REC-SVG-
20010904/DTD/svg10.dtd">
<svg width="400" height="200">
  <title>Simple Shapes</title>
  <defs>
    <style type="text/css"><![CDATA[
      circle, rect {
        stroke: #000;
        fill: #999;
        }
    ]]><style>
  </defs>
  <g id="mycircle">
    <circle  cx="60" cy="60" r="50" />
    <text x="45" y="125">Circle</text>
  </g>
  <g id="mysquare">
    <rect x="150" y="10" r="50" width="100" height="100" />
    <text x="150" y="125">Rectangle</text>
  </g>
</svg>
```

Listing 7.8   The External CSS for the SVG

```
circle, rect {
        stroke: #000;
        fill: #999;
        }
```

Listing 7.9   The SVG Pulling in the External CSS

```
<?xml version="1.0"?>
<?xml-stylesheet href="external.css" type="text/css" />
<!DOCTYPE svg PUBLIC "-//W3C//DTD SVG 1.0//EN""http://www.w3.org/TR/2001/REC-SVG-
20010904/DTD/svg10.dtd">
<svg width="400" height="200">
  <title>Simple Shapes</title>
  <g id="mycircle">
    <circle  cx="60" cy="60" r="50" />
    <text x="45" y="125">Circle</text>
  </g>
  <g id="mysquare">
    <rect x="150" y="10" r="50" width="100" height="100" />
```

continues

Listing 7.9   The SVG Pulling in the External CSS   (Continued)

```
    <text x="150" y="125">Rectangle</text>
  </g>
</svg>
```

Now that you know how to apply a style to an SVG image file, you probably want to know which elements in SVG can have style applied to them, and of those elements, you probably want to know what types of styles to use—beyond just strokes and fills. For more information, check out the comprehensive property listing at `http://www.w3.org/TR/SVG/propidx.html`.

Reality Check for SVG Development

An important benefit of SVG is that it is open for developers to hand code. Developers can manipulate the code through lines of code in a text editor and add in some interactivity. However, for most designers, that's too extreme. Sure, SVG is an interesting file format, but typically, a visually oriented person isn't going to enjoy hacking together an SVG experience by hand.

Print designers don't hand-code their layouts in PostScript. They tend to use WYSIWYG editors to place their images, flow their copy, and send their designs to the printer. The thought of hand-coding a PostScript file to create those designs never crosses their minds during the workday. Thanks to technology, they don't have to. They can save their files in Adobe Illustrator, QuarkXPress, Adobe InDesign, or other page layout programs and be done with it.

The same is soon going to be said for SVG. Developers will either use tools like Adobe's Illustrator or LiveMotion to create rich SVG images and animation. Don't feel you have to learn how to code valid XML SVG files by hand. Do the world a favor and spend that time on the design instead.

Reality Check for SVG Usage

Macromedia claims to have 436 million users with a Flash player installed in their browser. By even the most conservative estimates, that's a lot more users than those who have the compatibility to view SVG. Adobe provides an SVG plug-in at their site (see `http://www.adobe.com/svg/viewer/install/main.html`). However, people tend not to go out of their way to get a plug-in.

If a majority of the Web surfing world can't see your beautiful SVG file, should you still build for SVG? That depends on your audience. If you know your audience well enough to do so, then by all means do it. If you are not sure and still desire to create vector-based animations, then Flash is the way to go.

The roadblock to SVG's future rests primarily in the hands of the browser vendors. Until there are majority of browsers with the ability to render SVG built-in, most designers will opt to stay with Flash, which by its sixth release (at the time of this writing) is a mature technology in its own right.

For More Information

To learn more about harnessing the innate power of SVG, look to these resources:

- SVG Developers mailing list—`http://groups.yahoo.com/group/svg-developers/`

- XMLization of Graphics—`http://tech.irt.org/articles/js209/index.htm`

- SVG Frequently Asked Questions—`http://www.svgfaq.com/`

The Future of PNG and SVG

In the coming months and years, as we see CSS grow in usage and mature even further as a design language, other technologies like PNG and SVG will allow designers to create enhanced designs that also allow for better accessibility and forward compatibility. Until that time, use of PNG and SVG is limited to specific audiences who can view the images. However, even though these technologies aren't quite ready for prime time, it is good to be aware of them and how to best employ them in your designs.

Part IV

Launching Progressive Design with CSS: Deconstructions

Chapter 8

Business Publishing

This is the first chapter in our gallery of progressive designs. These next few chapters look at how to approach different Web publishing scenarios and how to use CSS to solve their respective design problems.

Business publishing refers to pages that are associated with making money on the Web. Whether a company has a merchant account or pushes out press releases onto your division's part of the intranet, you can use CSS to effectively handle the design of your Web site.

This chapter focuses on typical Web pages that are often found on business sites, such as a company news page, an e-commerce shopping cart page, and a page from an online news magazine.

A Company News Page

Signal vs. Noise (SvN) is a "relaxed voice" page (not stuffy public relations filler) from 37 signals, a Web firm specializing in simplicity in interface design and usability (see http://www.37signals.com/svn/). This page touches on musings and dialogue that cross the staff's mind and relate to the Web development industry. The topics range from pop Internet culture phenomenon to design and usability issues. Sometimes topics aren't even related to the Internet, such as Will Ferrell leaving *Saturday Night Live* (May 8, 2002 entry).

Figure 8.1 shows the SvN site in CSS. Figure 8.2 shows the same site without CSS. You can see in the comparison how much CSS affects the design and layout of the page. Although the change is not drastic, the CSS page does provide a cleaner presentation.

Figure 8.1

Company news page layout with CSS.

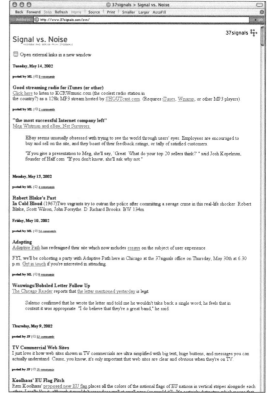

Figure 8.2

Company news page without CSS.

Minor Bugs

Although this page is a good example of how minimalism can be applied to a Web page, the code that supports it isn't a solid example of HTML markup. Let's look at the code that makes this page possible and see where improvements could be made.

Structured Markup in Real Life

Whatever you do with your CSS, make sure you structure your content correctly. As discussed in Chapter 3, "Setting Up Style," using markup content saves you from problems later on in the lifetime of a Web document. Remember that you want to use HTML elements to create an *inherent* presentational meaning in your content; don't use HTML elements inappropriately.

The header for each entry in the SvN page is formed by inserting a br after a strong element. The header isn't defined by a block-level element, but rather the use of strong, which should be used to highlight a phrase—not a heading.

Put the title for each entry as its own block level element, such as h7, instead of wrapping it in a strong container.

From:

```
<strong>GetReal</strong><br /> Hey GetNYTimes.com:
If you're…
```

To:

```
<h7>Get Real<h7>
<p> Hey GetNYTimes.com: If you're…
```

An Unordered List Is Not Messy

For the link listing that appears at the end of the page, make the list an unordered list, ul, instead of wrapping it up in a paragraph element and using a br.

From:

```
<h5>Affiliated Sites</h5>
<p class="post">
  <a href="http://www.37signals.com/">37signals</a>: We
are interface and on-line experience designers who have
a passion for sophistication and simplicity.<br /><br />
  <a href="http://www.37signals.com/dnf">Design Not Found
</a>:
The best and worst of Contingency Design (design for
when things go wrong).<br /><br />
  <a href="http://www.enormicom.com/">eNormicom</a>:
Look, we don't want to waste your time...or ours. You
must be determined to create massive economic results in
the next 10 minutes. Ready? Then read on. [featured in t
he N.Y. Times]
</p>
```

To:

```
<h5>Affiliated Sites</h5>
<ul>
  <li> <a href="http://www.37signals.com/">37signals</a>:
We are interface and on-line experience designers who
have a passion for sophistication and simplicity.</li>
  <li> <a href="http://www.37signals.com/dnf">Design
Not Found</a>: The best and worst of Contingency Design
(design for when things go wrong).</li>
```

```
<li> <a href="http://www.enormicom.com/">eNormicom</a>:
Look, we don't want to waste your time...or ours. You must
be determined to create massive economic results in the
next 10 minutes. Ready? Then read on. [featured in the
N.Y. Times]</li>
</ul>
```

When you have a set of links, they have meaning in their grouping with-out a specific or implied order. If you did have an order, it would mean using an ordered list, ol, which would mean seeing a sequence of numbers or letters (for example, 1, 2, 3 or a, b, c) before each item.

Using ul is a lot simpler to deal with in terms of markup. You can drop the excessive brs or divs and reach for ul and li.

Valid Hacks and Workarounds

Listing 8.1, one of the style sheets for the SvN page, contains markup that uses what's referred to as the *box model hack*. See the bold code for a close-up look at this hack.

Listing 8.1   The Code for the sophisto.css
(from http://www.37signals.com/svn/styles/sophisto.css)

```
/* redundant rules for bad browsers  */

body {
  font-size: small;
  voice-family: "\"}\"";
  voice-family: inherit;
  font-size: medium; }

html>body {
  font-size: medium;}


/* Layout Information */

#Content>p {margin: 0px;}
#Content>p+p {text-indent: 0px;}

#Header {
  margin: 10px 0px 10px 35px;
  padding: 0px 0px 0px 0px;
  height: 42px;
  voice-family: "\"}\"";
  voice-family: inherit;
  height:22px; }
```

```
#Title {
  margin: 0px 0px 0px 25px;
  padding: 0px 0px 0px 0px;
  height: 28px;
  voice-family: "\"}\"";
  voice-family: inherit;
  height:28px; }

body>#Header { height:22px; }
body>#Title { height:28px; }

#Content {
  margin: 39px 30px 100px 250px;
  padding: 0px 0px 0px 0px;
  font-size:12px; }

#Footer {
  margin: 30px 30px 0px 250px;
  padding: 0px 0px 0px 0px }

#Key {
  padding: 0px;
  font-size: 10px;
  line-height: 12px;
  padding: 0px 0px 20px 35px; }

#Sidebar {
  position: absolute;
  top: 110px;
  left: 35px;
  width: 190px;
  padding: 0px 0px 0px 0px;
  font-size: 10px;
  line-height: 12px; }

body>#Sidebar { width:190px; }

#toTop {
  margin: 20px 0px 0px 0px;
  padding: 6px 0px 0px 0px;
  border-top: 1px solid #ccc;
  font-size: 12px;
  line-height: 18px;
  text-align: right; }
```

continues

Listing 8.1   The Code for the sophisto.css *(from*
http://www.37signals.com/svn/styles/sophisto.css)   **(Continued)**

```
#form {
  margin: 0px 0px 0px 0px;
  padding: 0px 0px 10px 0px;
  font-size: 12px; }
```

Originally, Tantek Çelik demonstrated the hack to work around a bug in how Windows Internet Explorer 5 and 5.5 handled the box model. Thus, the name for the workaround is box model hack. But this particular hack is really a way to get certain browsers to ignore a given set of declarations.

The hack can be applied to making other selectors invisible to Windows Internet Explorer 5 and 5.5. In this workaround, we are shielding Windows Internet Explorer versions 5 and 5.5 from seeing that we set the font size to medium for other browsers.

The reason the designers of this page put this hack in their CSS is because Windows Internet Explorer 5+ uses the small value as the default font size instead of the medium value. Specifying medium in Windows Internet Explorer 5+ results in text that is one step larger than the default setting.

For more information about this workaround, see
`http://www.tantek.com/CSS/Examples/boxmodelhack.html`.

Following are some other workarounds to hide certain CSS rules from various browsers:

- **Macintosh Internet Explorer 5 Hack**—`http://www.sam-i-am.com/testsuite/css/mac_ie5_hack.html`
- **Hide CSS from Netscape Navigator 4**—`http://www.v2studio.com/k/css/n4hide/`
- **High Pass Filter (for Macintosh Internet Explorer 5+, Windows Internet Explorer 6+, Netscape Navigator 6+, Opera 5+)**—`http://www.tantek.com/CSS/Examples/highpass.html`

Why use hacks in the first place? Why not let the bad browsers continue to produce bad presentations? Well, for one reason, our clients who pay us to produce quality work might not like it. Another reason is that, as designers, our designs need to look their best. If we learn a bit about how to work around a browser's poor implementation to get everything perfect (not pixel perfect, mind you, but "close enough perfect" for the Web), then that's what Web builders do. Quality is about going that extra distance.

E-Commerce Shopping Cart Page

After the boom years of the Internet, the term *e-commerce* latched into the vernacular. E-commerce is such a part of the Internet vernacular that I would be remiss if I didn't put an online shopping cart page stylized through CSS in this chapter.

Listing 8.2 shows you the markup of a hypothetical shopping cart that doesn't use CSS.

Listing 8.2—The HTML Markup for the E-Commerce Page

```
<!DOCTYPE HTML PUBLIC [sr]
"-//W3C//DTD HTML 4.01 Transitional//EN" "http://www.w3.org/TR/html4/loose.dtd">
<html lang="en">
  <head>
    <meta http-equiv="content-type"
content="text/html; charset=iso-8859-1">
    <title>
      Great Stuff Online : Shopping Cart
    </title>
<style type="text/css" media="all">@import
"shoppingcart.css";</style>
  </head>
  <body>
    <div id="header">
      <h1>
        Great Stuff Online
      </h1>
      <p class="tagline">
        Same stuff you can get at your local store,
but online
      </p>
      <p class="no">
        Main Navigation:
      </p>
      <div id="nav">
        <ul>
          <li>
            <a href="/about/">
              About</a>
          </li>
          <li>
            <a href="/shop/">
              Continue shopping</a>
          </li>
          <li>
```

---

continues

Listing 8.2—The HTML Markup for the E-Commerce Page   (Continued)

```
              <a href="/search/">
                Search</a>
          </li>
          <li>
            <a href="">
              Sitemap</a>
          </li>
          <li>
            <a href="/contactus/">
              Contact Us</a>
          </li>
        </ul>
      </div>
  </div>
  <div id="content">
    <h4>
      Checkout path:
    </h4>
    <ol class="checkout">
      <li>
        Shipping address
      </li>
      <li>
        Confirm item
      </li>
      <li>
      Shipping method
      </li>
      <li>
        Pay up
      </li>
      <li>
        <strong>
          Place order</strong>
      </li>
    </ol>
    <p class="order">
      Your order does not go through until you press the
      <input type="button" value="Place your order">
      button.
    </p>
    <div class="shopticket">
      <h4>
        Online Shopping Cart
      </h4>
```

```
<form action="checkout.asp" method="post">
  <table summary="Checkout cart">
    <tr>
      <th>
        Product SKU
      </th>
      <th>
        Description
      </th>
      <th>
        Price $US
      </th>
      <th>
        Qty
      </th>
    </tr>
    <tr>
      <td>
        MU1203
      </td>
      <td>
        Eat at Joe's Restaurant Soundtrack
      </td>
      <td>
        $14.95
      </td>
      <td>
        <input type="text" size="2" value="1">
        <input type="button" value="update qty.">
      </td>
    </tr>
    <tr>
      <td>
        BK4501
      </td>
      <td>
        Mammoth Mistake: Forgetting Opera Tix
      </td>
      <td>
        $9.98
      </td>
      <td>
        <input type="text" size="2" value="1">
        <input type="button" value="update qty.">
      </td>
    </tr>
```

continues

Listing 8.2—The HTML Markup for the E-Commerce Page   (Continued)

```
        <tr>
          <td>
            BK5551
          </td>
          <td>
            Don't Make My Web Site
          </td>
          <td>
            $7.77
          </td>
          <td>
            <input type="text" size="2" value="1">
            <input type="button" value="update qty.">
          </td>
        </tr>
        <tr>
          <td>
          </td>
          <td class="shiphand">
            <strong>
              <select>
                <option>
                  Standard shipping (2-7 business days)
                </option>
                <option>
                  Two day shipping (2 business days)
                </option>
                <option>
                  One day shipping (1 business day)
                </option>
              </select>
            </strong>
          </td>
          <td class="shiphand">
            <strong>
              $4.96</strong>
          </td>
          <td>
          </td>
        </tr>
        <tr>
          <td>
          </td>
          <td class="total">
            <strong>
```

```
                  Total</strong>
            </td>
            <td class="total">
               <strong>
                  $32.70</strong>
            </td>
            <td>
            </td>
         </tr>
      </table>
   </form>
</div>
<p class="order">
   Your order does not go through until you press the
   <input type="button" value="Place your order">
   button.
</p>
<form action="addresschange.asp" method="post">
<div class="addresses">
   <div class="floatl">
      <h4>
         Shipping to:
      </h4>
      <p>
         John Smith
         <br>
         123 Saltwater Dr.
         <br>
         Orlando, FL 55555
         <br>
         <input type="button" value="change">
      </p>
   </div>
   <div class="floatr">
      <h4>
         Payment Method:
      </h4>
      <p>
         Visa: ***-55555
         <br>
         Exp: 05/2006
         <br>
         <input type="button" value="change">
      </p>
      </div>
   <div class="floatr">
      <h4>
```

continues

Listing 8.2—The HTML Markup for the E-Commerce Page   (Continued)

```
            Billing Address:
        </h4>
        <p>
            John Smith
            <br>
            123 Saltwater Dr.
            <br>
            Orlando, FL 55555
            <br>
            <input type="button" value="change">
        </p>
    </div>
  </div>
  </form>
</div>
<br style="clear: both;">
<div id="footer">
  <ul>
    <li>
      <a href="/faq/">
        FAQ</a>
    </li>
    <li>
      <a href="/sitemap/">
        Sitemap</a>
    </li>
    <li>
      <a href="/search/">
        Search</a>
    </li>
    <li>
      <a href="/contactus/">
        Contact Us</a>
    </li>
  </ul>
  <ul>
    <li>
      <a href="/privacypolicy/">
        Privacy Policy</a>
    </li>
    <li>
      <a href="/terms/">
        Terms of Use</a>
    </li>
  </ul>
```

```
    </div>
    <p>
      Copyright &copy; 2002 Big Company. All rights
reserved.
    </p>
  </body>
</html>
```

Figure 8.3 shows you what the markup from Listing 8.2 looks like on the Web.

Figure 8.3

Shopping cart page without CSS.

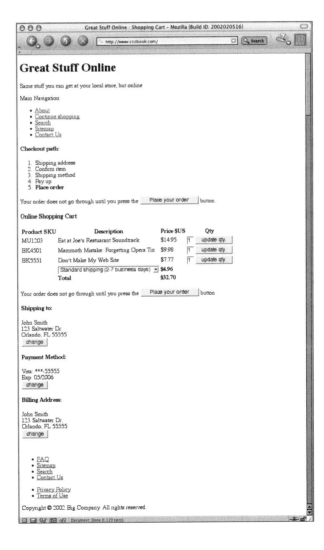

Listing 8.3 shows you the markup of the same hypothetical shopping cart, but this time the example uses CSS. This type of example probably works for most of the sites on the Web that have a shopping cart for their examples. Sites like Amazon.com still want to tailor their content to Netscape 2.0. However, if you don't have the venture capital of an international bookseller, you can use CSS without resorting to nested HTML tables.

Listing 8.3   CSS for the E-Commerce Page, Linked into the Document

```css
.no {
  display: none;
  }

a {
  font-family: Verdana;
  font-size: 0.9em;
  color: #666;
  }

body {
  font-family: Verdana;
  font-size: 0.9em;
  }

#content {
  margin-bottom: 5em;
  }

h1 {
  font-family: Georgia, Times, serif;
  font-size: 2.5em;
  margin: 15px 0 0 10%;
  padding: 0;
  }

h4 {
  margin: 0 0 0 0;
  padding: 1em 0 10px 10%;
  }

p {
  margin: 0 0 0 0;
  padding: 0 0 0 10%;
  }
```

```
.tagline  {
  font-family: Georgia, Times, serif;
  font-style: italic;
  margin: 0 0 1em 10%;
  padding: 0;
  }

#nav  {
  margin-left: 10%;
  }

#nav ul {
  display: inline;
  padding: 0;
  margin: 0;
  }

#nav ul li:first-child  {
  border: none;
  padding-left: 0;
  }

#nav ul li  {
  display: inline;
  padding: 0 1em 0 1em;
  border-left: 1px dashed #666;
  font-size: 0.9em;
  }

#nav ul li a  {
  border: 0;
  margin: 0;
  padding: 0;
  }

.checkout  {
  margin: 0 0 1.5em 0;
  padding: 0 0 0 10%;
  }

.checkout ul  {
  display: inline;
  margin: 0;
  padding: 0;

  }
```

continues

Listing 8.3   CSS for the E-Commerce Page, Linked into the Document (Continued)

```css
.checkout li  {
  display: inline;
  padding: 5px 5px 5px 15px;
  border-bottom: 1px solid #666;
  margin: 0;
  width: 20%;
  }

.addresses  {
  padding-left: 10%;
  padding-right: 5%;
  }

.checkout li:first-child  {
  border-bottom: 1px solid #666;
  padding-left: 0;
  }

.checkout li strong  {
  background-color: #fff;
  border-bottom: 5px solid #666;
  padding: 0;
  margin: 0;
  }

table  {
  margin: 0 0 0 0.5em;
  }

th  {
  text-align: left;
  padding: 5px 0 5px 0;
  }

td  {
  padding: 2px 0 2px 0;

  }

.shopticket  {
  margin: 0.5em 5% 7px 10%;
  border: 1px solid #666;
  padding:  0 0 0 0;
  }
```

```
.shopticket h4  {
  padding: 0.5em;
  margin: 0;
  background-color: #000;
  color: #fff;
  }

.order  {
  margin: 1em 0 1em 0;
  }

.shiphand  {
  font-weight: bold;
  }

.total  {
  font-weight: bold;
  }

.floatr  {
  float: right;
  width: 33%;
  margin: 1em 0 0 0;
  border-top: 1px solid #000;
  border-left: 1px solid #000;
  }

.floatl {
  float: left;
  width: 33%;
  margin: 1em 0 0 0;
  padding: 0;
  border-top: 1px solid #000;
  border-left: 1px solid #000;
  }

#footer  {
  clear: both;
  margin: 1em 0 1em 10%;
  }

#footer ul  {
  display: block;
  padding: 0;
  margin: 0.5em 0 0 0;
  }
```

continues

Listing 8.3   CSS for the E-Commerce Page, Linked into the Document

```
#footer ul li  {
  display: inline;
  padding: 0 1em 0 1em;
  border-left: 1px dashed #666;
  font-size: 0.9em;
  }

#footer ul li:first-child  {
  border: none;
  padding-left: 0;
  }
```

Figure 8.4 shows you what the CSS version from Listing 8.3 looks like on the Web.

Figure 8.4

Shopping cart page with CSS.

Horizontal Navigation Through CSS

Listing 8.4 shows you how to convert an unordered list into a horizontal navigation bar. (Check the header and footer in Figure 8.4.) This is done by making the unordered list and list items inline. In other words, they lose their "block level" feature of forcing a break. The items appear right after each other in a row.

Sometimes, you don't want to have a vertical list of links for your navigation scheme. In traditional Web design methods, you could put links into a row of table cells. Because we are stopping those bad Web development practices, we need to find a new way to achieve a horizontal navigation sequence. We can burst out of that prison by using this method in CSS. And because it's CSS, it degrades gracefully into Web devices that don't use CSS.

Listing 8.4   Converting an Unordered List into a Horizontal Navigation Bar

```
#nav ul {
   display: inline;
   padding: 0;
   margin: 0;
   }

#nav ul li:first-child  {
   border: none;
   padding-left: 0;
   }

#nav ul li  {
   display: inline;
   padding: 0 1em 0 1em;
   border-left: 1px dashed #666;
   font-size: 0.9em;
   }
```

Online News Magazine Layout

Try this example of an online news magazine layout for those times when you have content floating around on your hard drive and you want to publish it in an online magazine. With magazines, you can focus more attention on the visual than on just the text. Use this example if you have great imagery to work with and the types of stories to compliment them.

Listing 8.5 shows you the markup of a hypothetical magazine layout that doesn't use CSS.

Listing 8.5   Markup for the Magazine Layout

```html
<!DOCTYPE HTML PUBLIC
"-//W3C//DTD HTML 4.01 Transitional//EN" "http://www.w3.org/TR/html4/loose.dtd">
<html lang="en">
  <head>
    <meta http-equiv="content-type"
content="text/html; charset=iso-8859-1">
    <title>
      People in Life
    </title>
    <link href="style.css" type="text/css"
rel="stylesheet">
  </head>
  <body>
    <div id="header">
      <h1>
        <img src="maghed.gif" alt="People in Life
Magazine">
      </h1>
      <p class="tagline">
        The magazine about people and life. No kidding.
      </p>
      <p class="no">
        Main Navigation:
      </p>
      <div id="nav">
        <ul>
          <li>
            <a href="/about/">
              About</a>
          </li>
          <li>
            <a href="/search/">
              Search</a>
          </li>
          <li>
            <a href="/sitemap/">
              Sitemap</a>
          </li>
          <li>
            <a href="/contact/">
              Contact Us</a>
          </li>
          <li>
            <a href="/archive/">
              Archive</a>
```

```
          </li>
        </ul>
      </div>
    </div>
    <div id="content">
      <h2>
        Current Issue -
        <strong>
          February 2002</strong>
      </h2>
      <h3>
        <a href="/2002/02/mainstory/">
          How People Cope with Reality</a>
      </h3>
      <p class="caption">
        Caption goes here. Usually a couple of words.
      </p>
      <p class="desc">
        Lorem ipsum dolor sit amet, consetetur sadipscing
elitr, sed diam nonumy eirmod tempor invidunt ut labore et
dolore magna aliquyam erat, sed diam voluptua. At vero eos
et accusam et justo duo dolores et ea rebum.
      </p>
      <p class="prompt">
        <a href="/2002/02/mainstory/">
          Read more</a>
      </p>
<!-- Insert ad banner, large - if you want -->
      <div id="substory1">
        <h4>
          <a href="/2002/02/substory1/">
            Sunglasses are winning the war</a>
        </h4>
        <p class="desc">
          Lorem ipsum dolor sit amet, consetetur sadipscing
elitr, sed diam nonumy eirmod tempor invidunt ut labore et
dolore magna aliquyam erat, sed diam voluptua. At vero eos
et accusam et justo duo dolores et ea rebum.
        </p>
        <p class="prompt">
          <a href="/2002/02/mainstory/">
            Read more</a>
        </p>
      </div>
      <div id="substory2">
        <h5>
```

continues

Listing 8.5   Markup for the Magazine Layout   (Continued)

```
                <a href="/2002/02/substory2/">
                    Stayed up late, lately?</a>
            </h5>
            <p class="desc">
                Lorem ipsum dolor sit amet, consetetur sadipscing
elitr, sed diam nonumy eirmod tempor invidunt ut labore et
dolore magna aliquyam erat, sed diam voluptua. At vero eos
et accusam et justo duo dolores et ea rebum.
            </p>
            <p class="prompt">
                <a href="/2002/02/mainstory/">
                    Read more</a>
            </p>
        </div>
        <br style="clear: both;">
<!-- Insert ad banner, small -->
        <div class="quickpoll">
            <fieldset>
                <legend align="left">
                    Quick Poll
                </legend>
                <p>
                    How many times have you thought about your
sunglasses today?
                </p>
                <form action="pollday.php" method="post">
                    <input type="radio" value="timevalue">
                    Once a minute
                    <br>
                    <input type="radio" value="timevalue">
                    Once an hour
                    <br>
                    <input type="radio" value="timevalue">
                    Once a day
                    <br>
                    <input type="radio" value="timevalue">
                    Once a month
                    <br>
                    <input type="submit" value="submit"
class="submit">
                </form>
            </fieldset>
        </div>
    </div>
    <div id="footer">
```

```
      <ul>
        <li>
          <a href="/faq/">
            FAQ</a>
        </li>
        <li>
          <a href="/sitemap/">
            Sitemap</a>
        </li>
        <li>
          <a href="/search/">
            Search</a>
        </li>
        <li>
          <a href="/contactus/">
            Contact Us</a>
        </li>
      </ul>
      <br>
      <ul>
        <li>
          <a href="/privacy/">
            Privacy Policy</a>
        </li>
        <li>
          <a href="/tos/">
            Terms of Use</a>
        </li>
        <li>
          <a href="/reprints/">
            Reprints &amp Permission</a>
        </li>
      </ul>
      <p>
        Copyright &copy; 2002 People in Life, Inc. All
rights reserved.
      </p>
    </div>
  </body>
</html>
```

Figure 8.5 shows you what the markup from Listing 8.5 looks like on
the Web.

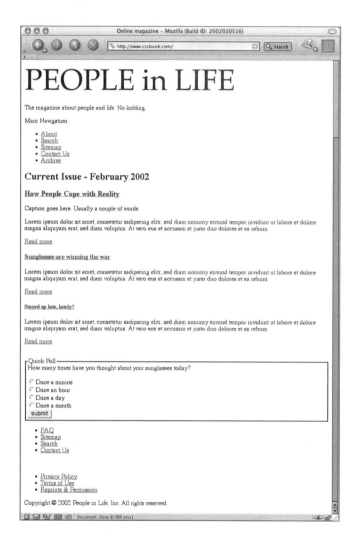

Figure 8.5

Online magazine layout
without CSS.

Listing 8.6 shows you the markup of the same hypothetical magazine layout, but this time the example uses CSS. With the power of CSS at your disposal, you can transform a boring Web page into one with instant visual appeal.

Listing 8.6   CSS for the Magazine Layout

```
html  {
  width: 97%;
  }


h1   {
    margin: 10px 0 0 0;
  }
```

```
.tagline {
    text-align: right;
    margin: 0 0 1em 0;
    font-style: italic;
    font-weight: bold;
    font-size: 1.1em;
  }

body  {
    margin: 0 0 0 125px;
  }

a  {
    color: #777;
  }

#content  {
  border-left: 1px solid #999;
  }

#nav  {
  position: absolute;
  width: 100px;
  top: 10px;
  left: 10px;
  }

#nav ul {
  list-style: none outside;
  width: 100px;
  padding: 0;
  margin: 0 15px 10px 0;
  background-color: #b50;
  color: #ffc;
  border: solid 1px #333;
  font-family: Verdana, Arial, Helvetica, sans-serif;
  text-align: center;
  }

#nav ul li {
  padding: 0;
  margin: 0;
  border: none;
  display: block;
  font-family: Verdana, Arial, Helvetica, sans-serif;
  }
```

continues

Listing 8.6   CSS for the Magazine Layout   (Continued)

```css
#nav ul li a {
  display: block;
  padding: 5px;
  margin: 0;
  background-color: #ccc;
  color: #333;
  border-top: solid 1px #999;
  border-bottom: solid 1px #bbb;
  font-family: Verdana, Arial, Helvetica, sans-serif;
  text-decoration: none;
  }

#nav ul li a:hover {
  background-color: #666;
  color: #fff;
  border-top: solid 1px #999;
  border-bottom: solid 1px #bbb;
  font-family: Verdana, Arial, Helvetica, sans-serif;
  text-decoration: none;
  }

#nav ul li a:active {
  background-color: #000;
  color: #999;
  border-top: solid 1px #999;
  border-bottom: solid 1px #bbb;
  font-family: Verdana, Arial, Helvetica, sans-serif;
  text-decoration: none;
  }

#footer  {
  margin: 2em 0 0 0;
  }

#footer ul {
  margin: 0 0 0 0;
  padding: 0;
  display: inline;
  }

#footer ul li  {
  display: inline;
  padding-right: 15px;
  font-family: Verdana, Arial, Helvetica, sans-serif;
  font-size: .8em;
  }
```

```
.no  {
  display: none;
  }

h2  {
  font-family: Georgia, Times, serif;
  font-size: 0.9em;
  margin: 0;
  padding: 10px;
  font-weight: normal;
  background-color: #999;
  }

h3   {
  background-position: 0 0;
  background-repeat: no-repeat;
  background-image: url("mag.jpg");
  width: 100%;
  height: 300px;
  padding: 0 0 0 10px;
  margin: 0;
  }

h3  a {
  background-color: #fff;
  color: #000;
  padding: 0 1em 1em 0;
  margin: 0;
  text-transform: uppercase;
  text-decoration: none;
  font-family: Verdana, Arial, Helvetica, sans-serif;
  }

h4   {
  background-position: top right;
  background-repeat: no-repeat;
  background-image: url("mag1.jpg");
  width: 100%;
  height: 200px;
  padding: 0;
  margin: 0;
  }

h4, h5  {
  font-size: 0.9em;
  font-weight: bold
  margin: 0 0 1em 0;
  }
```

continues

Listing 8.6   CSS for the Magazine Layout   (Continued)

```css
h4  a  {
  background-color: #fff;
  color: #000;
  padding: 0 1em 1em 0;
  margin: 0 0 0 10px;
  text-transform: uppercase;
  text-decoration: none;
  font-family: Verdana, Arial, Helvetica, sans-serif;
  }

h5    {
  background-position: 0 0;
  background-repeat: no-repeat;
  background-image: url("mag2.jpg");
  width: 100%;
  height: 200px;
  padding: 0;
  margin: 0;
  }

h5  a  {
  background-color: #fff;
  color: #000;
  padding: 0 1em 1em 0;
  margin: 0 0 0 10px;
  text-transform: uppercase;
  text-decoration: none;
  font-family: Verdana, Arial, Helvetica, sans-serif;
  }

.quickpoll  {
  width: 33%;
  }

form {
  margin-left: 10px;
  }

fieldset  {
  border: 1px solid #000;
  margin: 0 0 0 10px;
  background-color: #ccc;
  color: #333;
  }
```

```
fieldset legend  {
  background-color: #fff;
  padding: 0 1em 0 1em;
  }

fieldset p  {
  margin: 0;
  padding: 0;
  }

.submit  {
  border: 1px solid #000;
  padding: 0.2em;
  }

#substory1  {
  width: 500px;
  margin: 3em 0 3em 0;
  }

#substory2  {
  width: 500px;
  margin: 1em 0 1em 0;
  }

#substory1, #substory2  {
  }

#substory1 .desc, #substory2 .desc {
  font-size: 0.9em;

  }

.caption  {
  font-family: Verdana, Arial, Helvetica, sans-serif;
  font-size: 0.8em;
  padding: 0 0 0 0;
  margin: 0 0 0 10px;
  }

.desc  {
  font-size: 1.1em;
  font-weight: normal;
  font-family: Georgia, Times, serif;
  padding: 0 0 0 0;
  margin: 1em 0 0 10px;
  display: inline;
```

continues

Listing 8.6   CSS for the Magazine Layout   (Continued)

```
  }

.prompt  {
  display: inline;
  margin: 0;
  padding: 0;
  font-family: Verdana, Arial, Helvetica, sans-serif;
  font-size: 0.8em;
  font-weight: bold;
  }
```

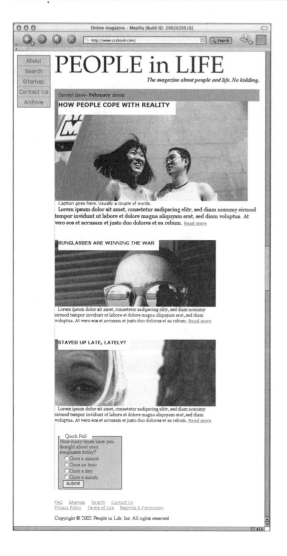

In Listing 8.6, notice the titles for the stories that are in bold. The lead story is wrapped up in an h4 element. That h4 element contains the background image for the article. The anchor element has a background color set to white and text set to black to make it legible. This is a great way to design elements using CSS.

Figure 8.6 shows you what the CSS version from Listing 8.6 looks like on the Web.

These examples have shown that Web pages for business-related pages do not have to resort to traditional Web development methods or sacrificing anything from your designs. Use the examples as jumping-off points for your needs, or better yet, start off in a totally new direction with CSS. You'll be able to stretch your designs more than you ever could with an HTML table or a stretched single pixel.

Figure 8.6

Online magazine layout using CSS.

Chapter 9

Independent Publishing

If you tried to reach the millions online that you can offline by creating your own print newspaper or magazine, you would probably go broke just trying to figure out the logistics of it all. In contrast, the reason why the Web grew so fast was the ease of publishing. The sites that popped up in the early 1990s Web boom were often quirky, off-the-wall, irreverent, and created with a fresh voice not found in print media.

That's what I love about the Web. You can still get an ISP's hosting package and crank out your own online publication on an old PC. Your independent voice can sit online next to IBM's, Levi's, or McDonald's.

This chapter shows you two different examples of independent publishing—a personal site example and an e-zine example. With two examples, you will see the breadth of power in CSS. CSS can be used to enhance the presentation slightly in a two-column layout or completely overhaul the presentation in an avant-garde design.

> **Note**
>
> **A worldwide project called "Independents Day" recognizes and celebrates the online independent publisher. If you create your own online world, you might want to think about joining them. See** http://www. independentsday. org/.

Personal Site

A personal site can be many things. It can be a place for business where you can post your résumé for potential recruiters. Alternatively, it can be an online journal recording your thoughts about current events, what you had for lunch, other social interactions, or individual misadventures. The possibilities are endless when you are your own content producer.

Privacy Online

Be careful what you put online, and keep your privacy in mind before publishing personal information online. This might be an obvious suggestion, but it is worth stating. At the least, keep your home address and phone number off the Web site.

You might want to avoid pictures of children or other specific family information online. Some people might consider the risks low, but you never know for sure who will be visiting your site after you post it online, so it is usually best to err on the side of caution.

For this CSS design example of a personal site, we will use a hypothetical version of my site. Your personal site will no doubt cater to your unique tastes. For this personal site, I want to keep a journal (sometimes referred to as a Web log or blog, for short). I also want to include a hot list—a list of sites I like, links to my recent work, a sign-up form for a newsletter announcing the infrequent updates about my life or site, and a link to a form for contacting me via email.

Figure 9.1 and Figure 9.2 both show the hypothetical version of my personal site. You can see that they look a little different. This is because I styled one in CSS (Figure 9.1) and one in just plain HTML (Figure 9.2).

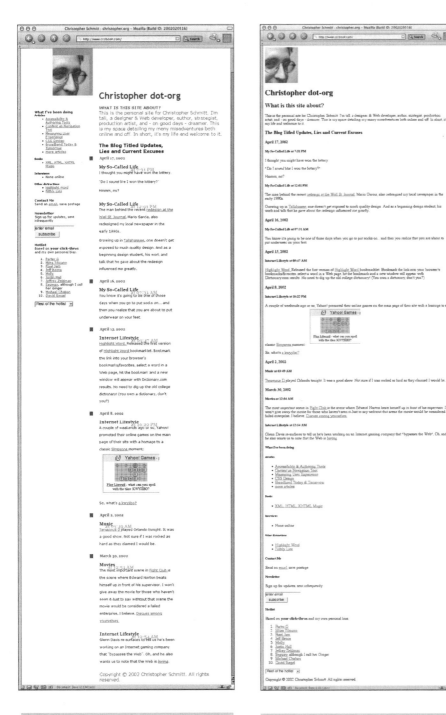

Figure 9.1

The personal site styled with CSS.

Figure 9.2

The personal site styled with HTML is bland without the CSS spice.

Creating the Daily Blog Entry Design

Let's look at a couple of items in this design in detail. The first thing I want to look at it is how the daily entries for the blog were created. Listing 9.1 is the HTML sample of a journal entry, and Figure 9.3 shows what it would look like on the screen.

Listing 9.1   HTML Sample of a Journal "Blog" Entry

```
<div class="daily">
  <h4>
    April 17, 2002
  </h4>
  <div class="entry">
    <h5 class="subject">
      <span class="cat">
        My So-Called Life
      </span>
      at 7:31 PM
    </h5>
    <p>
      I thought you might have won the lottery.
    </p>
    <p>
      "Do I
      <em>
        sound
      </em>
      like I won the lottery?"
    </p>
    <p>
      Hmmm, no?
    </p>
  </div>
</div>
```

April 17, 2002

My So-Called Life
at 7:31 PM
I thought you might have won the lottery.

"Do I *sound* like I won the lottery?"

Hmmm, no?

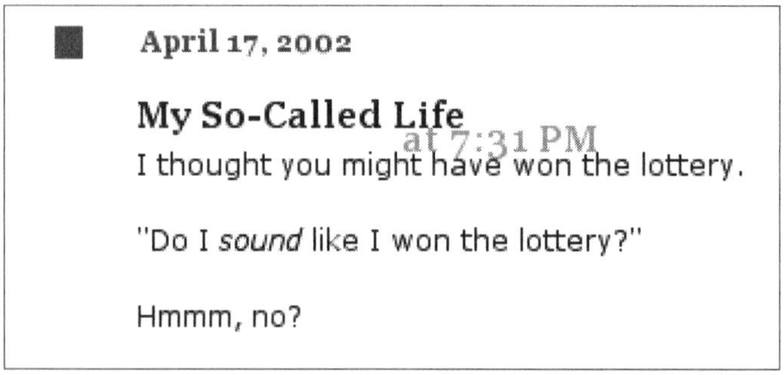

Figure 9.3

Detail of a journal entry.

You can create the bullet on the left side of the date by defining the left side of the border in the CSS rule shown in Listing 9.2.

Listing 9.2   Defining the Bullet with CSS

```
.daily h4 {
  position: relative;
  font-size: 1em;
  font-family: Georgia, Times, serif;
  margin: 0 0 1em 0;
  padding: 0 0 0 1em;
  color: #444;
  border-left: 1em solid #444;
  line-height: 1em;
}
```

This rule is an attempt to get the bullet to be precisely square. The widths of the left and right sides equal the widths of the top and bottom. This attempt at a square through a *perfect* method is something I know to be more of a fruitless exercise because font sizes won't be the same from browser to browser or computer to computer, but it makes me feel better for trying. You might see a rectangle instead of a square in your browser, and that's fine, too. It makes me feel better knowing that I coded for a square. And with the `line-height`, `font-size`, `border-left`, and `padding-right` properties all equal to one em unit, it should work across all major browsers.

Moving down from the date to the category and time stamp of the blog entry, we use the type of setup shown in Listing 9.3.

Listing 9.3   Setting Up the Category Label

```
<h5 class="subject">
  <span class="cat">
    My So-Called Life
  </span>
  at 7:31 PM
</h5>
```

Because we know the width of the "date" border (one em) and the "date" width of the left-hand padding (one em), we set the padding to a total of two ems. We do this to align the category label with the date of the entry (see Listing 9.4).

Listing 9.4 CSS Rule for the Category Label

```
.daily h5 {
  position: relative;
  font-size: 1em;
  font-weight: bold;
  color: #999;
  font-family: Georgia, Times, serif;
  padding: 0 0 0 1em;
  margin: 0;
  top: 0.7em;
}
```

Notice the way the time stamp is tucked underneath the category title in Figure 9.3. This effect is achieved mainly by positioning the element to be relative (see Listing 9.5). Positioning elements to be relative means that you can move an element to a new place in the Web page—comparative to its original placement on the page.

Listing 9.5 CSS Rule for the Category Text

```
.cat  {
  position: relative;
  color: #000;
  top: -0.6em;
  margin-right: -2em;
}
```

Note

For more information about personal site features such as Weblogs (or if you want to find out what a Weblog is), pick up *Blogging: Genius Strategies for Instant Web Content* by Biz Stone (New Riders, 2002).

Using the span tag around the category "My So-Called Life," we move in the margin by 2em units. This brings in the rest of the headline—the time stamp. Now we raise the category up by 0.6em units, which makes the time stamp legible.

The bad part is that Windows Internet Explorer 5+ gets this effect wrong. The timestamp background element overlaps the category (see Figure 9.4). A quick fix for this would be to take out the margin-right: -2em to eliminate the overlap altogether. (I hope Microsoft gets this right in the next Windows version of their browser.)

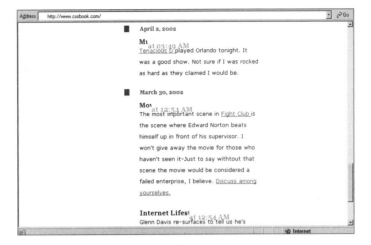

Figure 9.4

Two steps forward,
one step back.

Listing 9.6 is the personal site code, trimmed a bit for publishing purposes. To get the full code listing, check out this book's companion Web site (www.cssbook.com) to download this and other examples.

Note

Listing 9.6 uses the two-column layout as seen in Chapter 4, "Laying Out Pages."

Listing 9.6   Edited Personal Site Example

```
<!DOCTYPE HTML PUBLIC "-//W3C//DTD HTML 4.01 Transitional//EN"
  "http://www.w3.org/TR/html4/loose.dtd">
<html lang="en">
  <head>
    <meta http-equiv="content-type" content="text/html;charset=iso-8859-1">
    <title>
      Christopher Schmitt : christopher.org
    </title>
<style type="text/css">

  p, ol, ul, li {
    margin-top: 0;
    padding-top: 0;
    font-family: Verdana, "Myriad Web", Syntax, Arial, Helvetica, sans-serif;
  }

  h1, h2, h3, h4, h5 {
    margin-bottom: 0;
    padding-bottom: 0;
  }
```

continues

Listing 9.6   Edited Personal Site Example   (Continued)

```css
h1 {
    padding: 125px 0 0.5em 0;
    margin: 0;
    font-size: 2em;
    font-family: "Trebuchet MS", Verdana, "Myriad Web", Syntax, sans-serif;
    }

h2  {
    padding: 0;
    margin: 0;
    font-size: 0.9em;
    text-transform: uppercase;
    font-family: Verdana, "Myriad Web", Syntax, Arial, Helvetica, sans-serif;
    color: #333;
    }

h3  {
    font-size: 0.8em;
    padding: 0.2em 0 0.5em 0;
    margin: 0;
    font-family: Verdana, "Myriad Web", Syntax, Arial, Helvetica, sans-serif;
    }


ol, li, .colside li, .colside ul  {
    padding-top: 0;
    margin-top: 0;
    }

b {
    font-weight: bold;
    }

em, i {
    font-style: italic;
    }

body  {
    margin: 25px 0 3em 250px;
    }

.colmain  {
    margin-right: 40%;
    }
```

```
.colmain h3  {
  margin-left: 35px;
  font-size: 1.1em;
  }

.colside  {
  position: absolute;
  top: 200px;
  left: 50px;
  width: 175px;
  font-family: Verdana, "Myriad Web", Syntax, Arial, Helvetica, sans-serif;
  font-size: 0.9em;
  }

.colside p, .colside li  {
  font-size: 0.8em;
  }

.colside h6  {
  padding-top: 0;
  margin-top: 0;
  padding-bottom: 0;
  margin-bottom: 0;
  }

.daily p {
  margin: 0 0 0.5em 35px;
  line-height: 2em;
  font-family: Verdana, "Myriad Web", Syntax, Arial, Helvetica, sans-serif;
  font-size: 0.8em;
  }

.daily h4 {
  position: relative;
  font-size: 1em;
  font-family: Georgia, Times, serif;
  margin: 0 0 1em 0;
  padding: 0 0 0 1em;
  color: #444;
  border-left: 1em solid #444;
  line-height: 1em;
  }

.daily h5 {
  position: relative;
  font-size: 1em;
```

continues

Listing 9.6   Edited Personal Site Example   (Continued)

```
      font-weight: bold;
      color: #999;
      font-family: Georgia, Times, serif;
      padding: 0 0 0 35px;
      margin: 0;
      top: 0.7em;
      }

   .cat  {
      position: relative;
      color: #000;
      top: -0.6em;
      margin-right: -2em;
      }

   .entry  {
      margin: 0 0 1.5em 0;
      }

   #header, #footer  {
      margin-left: 35px;
      margin-right: 1.5em;
      color: #333;
      }

   #mugshot  {
      position: absolute;
      left: 116px;
      top: 0;
      border-top: 25px solid #999;
      border-right: 12px solid #999;
      }

   </style>
   </head>
   <body>
      <div id="header">
         <img src="christopher_schmitt.jpg" alt="Head of Christopher Schmitt"
         ➥id="mugshot">
         <h1>
            Christopher dot-org
         </h1>
         <h2>
            What is this site about?
         </h2>
```

```
    <p>
        This is the personal site for Christopher Schmitt. I'm tall, a designer
&amp; Web developer, author, strategist, production artist, and - on good days -
dreamer. This is my space detailing my many misadventures both online and off. In
short, it's my life and welcome to it.
    </p>
  </div>
  <div class="colmain">
    <h3>
      The Blog Titled Updates, Lies and Current Excuses
    </h3>
    <div class="daily">
      <h4>
        April 17, 2002
      </h4>
      <div class="entry">
        <h5 class="subject">
          <span class="cat">
            My So-Called Life
          </span>
          at 7:31 PM
        </h5>
        <p>
          I thought you might have won the lottery.
        </p>
        <p>
          "Do I
          <em>
            sound
          </em>
          like I won the lottery?"
        </p>
        <p>
          Hmmm, no?
        </p>
      </div>
      <div class="entry">
        <h5 class="subject">
          <span class="cat">
            My So-Called Life
          </span>
          at 12:01 PM
        </h5>
        <p>
          The man behind the recent
          <a href="http://www.poynter.org/centerpiece/040902_mario.htm">
```

continues

Listing 9.6   Edited Personal Site Example   (Continued)

```
                redesign at the Wall St. Journal</a>, Mario Garcia, also
                redesigned my local newspaper in the early 1990s.
            <p>
                Growing up in
                <a href="http://www.christopher.org/tallahassee/">
                    Tallahassee</a>, one doesn't get exposed to much quality design.
When I was a beginning design student, his work and lectures that he gave about
the redesign influenced me greatly.
            </div>
        </div>
        <div class="daily">
            <h4>
                April 16, 2002
            </h4>
            <div class="entry">
                <h5 class="subject">
                    <span class="cat">
                        My So-Called Life
                    </span>
                    at 07:31 AM
                </h5>
                <p>
                    You know it's going to be one of those days when you go to put
socks on... and then you realize that you are about to put underwear on your
feet.
            </div>
        </div>
        <div class="daily">
            <h4>
                April 15, 2002
            </h4>
            <div class="entry">
                <h5 class="subject">
                    <span class="cat">
                        Internet Lifestyle
                    </span>
                    at 09:47 AM
                </h5>
                <p>
                    <a href="http://www.roundsearch.com/highlightword/" target="_top">
                        Highlight Word.
                    </a>
                    Released the first version of
                    <a href="http://www.roundsearch.com/highlightword/" target="_top">
                        Highlight Word
```

```
            </a>
                bookmarklet. Bookmark the link into your browser's
bookmarks/favorites, select a word in a Web page, hit the bookmark and a new win-
dow will appear with Dictionary.com results. No need to dig up the old college
dictionary! (You do own a dictionary, don't you?)
        </div>
      </div>
</div>

    <div style="clear: both;"></div>
      <div class="colside">
        <h5>
          What I've been doing
        </h5>
        <h6>
          Articles
        </h6>
        <ul>
          <li>
            <a href="http://www.alistapart.com/stories/tools/">
              Accessibility &amp; Authoring Tools
            </a>
          </li>
          <li>
            <a href="http://www.digital-Web.com/features/feature_2001-11.shtml">
              Content as Navigation Tool
            </a>
          </li>
          <li>
            <a href="http://www.digital-Web.com/features/feature_2001-9.shtml">
              Measuring User Experience
            </a>
          </li>
          <li>
            <a href="http://www.Webreview.com/2001/03_09/Webauthors/index03.shtml">
              CSS Design
            </a>
          </li>
          <li>
            <a href="http://www.Webreview.com/2001/03_30/strategists/index01.shtml">
              Broadband Today &amp; Tomorrow
            </a>
          </li>
          <li>
            <a href="/articles/">
              more articles
            </a>
```

continues

Listing 9.6   Edited Personal Site Example   (Continued)

```
        </ul>
        <h6>
          Books
        </h6>
        <ul>
          <li>
            <a href="http://www.xhtml-resources.com/magic/">
              XML, HTML, XHTML Magic
            </a>
          </li>
        </ul>
<h5>

          Contact Me
        </h5>
        <p>
          Send an
          <a href="/contact/index.html">
            email</a>, save postage

        <h5>
          Hotlist
        </h5>
        <p>
          Based on
          <b>
            your click-thrus
          </b>
          and my own personal bias.
        </p>
        <ol>
          <li>
            <a href="http://www.serve.com/apg">
              Porter G
            </a>
          <li>
            <a href="http://www.Webhole.com/">
              Miles Tilmann
            </a>
          <li>
            <a href="http://www.pixeljam.com/">
              Pixel Jam
            </a>
          <li>
            <a href="http://www.amazon.com/">
              Jeff Bezos
```

```
        </a>
    <li>
      <a href="http://www.molly.com/">
        Molly
      </a>
    <li>
      <a href="http://www.links.net/">
        Justin Hall
      </a>
    <li>
      <a href="http://www.zeldman.com/">
        Jeffrey Zeldman
      </a>
    <li>
      <a href="http://www.segway.com/" target="_new">
        Segway</a>, although I call her Ginger
    <li>
      <a href="http://www.michaelchabon.com/" target="_new">
        Michael Chabon
      </a>
    <li>
      <a href="http://www.dsiegel.com/">
        David Siegel
      </a>
    </ol>
    <form action="/services/ranking.html" method="post">
      <select>
        <option>
          Rest of the hotlist
        </option>
      </select>
    </form>
  </div>
  <div id="footer">
    <p>
      Copyright &copy; 2002 Christopher Schmitt. All rights reserved.
    </p>
  </div>
</body>
</html>
```

E-Zine

If you were creating a traditional print magazine, you would need to follow some traditional design and publication guidelines, such as having a legible table of contents. Thankfully, you don't need to follow those rules when you publish material online. For instance, you can engage in developing an "off-the-wall" or avant-garde style for your presentation—a presentation that wouldn't sit right with most, if not all, nationally distributed magazines.

An *e-zine* is a (sometimes) self-published, underground magazine that's published electronically. It's usually done on the cheap, too, but on the Web, no one needs to know that.

For this CSS design example, we will use my fictional e-zine called *Likely Stories*. *Likely Stories* provides commentary on local and sometimes national stories to a community of readers.

Listing 9.7 is the code that makes this example e-zine design happen.

Listing 9.7   E-Zine Example

```html
<!DOCTYPE HTML PUBLIC "-//W3C//DTD HTML 4.01 Transitional//EN"
  "http://www.w3.org/TR/html4/loose.dtd">
<html lang="en">
  <head>
    <meta http-equiv="content-type" content="text/html; charset=iso-8859-1">
    <title>
      Likely Stories
    </title>
<style type="text/css">

html {
  width: 97%;
  }

body {
  background-image: url(bkgd_sidebar.jpg);
  background-repeat: repeat-y;
  background-position: bottom left;
  font-family: Verdana, Arial, Helvetica, sans-serif;
  margin: 0 0 0 151px;;
}

#header  {
  position: absolute;
  left: 191px;
  top: -1em;
}

#header p {
  margin: -1em 0 0 0;
  padding: 0;
```

```
    color: #06c;
    font-family: Courier, monospace;
}

#footer  {
  padding: 3em 0 3em 200px;
  width: 200px;
  font-size: 0.8em;
  color: #666;
  }

.nav  {
  position: absolute;
  width: 150px;
  left: -0.4em;
  top: -0.4em;
}

.nav p  {
  margin: 0;
  padding: 0;
  font-weight: bold;
  font-size: 0.9em;
}

.nav p a  {
  color: white;
  text-decoration: none;
}

.current  {
  background-image: url(bkgd_content.jpg);
  background-repeat: no-repeat;
  height: 428px;
  background-color: transparent;
}

.current img  {
  padding-top: 120px;
  margin-left: -44px;
}

.current p  {
  margin-top: .25em;
  margin-left: 40px;
  width: 300px;
  color: #fff;
```

continues

Listing 9.7   E-Zine Example   (Continued)

```
  font-weight: bold;
  line-height: 1.5em;
  background-color: transparent;
  margin-bottom: 0;

}


h1  {
  margin: 0;
  padding: 0;
  font-size: 3em;
  color: #fff;
  background-image: none;
  }

h3 {
  background-image: url(bkgd_barrier.gif);
   margin: 0;
  padding: 0.5em 0 0 40px;
  color: #c99;
  background-color: transparent;

}

.past ul  {
  margin: 0;
  padding: 50px 0 0 200px;
  color: #630;
  background-image: url(bkgd_otherstories.jpg);
  background-repeat: no-repeat;


  }

.past li {
  background-color: #fff;
  color: #06c;
  font-family: Courier, monospace;
  }


</style>
  </head>
  <body>
```

```
<div id="header">
  <h1>
    Likely Stories
  </h1>
  <p>
    The irreverent ezine published irregularly
  </p>
</div>
<div class="nav">
  <p>
    <a href="/archives/">
      Archives
    </a>
  </p>
  <p>
    <a href="/about/">
      About
    </a>
  </p>
  <p>
    <a href="/editors/">
      Our Editors
    </a>
  </p>
  <p>
    <a href="/writers/">
      Our Writers
    </a>
  </p>
  <p>
    <a href="/writeforus/">
      Write for us?
    </a>
  </p>
  <p>
    <a href="/contact/">
      Contact Us
    </a>
  </p>
</div>
<div class="current">
  <img src="hed_title.jpg" alt="" width="398" height="84">
  <p>
    How theme parks aren't everyone's happy utopia they portray inside the moat
  </p>
</div>
<div class="past">
```

continues

Listing 9.7   E-Zine Example   (Continued)

```
      <h3>
         Recent stories from past issues
      </h3>
      <ul>
         <li>
            <a href="/stories/badbreath/">
               Bad breath, bad business
            </a>
         </li>
         <li>
            <a href="/stories/arena/">
               Sports arena? No mas!
            </a>
         </li>
         <li>
            <a href="/stories/homefront/">
               Terrorism lawn care
            </a>
         </li>
         <li>
            <a href="/stories/eggseggseggs/">
               Eggs, eggs, irradiated eggs
            </a>
         </li>
      </ul>
   </div>
   <div id="footer">
      <p>
         Buy
         <a href="/back/">
            back issues,
         </a>
         or hit our
         <a href="/sitemap/">
            site map
         </a>
         for better directions.
      </p>
   </div>
</body>
</html>
```

Figure 9.5 shows you what Likely Stories looks like in CSS, and Figure 9.6 shows you what it looks like in plain HTML. These two examples showcase the power of CSS—the ability to completely transform the presentation of a Web page.

Figure 9.5

An e-zine cover design through CSS.

Figure 9.6

An e-zine site without the cover design (without the CSS).

This Web layout uses one image, a promotional photo for a tour, and manipulates it in several ways. The photo, an image of tourists being led by a tour guide in front of a pineapple water tower, matches the make-believe story in my e-zine (see Figure 9.7).

Figure 9.7

"Do you see something strange over there?"

I liked the man's expression and hat in the photo, so I used that to carry the main link to the main story. However, to make sure that visitors would know whose face it was, I put the man on the side so people could see an unobstructed view of it.

Below the real estate for the cover story are links to the past stories. I loved the part of the image with the tour guide pointing to the pineapple water tower, so I associated that part with the archives.

Before we get into the CSS, Figure 9.8 shows the images used to create the design.

Figure 9.8

The images used to create the design.

One of the pushpins, or centers of origin, for the design is the background image being positioned from the bottom. This is done with the CSS rule in Listing 9.8 for the body.

Listing 9.8   Code for a Pushpin

```
body {
  background-image: url(bkgd_sidebar.jpg);
  background-repeat: repeat-y;
  background-position: bottom left;
}
```

Design to Personal Taste

In MacIE, this body style causes a rendering error when visitors scroll. The resulting effect, however, adds to the experience in giving it an unusual design edge that is only seen in viewing the material online (see Figure 9.9). If you don't agree it's a nice touch, you can change the background position to top left (see Listing 9.9), and the side background will be positioned to start from the upper-left corner to get rid of the scrolling effect.

Listing 9.9   Changing the Start of the Background Tile

```
body {
  background-image: url(bkgd_sidebar.jpg);
  background-repeat: repeat-y;
  background-position: top left;
}
```

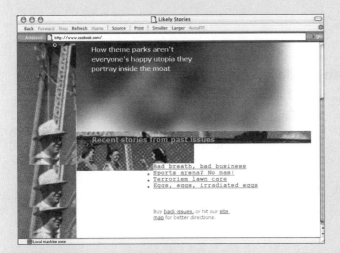

Figure 9.9

Notice the repetition of the man's head.

Main Navigation

For the site's main navigation, we wrapped around a `div` with a class of `nav`. Using positioning, we are able to move the links to the upper-left corner. This time, we won't flush the navigation with the top and left corner. Instead, we want it to be a little out of the way—again, to be slightly irreverent to match the e-zine's tagline. We apply a negative value to `top` and `left` and tuck a bit of the navigation away by using the CSS rules in Listing 9.10.

Listing 9.10   Laying Out the Navigation Links

```
.nav  {
  position: absolute;
  width: 150px;
  left: -0.4em;
  top: -0.4em;
}

.nav p  {
  margin: 0;
  padding: 0;
  font-weight: bold;
  font-size: 0.9em;
}

.nav p a  {
  color: white;
  text-decoration: none;
}
```

The Site's Title

For the title of the site, we want to be on the level of navigation. Therefore, we will tuck the top part away like the navigation, but we want it to be aligned, in part, with the cover story blurb. To do this, we take the tuck 1em out of sight to the visitor and then move the title 191 pixels left of the far left (see Listing 9.11).

Listing 9.11   CSS Rules for the Header

```
#header  {
  position: absolute;
  left: 191px;
  top: -1em;
}
```

```
#header p {
  margin: -1em 0 0 0;
  padding: 0;
  color: #06c;
  font-family: Courier, monospace;
}
```

I used 191 pixels because I knew how wide the background image for the body was (151 pixels). That gave me 40 pixels of white space.

The Background Image

Now we can tuck our background image, which will be the sidebar image, into the document (see Listing 9.12). We are placing the image at the bottom left of the browser viewport. (The default placement of a background image is in the upper right.)

Listing 9.12   The CSS Rules for the Background Image

```
body {
  background-image: url(bkgd_sidebar.jpg);
  background-repeat: repeat-y;
  background-position: bottom left;
  margin: 0 0 0 151px;;
}
```

Main Image

Now let's work on the main story's image. We want to apply a large enough area of screen real estate to make an impact with the reader. It needs to be the first thing the reader sees. We wrap the information containing the blurb about the current story "Tourism & the Local Economy" a height of 428 pixels; then we apply a background image (see Listing 9.13).

Listing 9.13   Bringing the Impact to the Main Story

```
.current  {
  background-image: url(bkgd_content.jpg);
  background-repeat: no-repeat;
  height: 428px;
  background-color: transparent;
}
```

The Header

The header for the story is a hanging indent, so we apply a negative margin to the image header. The CSS rule in Listing 9.14 sticks the image beyond the confines of the block element 44 pixels to the left.

Listing 9.14   Placing the Header

```
.current img  {
  padding-top: 120px;
  margin-left: -44px;
}

.current p  {
  margin-top: .25em;
  margin-left: 40px;
  width: 300px;
  color: #fff;
  font-weight: bold;
  line-height: 1.5em;
  background-color: transparent;
  margin-bottom: 0;
}
```

The Rest of the Layout

The rest of the layout is accomplished by allowing the other elements to "fall" below the current issue blurb.

This design effect was possible thanks to using pixels and measuring out how much space was used from element to element, but also giving enough space in case fonts grew or shrank from browser to browser.

Because we are using pixels and not a percentage, we know precisely how far the cover story elements have to be to flush our design elements together.

Chapter 10

Underground Styles

These examples look at some of the more unconventional styles so that you can see how technologies like SVG can help facilitate their production.

Drafting Table/Transformer Stylized with SVG

The Drafting Table/Transformer styles have the earmarks of an isometric view of drafting, the futuristic essence as expressed in the Transformer universe and often with a trademark of using 3D objects. This style is usually for images in which you want to carry a futuristic and hip look with a slight edge. For an example, check out the British MTV2 site www.mtv2.co.uk (see Figure 10.1).

NOTE

For more information on these "underground" styles, check out Curt Cloninger's *Fresh Styles for Web Designers* (New Riders Publishing, 2001), which goes further into styles similar to these, as well as many others.

Figure 10.1

The British MTV2's Web site decked out in drafting table/ transformer style.

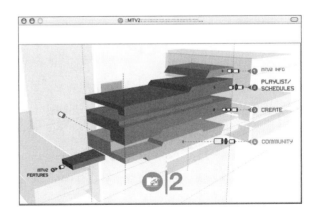

For this example, creating the site in SVG would be perfect because the pseudo-geometric effects could easily be pulled of using vector artwork.

However, I'm not about to code such complex vectors by hand! Heck, no! And you shouldn't either. The tool I used is Adobe Illustrator, which allows illustrations to be exported in SVG format (see Figure 10.2). Another popular tool for this type of work is Macromedia FreeHand. As a designer, build your elements like you normally would, and when you are ready to roll, simply export to SVG.

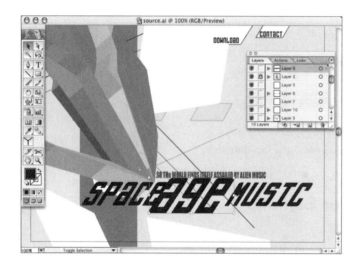

Figure 10.2

A scene from my Adobe Illustrator workspace.

After you have designed and created your SVG file (as well as installed the SVG plug-in from Adobe's Web site), you can embed it into your Web page as in Listing 10.1.

Listing 10.1   HTML Document That Embeds the SVG File

```
<!DOCTYPE HTML PUBLIC
"-//W3C//DTD HTML 4.01 Transitional//EN"
  "http://www.w3.org/TR/html4/loose.dtd">
<html lang="en">
<head>
  <meta http-equiv="content-type" [sr]
content="text/html; charset=iso-8859-1">
  <title>Transfomer Style</title>
  <style type="text/css">

  body {
    margin: 0;
    width: 100%;
  }
```

```
embed   {
   width: 800px;
   height: 550px;
   z-index: 1;
   }

  </style>
</head>
<body>
<embed src="source.svgz" type="image/svg+xml"
pluginspace="http://www.adobe.com/svg/viewer/install/"
id="background">
</body>
</html>
```

Figure 10.3 shows the end result.

Figure 10.3

The design in
the browser.

The SVG file is composed of 740 lines (see Figure 10.4).

Figure 10.4

Just the start of the code that was generated by Illustrator to create the SVG file.

Like I said, you shouldn't hand code 740 lines of SVG any more than you should hand code GIFs or JPEGs.

Of course, the reality of the situation is that this type of Web site is far from being practical in present-day Web development—even if you were only using an SVG for part of the design of a Web page. Today's browsers can't consistently handle SVG code or images. It's my hope that in the next couple of versions of the major browsers, that won't be the case.

HTMinimaList Stylized Site with a Mondrian Twist

The example for this section is another personal home page, but one that's not in a typical three-column layout. Typically, a three-column layout has a header, a footer, navigation in the left column, the main content in the middle, and supporting material and advertisements in the right column, such as this mundane example shown in Figure 10.5.

Figure 10.5

A traditional three-column layout with a visible header.

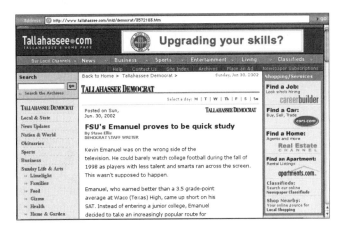

The example that we're going to look at doesn't have headers or footers. The left column is for the name of the site owner and some biographical information. The right column is for navigation—providing links to content in chronological order and sporting the most popular entries (see Figure 10.6). The only similarity to a "traditional" three-column layout is that the middle column is indeed used for the main content.

Figure 10.6

An HTMinimaList site with a twist.

This page is laid out using mostly text, which means it would usually fall under the HTMinimaList style of Web design—using HTML to structure the content of the page and CSS for positioning and formatting. This type of approach results in an often-Spartan page design. However, the use of solid white lines to divide areas of a photo of the journal owner gives it a twist of Mondrian influence.

Mondrian Influence

In case you are wondering what a *Mondrian influence* is, Piet Mondrian (1872–1944) was a Dutch abstract expressionist who, in his later years, used lines and solid areas of colors in his paintings (see Figure 10.7).

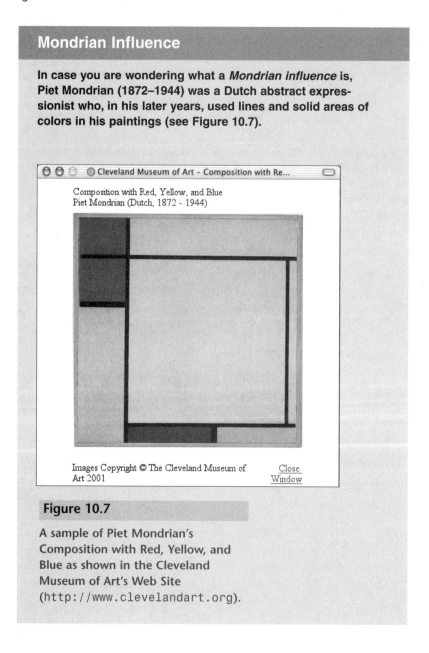

Figure 10.7

A sample of Piet Mondrian's Composition with Red, Yellow, and Blue as shown in the Cleveland Museum of Art's Web Site (http://www.clevelandart.org).

Figure 10.8 shows the same HTMinimaList page without the CSS for your reference. This screenshot shows you what the page looks like with the design transformation that's coming through CSS. In a traditional HTMinimaList design, the CSS would often just change the size, style, and location of the text that appears in a Web page that doesn't use CSS.

Figure 10.8

The site without CSS applied.

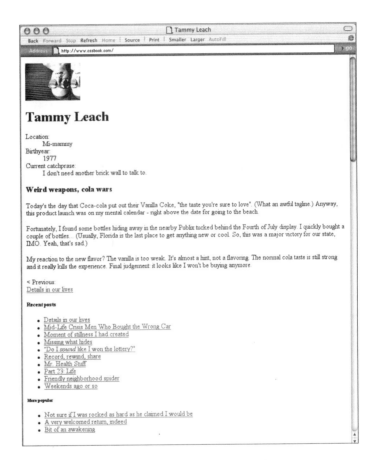

Breakdown of the CSS Used in This Site

This three-column layout is based on the code from Owen Briggs (see http://www.thenoodleincident.com/tutorials/box_lesson/basic3_ 3.html). In conjunction with a workaround to deal with the box model problems in Windows Internet Explorer, this three-column layout is similar to the two-column layout found in Chapter 4, "Laying Out Pages." The middle column has enough space in its side margins for the left and right columns to fit into by way of positioning "absolutely" (see Listing 10.2).

Listing 10.2   CSS Code for the Three-Column Layout

```css
.left {
  text-align: right;
  position: absolute;
  top: 0;
  left: 0;
  margin: 0 20px 20px 0;
  padding: 20% 10px 10px 0;
  width: 200px; /* ie5win fudge begins */
  voice-family: "\"}\"";
  voice-family:inherit;
  width: 170px;
}

html>body .left {
  width: 170px; /* ie5win fudge ends */
}


.middle {
  margin: 0px 210px 20px 190px;
  padding: 10px;
}

middle p.first    {
  text-indent: 0;
}

.right {
  font-size: 0.8em;
  position: absolute;
  top: 1em;
  right: 0px;
  margin:  0 20px 20px 20px;
  padding: 0px;
  background: #666;
  width: 200px; /* ie5win fudge begins */
  voice-family: "\"}\"";
  voice-family:inherit;
  width: 170px;
}

html>body .right {
  width: 170px; /* ie5win fudge ends */
}
```

The Background Images

Now let's add the Mondrian twist. One image will be the background for the left column and another will be the background of the main content area (see Listing 10.3). In the left column, we position the image in the top-right corner. In the middle column, we position it a bit off its default position, top-left corner, by 23 pixels from the top.

Listing 10.3   Adding the Mondrian Twist

```
.left {
  background-image: url("bkgd1.jpg");
  background-repeat: no-repeat;
  background-position: top right;
  background-color: #ccc;
}

.middle {
  background-image: url("bkgd2.jpg");
  background-repeat: no-repeat;
  background-position: 0 23px;
  background-color: #eee;
}
```

Then we apply a white background and a white border to the definition list, dl, to create a "dent" in the left background image.

Listing 10.4   Creating a Dent in the Left Background Image

```
dl {
  border: 10px solid #fff;
  margin: 10px;
  background-color: #fff;
  color: #999;
}
```

The Inline Image

Now, for the inline image, we create a line that goes around the image through the border property (see Listing 10.5).

Listing 10.5   Creating a Box Around the Image

```
img  {
  margin: 10px;
  border: 10px solid #fff;
}
```

The Rest of the Elements

Listing 10.6 has the code used to control formatting of the rest of the elements: fonts, margins, and padding.

Listing 10.6   The Rest of the CSS for the HTMinimaList Example

```
html {
  width: 97%;
}

body {
  margin: 0;
  font-family: Verdana, Arial, Helvetica, sans-serif;
  color: #666;
  background-color: #fff;
}

ul {
  margin-left: 2em;
  padding-left: 0;
}

li {
  padding-left: 0;
  list-style: square;
  margin-bottom: 1.5em;
}

h1 {
  font-size: 1em;
  font-weight: bold;
  font-family: Georgia, Times, "Times New Roman", serif;
  padding: 0;
```

```
   margin: 0 10px 0 20px;
   text-transform: uppercase;
   color: #333;
   background-color: #ccc;
}

dt, dd {
   font-size: 0.9em;
}

dt {
   font-weight: bold;
}

dd {
   display: inline;
   margin-left: 0;
}

h3 {
   font-family: Georgia, Times, "Times New Roman", serif;
   font-size: 1.5em;
   margin-bottom: 0;
}

h5, h6 {
   color: #000;
   margin: 0;
   padding: 0;
}


p {
   text-indent: 2.5em;
   padding: 0;
   margin: 0;
   line-height: 2em;
   font-family: Georgia, Times, "Times New Roman", serif;
   font-weight: bold;
   font-size: 0.9em;
}

.middle p.first    {
   text-indent: 0;
}

.blognav {
```

continues

Listing 10.6   The Rest of the CSS for the HTMinimaList Example   (Continued)

```
  padding: 3em;
}

a {
  color: #000;
  background-color: transparent;
}
```

With that last bit of CSS, we've taken an otherwise "dry" page design and given it a visual punch. It's a far cry from the standard HTMinimaList design style, but it's still related—even though it might be a distant, long-separated cousin.

When you're designing, try looking to the past artists in other media for inspiration in your designs. Don't just skim around surfing the Web to borrow ideas. That kind of practice stunts your design education and only serves to recycle design styles.

Don't Hesitate. Dive In.

Although it's a tad early to go crazy with SVG to do your entire site and expect people to view it properly (without a plug-in), you can *still* approach Web design without going for the typical, two- or three-column layout approach for your designs. CSS allows you to expand your designs.

Whatever you wind up doing in terms of style, try to use every facet of CSS that you can to push the limits. After you have marked up a Web page and applied CSS to it, create a whole new design without touching the markup. Push yourself to the edge creatively with that new style sheet. Have fun, and learn how far CSS will let you go.

Part V

Appendixes

Formatting Exercises

This Appendix consists of 50 examples of how to visually present text, a paragraph, and sometimes a headline through CSS. Listing A.1 is the basic HTML markup for the headline and paragraph that is used as the basis for all of the examples.

As you flip through this Appendix, you can simply pick and choose which design techniques you want to use in your pages. The code is paired with the screenshot so it's easy to transfer. The idea, however, is to inspire you to make your own variations of the headers or find your own ways of pulling a reader into your text.

Here's the general HTML document that the rest of the CSS examples will be based off of:

```
<!DOCTYPE HTML PUBLIC "-//W3C//DTD HTML 4.01
Transitional//EN" "http://www.w3.org/TR/html4/loose.dtd">
<html lang="en">
<head>
  <meta http-equiv="content-type" content="text/html;
charset=iso-8859-1">
  <title>Breaking Up Text</title>
</head>
<body>

<h3>
  Generic Headline
</h3>
<p>
  Lorem ipsum dolor sit amet, comsect quis nostrud exerci-
tation ullam corp consquet, vel illum dolore eu fugat exe-
ceptur sisint occaecat cupiri tat non. Nam liber tempor
cum soluta nobis. Tempor-ibud autem quinsud et aur delectus
ut ayt prefer endis dolorib. At ille pellit sensar luptae
epicur semp in indutial genelation.
</p>

</body>
</html>
```

Examples Available for Download

You can download all the code for the examples in this Appendix from this book's companion web site at http://www.cssbook.com/.

Example 1: Basic Headline and Paragraph

Listing A.1   The CSS for the Headline and Paragraph to Rest on Top of Each Other

```
body {
  margin: 5em 10% 10em 10%;
  }
h3 {
  padding-bottom: 0;
  margin-bottom: 0;
}
p {
  padding-top: 0;
  margin-top: 0;
  font-size: 1em;
}
```

Figure A.1 shows what happens when you simply take the default values of the h3 and p padding and margins and make them so that the headline rests on top of the paragraph.

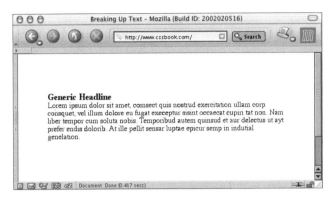

Figure A.1

The basic header and paragraph.

Example 2: How to Create a One-Pixel Headline Rule

Listing A.2   Creating a One-Pixel Headline Rule

```
body {
   margin: 5em 10% 10em 10%;
}

h3 {
   display: none;
}
p {
   padding-top: 0.5em;
   margin-top: 0;
   border-top: 1px solid #000;
   font-size: 1em;
}
```

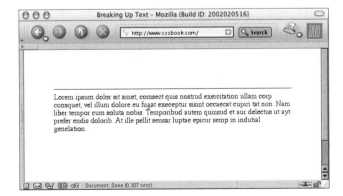

Figure A.2

A one-pixel headline rule is a classic style in traditional print media.

Example 3: How to Create a Ten-Pixel Headline Rule

Listing A.3   Creating a Ten-Pixel Headline Rule

```
body {
  margin: 5em 10% 10em 10%;
}

h3 {
  display: none;
}
p {
  padding-top: 0.5em;
  margin-top: 0;
  border-top: 10px solid #000;
  font-size: 1em;
}
```

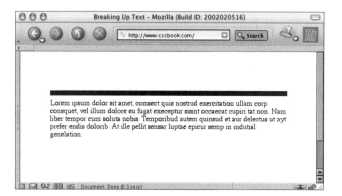

Figure A.3

A ten-pixel headline rule.

Example 4: How to Create a Dotted Line

Listing A.4   Creating a Dotted Line

```
body {
  margin: 5em 10% 10em 10%;
}
h3 {
  display: none;
}
p {
  border-top: 0.66em dotted #666;
  padding-top: 1em;
  margin-top: 0;
  font-size: 1em;
}
```

Figure A.4

Dotted rule over
a paragraph.

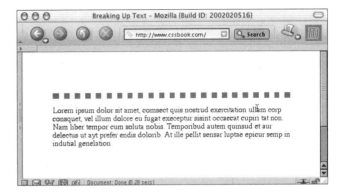

Example 5: How to Create Large, Bold, Type

Listing A.5   Creating Large, Bold Type

```
body {
   margin: 5em 10% 10em 10%;
}
h3 {
   display: none;
}
p {
   padding-top: 0;
   margin-top: 0;
}
.leader {
   text-transform: uppercase;
   font-family: Verdana, Helvetica, sans-serif;
   font-weight: bold;
}
```

Figure A.5

Large, bold type
attracts.

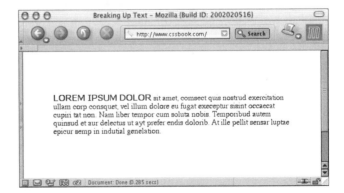

To get the first three words to be affected by the styles, we need to use a
span element (see Listing A.6).

Listing A.6   Using the span **Element**

```
<p>
  <span class="leader">Lorem ipsum dolor</span> sit amet, comsect quis nostrud
exercitation ullam corp consquet, vel illum dolore eu fugat execeptur sisint
occaecat cupiri tat non. Nam liber tempor cum soluta nobis. Temporibud autem
quinsud et aur delectus ut ayt prefer endis dolorib. At ille pellit sensar luptae
epicur semp in indutial genelation.
</p>
```

Example 6: How to Create Small, Bold Text

Listing A.7   Creating Small, Bold Text

```
body {
  margin: 5em 10% 10em 10%;
}
h3 {
  display: none;
}
p  {
  padding-top: 0;
  margin-top: 0;
  font-size: 1em;
}
.leader {
  font-weight: bold;
  text-transform: uppercase;
  font-size: 0.8em;
  font-family: Verdana, Helvetica, sans-serif;
}
```

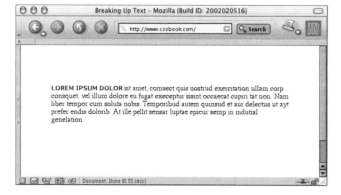

Figure A.6

Smaller type could be used, but legibility degrades depending on the typeface at that size.

Example 7: How to Create a Simple, Centered Headline

Listing A.8   Creating a Simple, Centered Headline

```
body {
    margin: 5em 10% 10em 10%;
}

h3 {
    padding-bottom: 0;
    margin-bottom: 0;
    text-align: center;
    font-weight: bold;
    text-transform: uppercase;
    font-size: 0.8em;
    font-family: Verdana, Helvetica, sans-serif;
}

p {
    padding-top: 0;
    margin-top: 0;
}
```

Figure A.7

The headline is uppercase, bold, centered, and smaller than the paragraph text.

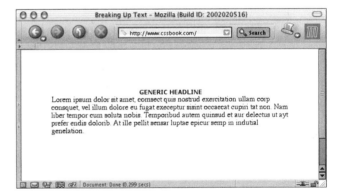

Example 8: How to Create a Right-Justified Heading

Listing A.9   Creating a Right-Justified Heading

```
body   {
    margin: 5em 10% 10em 10%;
}

h3     {
    padding-bottom: 0;
    margin-bottom: 0;
    text-align: right;
    font-weight: bold;
    text-transform: uppercase;
```

continues

Listing A.9   Creating a Right-Justified Heading   (Continued)

```
    font-size: 0.8em;
    font-family: Verdana, Helvetica, sans-serif;
}

p {
    padding-top: 0;
    margin-top: 0;
    text-align: justify;
}
```

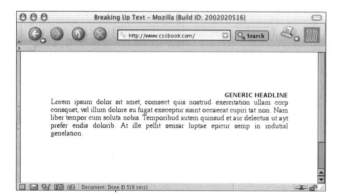

Figure A.8

Heading is justi-
fied to the right.

Example 9: Enclosing the Headline in a Thin Lined Box

Listing A.10   Creating a Thin Lined Box

```
body {
    margin: 5em 10% 10em 10%;
}

h3 {
    padding-bottom: 0;
    margin-bottom: 0;
    border: 0.1em solid #000;
    padding: 0.25em;
    text-align: right;
    font-weight: bold;
    text-transform: uppercase;
    font-size: 0.8em;
    font-family: Verdana, Helvetica, sans-serif;
}

p {
    padding-top: 0;
    margin-top: 0;
    text-align: justify;
}
```

Figure A.9

Enclose the
headline in
a thin
ruled box.

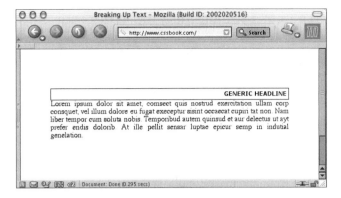

Example 10: Indenting the First Line of the Paragraph

Listing A.11   Indenting the First Line of the Paragraph

```
body {
  margin: 5em 10% 10em 10%;
}
h3 {
  padding-bottom: 0;
  margin-bottom: 0;
  font-weight: bold;
  text-transform: uppercase;
  font-size: 0.8em;
  font-family: Verdana, Helvetica, sans-serif;
}
p {
  padding-top: 0;
  margin-top: 0;
  text-indent: 3em;
}
```

Figure A.10

Bold, uppercase
headline with a
text indent on
the first line of
the paragraph.

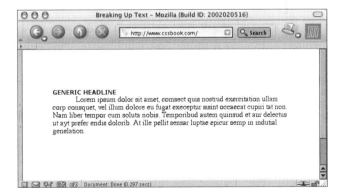

continues

Example 11: Indenting the Paragraph and the Headline

Listing A.12   Indenting in the Paragraph and the Headline

```
body {
  margin: 5em 10% 10em 10%;
}
h3 {
  padding-bottom: 0;
  margin-bottom: 0;
  font-weight: bold;
  text-transform: uppercase;
  font-size: 0.8em;
  font-family: Verdana, sans-serif;
  text-indent: 50px;
}
p {
  padding-top: 0;
  margin-top: 0;
  text-indent: 50px;
}
```

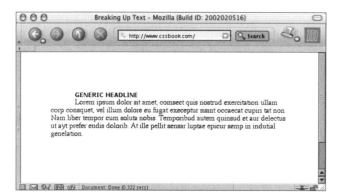

Figure A.11

Indent both the headline and the paragraph.

Example 12: How to Create a Hanging Indent

Listing A.13   Creating a Hanging Indent

```
body {
  margin: 5em 10% 10em 10%;
}
h3 {
  padding-bottom: 0;
  margin-bottom: 0;
  font-weight: bold;
  text-transform: uppercase;
  font-size: 0.8em;
  font-family: Verdana, Helvetica, sans-serif;
  text-indent: -50px;
}
```

```
}
p {
  padding-top: 0;
  margin-top: 0;
  text-indent: -50px;
}
```

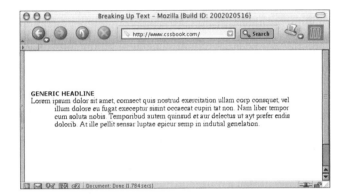

Figure A.12

Example of a
hanging indent.

Example 13: How to Create a Hanging Headline

Listing A.14   Creating a Hanging Headline

```
body {
  margin: 5em 10% 10em 10%;
}
h3 {
  padding-bottom: 0;
  margin-bottom: 0;   margin-left: -3em;
  font-weight: bold;
  text-transform: uppercase;
  font-size: 0.8em;

}
p {
  padding-top: 0;
  margin-top: 0;
}
```

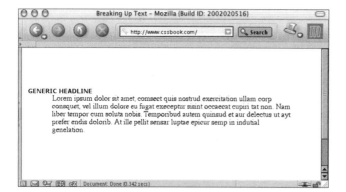

How the hanging
headline appears.

Example 14: How to Create a Variation of the Hanging Headline

Listing A.15   Creating a Variation of the Hanging Indent

```
body {
  margin: 5em 10% 10em 10%;
}
h3 {
  padding-bottom: 0;
  margin-left: -3em;
  margin-bottom: 1.5em;
  font-weight: bold;
  text-transform: uppercase;
  font-size: 0.8em;
  font-family: Verdana, Helvetica, sans-serif;
}
p {
  padding-top: 0;
  margin-top: 0;
  font-size: 1em;
}
```

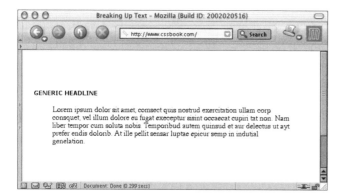

Figure A.14

A variation of
the hanging
indent.

Example 15: How to Insert Background Texture

Listing A.16   Inserting Background Texture

```
body {
  margin: 5em 10% 10em 10%;
}
h3 {
  padding-bottom: 0;
  margin-bottom: 0;
  margin-left: -3em;
  font-weight: bold;
  text-transform: uppercase;
  font-size: 0.8em;
  font-family: Verdana, Helvetica, sans-serif;
  background-image: url(examples.jpg);
  background-repeat: no-repeat;
}
p {
  padding-top: 0;
  margin-top: 0;
}
```

Figure A.15

Use an image
as background
texture.

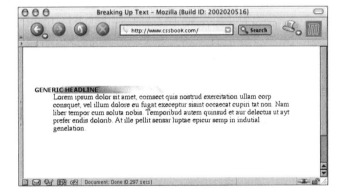

Example 16: How to Add Color to the Header's Background

Listing A.17   Adding Color to the Header's Background

```
body {
  margin: 5em 10% 10em 10%;
}
h3 {
  padding-bottom: 0;
  margin-bottom: 0;
  background-color: #999;
  padding: 0.3em;
  font-family: Verdana, Helvetica, sans-serif;
```

continues

Listing A.17 Adding Color to the Header's Background (Continued)

```
}
p {
  padding-top: 0;
  margin-top: 0.3em;
}
```

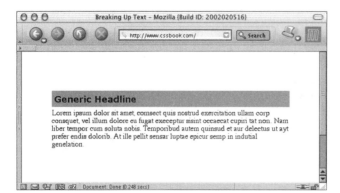

Figure A.16

Color in the header's background.

Example 17: How to Insert a Larger Background Image

Listing A.18 Inserting a Larger Background Image

```
body {
  margin: 5em 10% 10em 10%;
}
h3 {
  margin-bottom: 0;
  padding: 2em 0.5em 0.5em 0.5em;
  font-family: Verdana, Helvetica, sans-serif;
  background-image: url(examples.jpg);
  background-position: -20px -80px;
  background-repeat: no-repeat;
}
p {
  margin-top: 0;
  color: #333;
  padding: 0.25em 0 0 0.75em;
  font-family: Verdana, Helvetica, sans-serif;
}
```

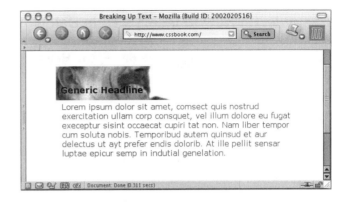

Figure A.17

The background image returns larger and less abstract.

Example 18: How to Insert a Rule Above the Header

Listing A.19   Inserting a Rule Above the Header

```
body {
   margin: 5em 10% 10em 10%;
}
h3 {
   padding-bottom: 0;
   margin-bottom: 0;
   border-top: 4px solid #000;
   font-family: Verdana, Helvetica, sans-serif;
   font-size: 1em;
}
p {
   padding-top: 0;
   margin-top: 0;
}
```

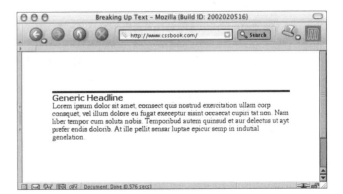

Figure A.18

A rule above the header.

Example 19: How to Insert a Rule Below the Header

Listing A.20   Inserting a Rule Below the Header

```
body {
   margin: 5em 10% 10em 10%;
}
h3 {
   padding-bottom: 0;
   margin-bottom: 0;
   border-bottom: 1px solid #000;
   font-family: Verdana, Helvetica, sans-serif;
   font-size: 0.8em;
}
p {
   padding-top: 0;
   margin-top: 0;

}
```

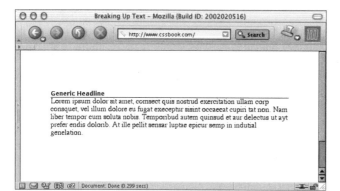

Figure A.19

A rule below
the header.

Example 20: How to Insert a Space Below the Header

Listing A.21   Inserting a Space Below the Header

```
body {
   margin: 5em 10% 10em 10%;
}
h3 {
   padding-bottom: 0.8em;
   margin-bottom: 0;
   border-top: 1px solid #000;
   font-family: Verdana, Helvetica, sans-serif;
   font-size: 0.8em;
}
p {
   padding-top: 0;
   margin-top: 0;
}
```

Figure A.20

Example of a space below the header.

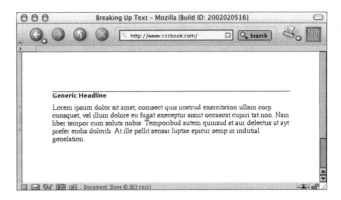

Example 21: How to Insert a Rule Below the Header with Some Padding

Listing A.22   Inserting a Rule Below the Header with Some Padding

```
body {
   margin: 5em 10% 10em 10%;
}
h3 {
   padding-bottom: 0.8em;
   margin-bottom: 0;
   border-bottom: 1px solid #000;
   font-family: Verdana, Helvetica, sans-serif;
   font-size: 0.8em;
}
p {
   padding-top: 0;
   margin-top: 0;
}
```

Figure A.21

Example of a rule below the header with some padding between the header and the rule.

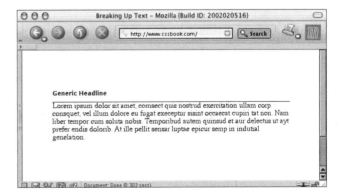

Example 22: How to Insert Two Rules

Listing A.23   Inserting Two Rules

```
body {
   margin: 5em 10% 10em 10%;
}
h3 {
   padding-bottom: 0;
   margin-bottom: 0;
   font-family: Verdana, Helvetica, sans-serif;
   font-size: 0.8em;
   border-top: 3px solid #000;
}
p {
   padding-top: 0;
   margin-top: 0;
}
.leader {
   border-bottom: 1px solid #000;
}
```

You need to apply a span tag around the first three words to achieve this visual affect (see Listing A.24).

Listing A.24   Applying the span Tag

```
<h3>
   Generic Headline
</h3>
<p>
   <span class="leader">Lorem ipsum dolor</span> sit amet, comsect quis nostrud
exercitation ullam corp consquet, vel illum dolore eu fugat execeptur sisint
occaecat cupiri tat non. Nam liber tempor cum soluta nobis. Temporibud autem
quinsud et aur delectus ut ayt prefer endis dolorib. At ille pellit sensar lup-
tae epicur semp in indutial genelation.
</p>
```

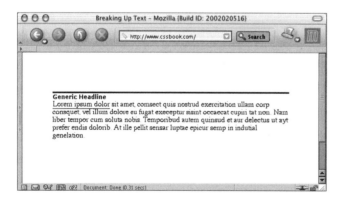

Figure A.22

When one rule just isn't enough, try two.

Example 23: How to Create a Larger Headline and Keep the Double Rule

Listing A.25   Creating a Larger Headline and Keeping the Double Rule

```
body {
  margin: 5em 10% 10em 10%;
}

h3 {
  padding-bottom: 0;
  margin-bottom: 0;
  display: inline;
  padding: 0 0 0.4em 0;
  margin-bottom: 0;
  font-family: Verdana, sans-serif;
  font-size: 2em;
  border-top: 3px solid #000;
  border-bottom: 1px solid #000;
}
p {
  padding-top: 0;
  margin-top: 0;
}
```

Figure A.23

How the larger headline, double rule looks.

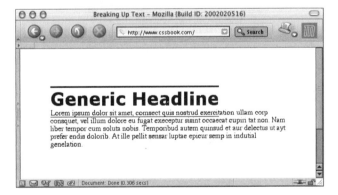

Example 24: How to Insert an Image Between the Double Rule

Listing A.26   Inserting an Image Between the Double Rule

```
body {
  margin: 5em 10% 10em 10%;
}
h3 {
  padding-bottom: 0;
  margin-bottom: 0;
  display: inline;
  font-family: Verdana, sans-serif;
  font-size: 2em;
```

continues

Listing A.26   Inserting an Image Between the Double Rule   (Continued)

```
    border-top: 3px solid #000;
    padding: 0 0 .4em 0;
    border-left: 1px solid #333;
    border-bottom: 1px solid #666;
    background-image: url(examples.jpg);
    background-position: -20px -80px;
    background-repeat: no-repeat;
}
p {
    padding-top: 0;
    margin-top: 0;
}
```

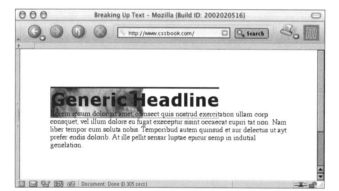

Figure A.24

Bring in an image for those times when extra emphasis is needed and you can't find your highlighter.

Example 25: How to Create a Stressed Headline Rule Under the Header

Listing A.27   Creating a Stressed Headline Rule Under the Header

```
body {
    margin: 5em 10% 10em 10%;
}
h3 {
    padding-bottom: 0;
    margin-bottom: 0;
    display: inline;
    font-family: Verdana, Helvetica, sans-serif;
    font-size: 0.8em;
    border-bottom: 3px solid #000;
}
p {
    padding-top: 0.8em;
    margin-top: 0;
    border-top: 1px solid #000;
}
```

Figure A.25

The stressed
headline rule
under the
header.

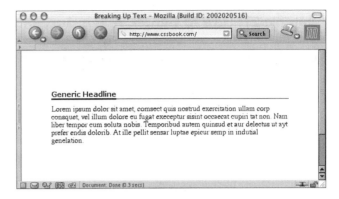

Example 26: How to Create a Right-Justified Stressed Header

Listing A.28   Creating a Right-Justified Stressed Header

```
body {
  margin: 5em 10% 10em 10%;
}
h3 {
  padding-bottom: 0;
  margin-bottom: 0;
  display: inline;
  text-align: right;
  font-family: Verdana, Helvetica, sans-serif;
  font-size: 0.8em;
  border-bottom: 3px solid #000;
}
p {
  padding-top: 0.8em;
  margin-top: 0;
  border-top: 1px solid #000;
}
```

Figure A.26

The right-justified
stressed header.

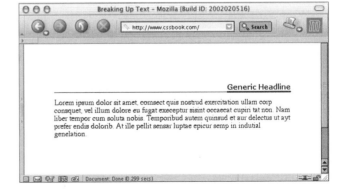

Example 27: How to Center, Add a Box, and Add an Image to the Headline

Listing A.29   Centering, Adding a Box, and Adding an Image to the Headline

```
body {
  margin: 5em 10% 10em 10%;
}
h3 {
  padding-bottom: 0;
  padding-top: 2em;
  display: inline;
  margin-bottom: 0;
  text-align: center;
  background-image: url(examples.jpg);
  border: 1px solid #000;
  background-repeat: no-repeat;
  background-position: -20px -80px;
  font-size: 1.2em;
  font-family: Verdana, Helvetica, sans-serif;
  border-bottom: 3px solid #000;
}
p {
  padding-top: 0.8em;
  margin-top: 0;
}
```

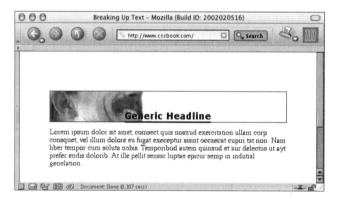

Figure A.27

Center the text and then wrap it in a box with an image.

Example 28: How to Insetting the Headline in the Text and Add a Rule

Listing A.30   Insetting the Headline in the Text and Adding a Rule

```
body {
  margin: 5em 10% 10em 10%;
}
h3 {
  padding: .5em;
  margin: -.5em 1em 1em 0;
  font-family: Verdana, sans-serif;
  font-size: 0.8em;
```

```
    float: left;
    width: 10em;
    text-align: left;
    background: #999;
    color: #000;
    text-transform: uppercase;
    border-top: 1.25px solid #fff;
}
p {
    margin-top: 1em;
    padding-top: 1em;
    border-top: 1px solid #999;
}
```

Figure A.28

Headline insetting in text with a thin rule.

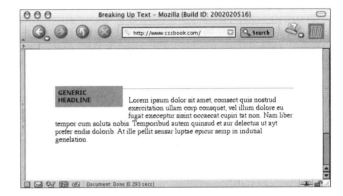

Example 29: How to Right-Align Example 28

Listing A.31   Right-Aligning Example 28

```
body {
    margin: 5em 10% 10em 10%;
}
h3 {
    padding: .5em;
    margin: -.5em 0 .5em 1em;
    font-family: Verdana, Helvetica, sans-serif;
    font-size: 0.8em;
    float: right;
    width: 10em;
    text-align: right;
    background: #999;
    color: #000;
    text-transform: uppercase;
    border-top: 1.25px solid #fff;
}
p {
    margin-top: 1em;
    padding-top: 1em;
    border-top: 1px solid #999;
}
```

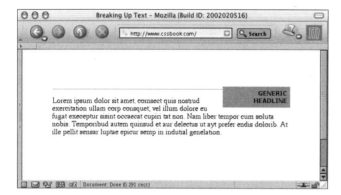

Figure A.29

Example 28
aligned to
the right.

Example 30: How to Create an Outlined Variation of Example 28

Listing A.32   Creating an Outlined Variation of Example 28

```css
body {
   margin: 5em 10% 10em 10%;
}
h3 {
   padding: .5em;
   margin: -.5em 1em 1em 0;
   font-family: Verdana, sans-serif;
   font-size: 0.8em;
   float: left;
   width: 10em;
   text-align: left;
   background: #999;
   color: #000;
   text-transform: uppercase;
   border: 1px solid #000;
}
p {
   padding: 1em 0.5em 0.5em 0.5em;
   margin-top: 1em;
   border: 1px solid #000;
}
```

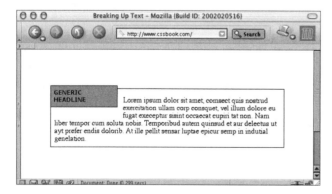

Figure A.30

A variation of
Example 28
that is similar
to a folder tab
design that's
popular on
e-commerce
sites.

Example 31: How to Create an Outlined Variation Flushed Right

Listing A.33   Creating an Outlined Variation Flushed Right

```
body {
   margin: 5em 10% 10em 10%;
}
h3 {
   padding: .5em;
   margin: -.5em 0 .5em 1em;
   font-family: Verdana, sans-serif;
   font-size: 0.8em;
   float: right;
   width: 10em;
   text-align: right;
   background: #999;
   color: #000;
   text-transform: uppercase;
 border: 1.25px solid #000;
}
p {
   padding-top: 1em;
   margin-top: 1em;
   border-top: 1px solid #000;
}
```

Figure A.31

The outlined variation flushed right.

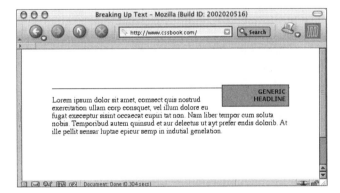

Lorem ipsum dolor sit amet, comsect quis nostrud exercitation ullam corp consquet, vel illum dolore eu fugat execeptur sisint occaecat eupin tat non. Nam liber tempor cum soluta nobis. Temporibud autem quinsud et aur deleetus ut ayt prefer endis dolorib. At ille pellit sensar luptae epicur semp in indutial genelation.

GENERIC HEADLINE

Example 32: How to Add a Background Image to a Paragraph

Listing A.34   Adding a Background Image to a Paragraph

```
body {
   margin: 5em 10% 10em 10%;
}
h3 {
   padding: .5em;
   margin: -1.5em 1em .5em 0;
   font-family: Verdana, sans-serif;
```

continues

Listing A.34   Adding a Background Image to a Paragraph   (Continued)

```
  font-size: 0.8em;
  float: left;
  width: 15em;
  text-align: left;
  background-color: #fff;
  color: #000;
  text-transform: uppercase;
  border-left: 0.15em solid #000;
  border-right: 0.15em solid #000;
}
p {
  padding: 2em 1.5em 1em 15em;
  margin-top: -0.5em;
  border: 0.1em solid #000;
  text-align: justify;
  background-image: url(examples.jpg);
  background-repeat: no-repeat;
  background-position: -.1em -.25em;
}
```

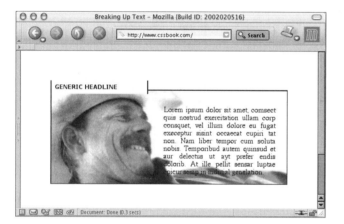

Figure A.32

A variation with a background image.

Example 33: How to Make Your Text Look Trapped

Listing A.35   Making Your Text Look Trapped

```
body {
  margin: 5em 10% 10em 10%;
}
h3 {
  padding: 0.5em;
  margin-bottom: 0;
  border-left: 1px solid #000;
  border-top: 1px solid #000;
  font-family: Verdana, sans-serif;
  font-size: 0.8em;
```

```
}
p {
  padding: 0.5em;
  margin-top: 0;
  border-left: 1px solid #000;
  border-top: 1px solid #000;
}
```

Figure A.33

One of my favorite formats: making the text look trapped.

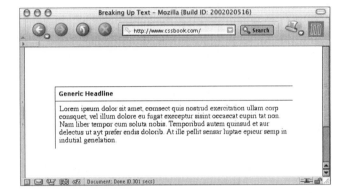

Example 34: How to Insert a Bold Box on the Left Side

Listing A.36   Inserting a Bold Box on the Left Side

```
body {
  margin: 5em 10% 10em 10%;
}
h3 {
  padding-bottom: 0;
  margin-bottom: 0;
  border-left: 1em solid #000;
  font-family: Verdana, Helvetica, sans-serif;
  padding-left: 0.8em;
  font-size: 0.8em;
  width: 40px;
}
p {
  padding-top: 0.5em;
  margin-top: 0;
  font-size: 1em;
  border-top: 0.1em solid #000;
}
```

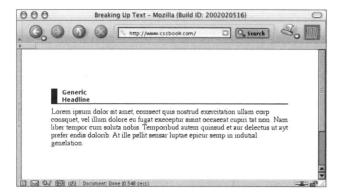

Figure A.34

A bold left side
is a flag to the
reader.

Example 35: How to Add a Thick Line

Listing A.37   Adding a Thick Line

```
body {
    margin: 5em 10% 10em 10%;
}
h3 {
    padding: 4em 0 1em 0.5em;
    margin-bottom: 0;
    border-left: 10px solid #000;
    border-top: 10px solid #000;
    font-family: Verdana, sans-serif;
    font-size: 0.8em;
}
p {
    padding-top: 0;
    margin-top: 0;
    border-left: 10px solid #000;
    padding-left: 0.5em;
}
```

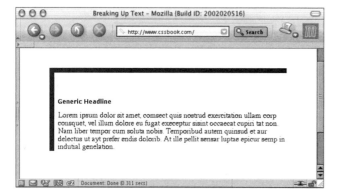

Figure A.35

A think line shelters
the headline and
text.

Example 36: How to Shelter the Header and Change the Leading and Typeface

Listing A.38   Sheltering the Header and Changing the Leading and Typeface

```
body {
  margin: 5em 10% 10em 10%;
}
h3 {
  padding: 4em 1em 0 0.5em;
  margin-bottom: 0.3em;
  border-left: 10px solid #000;
  border-top: 10px solid #000;
  font-family: Georgia, Times, serif;
  font-size: 1em;
}
p {
  padding-top: 0;
  margin-top: 0;
  font-family: Verdana, Helvetica, sans-serif;
  line-height: 2em;
}
```

Figure A.36

Shelter just the header, but break out paragraph text through leading and a change in typeface.

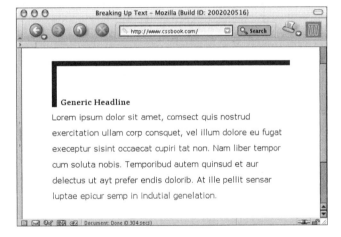

Example 37: How to Enclose the Heading in a Thin Line and Add Padding

Listing A.39   Enclosing the Heading in a Thin Line and Adding Padding

```
body {
  margin: 5em 10% 10em 10%;
}
h3 {
  padding: 4em 0 1em 0.5em;
  margin-bottom: .5em;
  border: 1px solid #000;
```

continues

Listing A.39   Enclosing the Heading in a Thin Line and Adding Padding   (Continued)

```
  font-family: Verdana, sans-serif;
  font-size: 0.8em;
}
p {
  padding-top: 0;
  margin-top: 0;
}
```

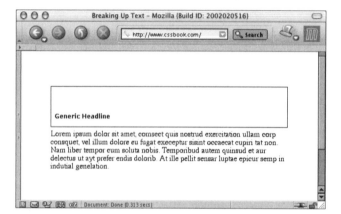

Figure A.37

Enclose the headline in a thin rule and play with the padding.

Example 38: How to Enclose the Heading with a Wide Width on the Side Borders

---

Listing A.40   Enclosing the Heading with a Wide Width on the Side Borders

```
body {
  margin: 5em 10% 10em 10%;
}
h3 {
  padding-top: 0.5em;
  padding-bottom: 0.5em;
  margin-bottom: 0;
  border-top: 1px solid #000;
  border-bottom: 1px solid #000;
  border-left: 20px solid #000;
  border-right: 20px solid #000;
  font-family: Verdana, Helvetica, sans-serif;
  font-size: 1em;
  text-align: center;
}
p {
  padding-top: 0.5em;
  margin-top: 0;
  font-size: 1em;
}
```

Figure A.38

Keep the headline enclosed with a wide width on the side borders.

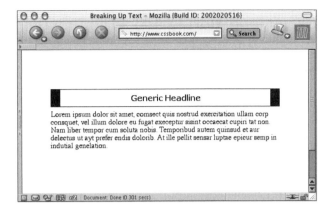

Example 39: How to Add a Thick Top Rule and a Thin Bottom Rule Around the Header

Listing A.41   Adding a Thick Top Rule and a Thin Bottom Rule Around the Header

```
body {
    margin: 5em 10% 10em 10%;
}
h3 {
    padding-bottom: 0;
    margin-bottom: 0;
    border-top: 0.8em solid #000;
border-bottom: 0.1em solid #000;
    font-family: Verdana, sans-serif;
    font-size: 0.8em;
    text-align: right;
    padding-top: 1em;
}
p {
    padding-top: .5em;
    margin-top: 0;
    font-size: 1em;
}
```

Figure A.39

Two rules: one thick and one thin.

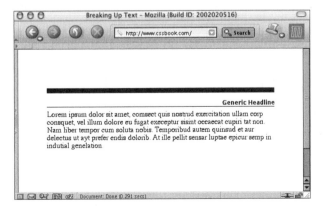

Example 40: How to Add a Thin Top Rule and a Bottom Dotted Line Around the Header

---

Listing A.42   Adding a Thin Top Rule and a Bottom Dotted Line Around the Header

```
body {
  margin: 5em 10% 10em 10%;
}
h3 {

  margin: 1em 0 1em 0;
  display: inline;
  text-align: center;
  border-top: 2px solid #000;
  border-bottom: 5px dotted #000;
  font-family: Georgia, Times, serif;
  font-size: 0.8em;
  padding: 0.5em 0 0.5em 0;
}
p {
  padding-top: 0;
  margin-top: 0;
  font-size: 1em;
}
```

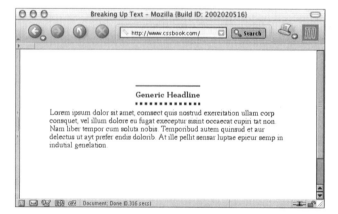

Figure A.40

A thin rule on top of the headline and a dotted line at the bottom.

Example 41: How to Make the Top Line Thicker

Listing A.43   Making the Top Line Thicker

```
body {
  margin: 5em 10% 10em 10%;
}
h3 {

  margin: 1em 0 1em 0;
  display: inline;
```

```
  text-align: center;
  border-bottom: 5px dotted #000;
  border-top: 1.5em solid #000;
  font-family: Georgia, Times, serif;
  font-size: 0.8em;
  padding: .5em 0 .5em 0;
}
p {
  padding-top: 0;
  margin-top: 0;
}
```

Figure A.41

Thin line at the top becomes thicker.

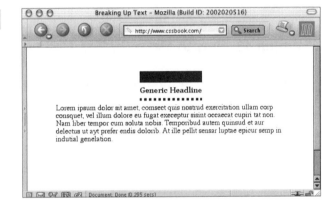

Example 42: How to Make the Bottom Line Thicker

Listing A.44   Making the Bottom Line Thicker

```
body {
  margin: 5em 10% 10em 10%;
}
h3 {

  margin: 1em 0 2em 0;
  display: inline;
  text-align: center;
  border-top: 5px dotted #000;
  border-bottom: 1.5em solid #000;
  font-family: Georgia, Times, serif;
  font-size: 0.8em;
  padding: .5em 0 .5em 0;
}
p {
  padding-top: 0;
  margin-top: 0;
}
```

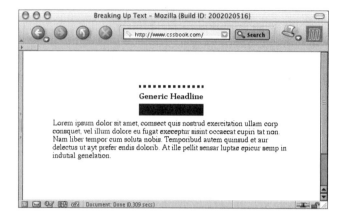

Figure A.42

Now the bottom
line is thicker.

Example 43: How to Make the Top Headline Rule Larger Than the Headline

Listing A.45   Making the Top Headline Rule Larger Than the Headline

```
body {
  margin: 5em 10% 10em 10%;
}
h3 {

  margin: 1em 0 0.25em 0;
  display: inline;
  border-top: 0.5em dotted #000;
  font-size: 1em;
  padding: 0.25em 15% 0.25em 0;
}
p {
  padding-top: 0;
  margin-top: 0;
  font-size: 1em;
}
```

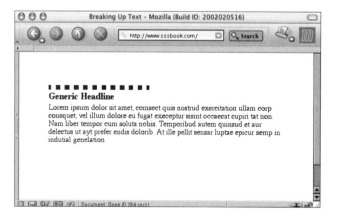

Figure A.43

The top dotted
line is longer
than the text of
the headline, but
not as long as
the width of the
paragraph.

Example 44: How to Make a Strong Initial Cap

Listing A.46   Making a Strong Initial Cap

```
body {
  margin: 5em 10% 10em 10%;
}
h3 {
  display: none;
}
p {
  padding-top: 0;
  margin-top: 0;
  text-indent: 33%;
}
p:first-letter {
  font-size: 666%;
  font-weight: bold;
  font-family: Verdana, Helvetica, sans-serif;
  line-height: 0.8em;
}
```

Modification for Current Browsers

Some of the current browsers don't render the pseudo-element first-letter. To make this effect work, you need to replace the p:first-letter selector with .initialcap and modify the markup a bit (see Listing A.47).

Listing A.47   Modifying the Current Browser

```
.initialcap {
  font-size: 666%;
  font-weight: bold;
  font-family: Verdana, Helvetica, sans-serif;
  line-height: 0.8em;
}

<p>
  <span class="initialcap">L</span>orem ipsum dolor sit
amet, comsect quis nostrud exercitation ullam corp con-
squet, vel illum dolore eu fugat execeptur sisint
occaecat cupiri tat non. Nam liber tempor cum soluta
nobis. Temporibud autem quinsud et aur delectus ut ayt
prefer endis dolorib. At ille pellit sensar luptae epi-
cur semp in indutial genelation.
</p>
```

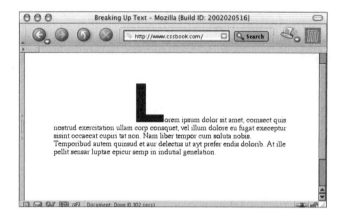

Indent the first line, but increase the size of the first letter to humongous proportions.

Example 45: How to Add the Header on Top of a Strong Initial Cap and Bold the First Word in the Paragraph

Listing A.48 Adding the Header on Top of a Strong Initial Cap and Bolding the First Word in the Paragraph

```
body {
  margin: 5em 10% 10em 10%;
}
h3 {
  padding: .25em 0 .25em 0;
  margin: 1em 0 .25em 0;
  text-align: center;
  border-bottom: 1px solid #000;
  font-family: Georgia, Times, serif;
  font-weight: bold;
  font-size: .9em;
}
p {
  text-indent: 40%;
  padding-top: 0;
  margin-top: 0;
  font-size: 1em;
}
p:first-letter{
  font-size: 666%;
  font-weight: bold;
  font-family: Verdana, Helvetica, sans-serif;
  line-height: 0.8em;
}
.firstword {
  font-size: 1.5em;
  font-weight: bold;
  font-family: Verdana, Helvetica, sans-serif;
  line-height: 0.8em;
  text-transform: capitalize;
}
```

Modify the HTML

To grab the first word in the paragraph through CSS, we need to wrap it in its own span tag (see Listing A.49).

Listing A.49   Modifying the HTML

```
<p>
  <span class="firstword">Lorem</span> ipsum dolor sit
amet, comsect quis nostrud exercitation ullam corp
consquet, vel illum dolore eu fugat execeptur sisint
occaecat cupiri tat non. Nam liber tempor cum soluta
nobis. Temporibud autem quinsud et aur delectus ut ayt
prefer endis dolorib. At ille pellit sensar luptae
epicur semp in indutial genelation.
</p>
```

Figure A.45

Bring back the headline and a thin rule to work with the initial caps. Then make the first word bold.

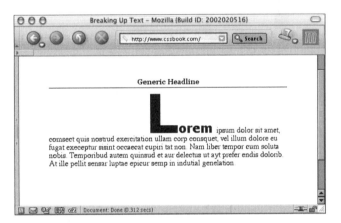

Example 46: How to Enclose the Headline in a Thick Ruled Box

Listing A.50   Enclosing the Headline in a Thick Ruled Box

```
body {
  margin: 5em 10% 10em 10%;
}
h3 {
  margin: 0 1.5em 0 0;
  text-align: center;
  border: 30px solid #000;
  font-family: Georgia, Times, serif;
  font-weight: bold;
  font-size: .9em;
  padding: 2em;
  float: left;
```

continues

Listing A.50   Enclosing the Headline in a Thick Ruled Box   (Continued)

```
  width: 5em;
}
p {
  padding-top: 0;
  margin-top: 0;
  font-size: 1em;
  font-family: Verdana, Helvetica, sans-serif;
}
```

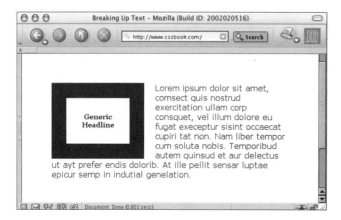

Figure A.46

Enclose the headline in a thick ruled box and place it to the left of the content.

Example 47: How to Insert an Image into the Thick Ruled Box

Listing A.51   Inserting an Image into the Thick Ruled Box

```
body {
  margin: 5em 10% 10em 10%;
}
h3 {
  padding: 0 2em 2em 0;
  margin: 0 1.5em 0 0;
  text-align: left;
  border: 30px solid #000;
  font-family: Georgia, Times, serif;
  font-weight: bold;
  font-size: 1em;
  float: left;
  width: 10em;
  height: 10em;
  background-image: url(examples.jpg);
}
p {
  padding-top: 0;
  margin-top: 0;
  font-size: 1em;
  font-family: Verdana, Helvetica, sans-serif;
}
```

Figure A.47

Place the image in the back-ground of the headline box.

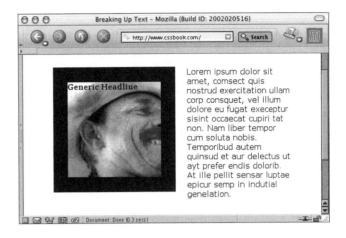

Example 48: How to Tuck the Header into the Paragraph

Listing A.52   Tucking the Header into the Paragraph

```css
body {
  margin: 5em 10% 10em 10%;
}
h3 {
  padding-bottom: 0;
  margin-bottom: 0;
  position: relative;
  top: 2.75em;
  left: -5%;
  font-size: .9em;
  font-weight: bold;
  font-family: Georgia, Times, serif;
  text-transform: uppercase;
}
p {
  padding-top: 0;
  margin-top: 0;
  font-size: 1em;
  line-height: 2.5em; font-family: Georgia, Times, serif;
}
p:first-line {
  font-weight: bold;
}
```

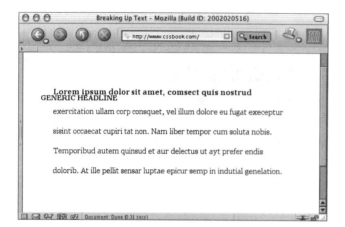

Figure A.48

The headline is a hanging indent tucked into the space between the first and second line of the paragraph.

Example 49: How to Tuck the Header and Indent the Paragraph to Add a Dynamic to an Otherwise Dull Layout

Listing A.53   Tucking the Header and Indenting the Paragraph to Add a Dynamic to an Otherwise Dull Layout

```
body {
   margin: 5em 10% 10em 10%;
}
h3 {
   padding-bottom: 0;
   margin-bottom: 0;
   position: relative;
   top: 2.75em;
   left: -5%;
   font-size: .9em;
   font-weight: bold;
   font-family: Georgia, Times, serif;
   text-transform: uppercase;
}
p {
   padding-top: 0;
   margin-top: 0;
   font-size: 1em;
   text-indent: 5%;
   line-height: 2.5em;
   font-family: Georgia, Times, serif;
}
p:first-line {
   font-weight: bold;
}
```

Figure A.49

Contrast an indent of the paragraph with the buried hanging indent.

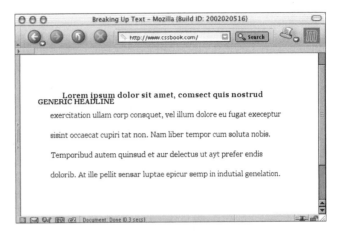

Example 50: How to Tuck the Header While Indenting Both the Header and Paragraph

Listing A.54   Tucking the Header While Indenting Both the Header and Paragraph

```
body {
  margin: 5em 10% 10em 10%;
}
h3 {
  padding-bottom: 0;
  margin-bottom: 0;
  position: relative;
  top: 2.75em;
  left: 5%;
  font-size: 1em;
  font-weight: bold;
  font-family: Georgia, Times, serif;
  text-transform: uppercase;
  margin: 0;
  padding: 0;
}
p {
  padding-top: 0;
  margin-top: 0;
  font-size: 1em;
  text-indent: 5%;
  line-height: 2.5em;
  font-family: Georgia, Times, serif;
}
```

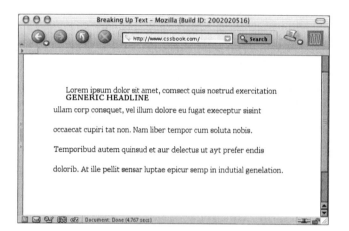

Figure A.50

Indent both the buried headline and the paragraph.

Appendix B

CSS Reference

This is the property index for the Cascading Style Sheet 2 specification. The World Wide Web Consortium (W3C) has set it as a level of Recommendation. That means it is the standard that browsers should implement when putting a rendering engine in their browser to handle CSS. However, the level of actual implementation varies from browser to browser.

Table B.1 shows you the properties that are available through CSS as well as the media, the values, the initial value, what the property applies to, and whether the property is inherited.

More Resources Available on the Web Site

These are brief and to-the-point resources for those times when you are away from a computer that has an Internet connection. If you are on the Web and want pointers to more complete resources, check out this book's Web site at `http://www.cssbook.com/`.

Table B.1   CSS2 Property Index[1]

Property Name	Media	Values	Initial Value	Applies To	Inherited
`azimuth`	Aural	`<angle>` | `[[ left-side` `| far-left | left` `| center-left` `| center | center-` `right | right |` `far-right | right-` `side ] | behind ]` `| leftwards |` `rightwards |` `inherit`	center	All elements	Y
`background`	Visual	`['background-` `color' ||` `'background-image'` `|| 'background-` `repeat' ||` `'background-` `attachment' ||` `'background-` `position'] |` `inherit`	See individual values	All elements	N
`background-attachment`	Visual	`scroll | fixed |` `inherit`	Scroll	All elements	N
`background-color`	Visual	`<color> |` `transparent |` `inherit`	Transparent	All elements	N
`background-image`	Visual	`<uri> | none |` `inherit`	None	All elements	N
`background-position`	Visual	`[ [<percentage> |` `<length> ]{1,2} |` `[ [top | center |` `bottom] || [left |` `center | right] ]` `] | inherit`	0% 0%	Block-level and replaced elements	N
`background-repeat`	Visual	`repeat | repeat-x` `| repeat-y | no-` `repeat | inherit`	Repeat	All elements	N
`border`	Visual	`[ 'border-width'` `|| 'border-style'` `|| <color> ] |` `inherit`	See individual properties	All elements	N
`border-collapse`	Visual	`collapse |` `separate |` `inherit`	Collapse	`'table'` and `'inline-table'` elements	Y
`border-color`	Visual	`<color>{1,4} |` `transparent |` `inherit`	See individual properties	All elements	N

Property Name	Media	Values	Initial Value	Applies To	Inherited
border-spacing	Visual	`<length>` `<length>?` `	inherit`	0	`'table'` and `'inline-table'` elements	Y
border-style	Visual	`<border-style>{1,4}` `	inherit`	See individual properties	All elements	N
border-top	Visual	`['border-top-width' || 'border-style' || <color>]	inherit`	See individual properties	All elements	N
border-right	Visual	`['border-right-width' || 'border-style' || <color>]	inherit`	See individual properties	All elements	N
border-bottom	Visual	`['border-bottom-width' || 'border-style' || <color>]	inherit`	See individual properties	All elements	N
border-left	Visual	`['border-left-width' || 'border-style' || <color>]	inherit`	See individual properties	All elements	N
border-top-color	Visual	`<color>	inherit`	The value of the 'color' property	All elements	N
border-right-color	Visual	`<color>	inherit`	The value of the 'color' property	All elements	N
border-bottom-color	Visual	`<color>	inherit`	The value of the 'color' property	All elements	N
border-left-color	Visual	`<color>	inherit`	The value of the 'color' property	All elements	N
border-top-style	Visual	`<border-style>	inherit`	None	All elements	N
border-right-style	Visual	`<border-style>	inherit`	None	All elements	N
border-bottom-style	Visual	`<border-style>	inherit`	None	All elements	N
border-left-style	Visual	`<border-style>	inherit`	None	All elements	N
border-top-width	Visual	`<border-width>	inherit`	Medium	All elements	N
border-right-width	Visual	`<border-width>	inherit`	Medium	All elements	N

continues

Table B.1 CSS2 Property Index[1] (Continued)

Property Name	Media	Values	Initial Value	Applies To	Inherited
border-bottom-width	Visual	`<border-width>` | `inherit`	Medium	All elements	N
border-left-width	Visual	`<border-width>` | `inherit`	Medium	All elements	N
border-width	Visual	`<border-width>` `{1,4}` | `inherit`	See individual properties	All elements	N
bottom	Visual	`<length>` | `<percentage>` | `auto` | `inherit`	Auto	Positioned elements	N
caption-side	Visual	`top` | `bottom` | `left` | `right` | `inherit`	Top	'table-caption' elements	Y
clear	Visual	`none` | `left` | `right` | `both` | `inherit`	None	Block-level elements	N
clip	Visual	`<shape>` | `auto` | `inherit`	Auto	Block-level and replaced elements	N
color	Visual	`<color>` | `inherit`	Depends on user agent	All elements	Y
content	All	`[ <string>` | `<uri>` | `<counter>` | `attr(X)` | `open-quote` | `close-quote` | `no-open-quote` | `no-close-quote ]+` | `inherit`	Empty string	:before and :after pseudo-elements	N
counter-increment	All	`[ <identifier> <integer>? ]+` | `none` | `inherit`	None	All elements	N
counter-reset	All	`[ <identifier> <integer>? ]+` | `none` | `inherit`	None	All elements	N
cue	Aural	`[ 'cue-before'` || `'cue-after' ]` | `inherit`	See individual values	All elements	N
cue-after	Aural	`<uri>` | `none` | `inherit`	None	All elements	N
cue-before	Aural	`<uri>` | `none` | `inherit`	None	All elements	N

Property Name	Media	Values	Initial Value	Applies To	Inherited
cursor	Visual, interactive	[[`<uri>` ,]* [auto | crosshair | default | pointer | move | e-resize | ne-resize | nw-resize | n-resize | se-resize | sw-resize | s-resize | w-resize| text | wait | help]] | inherit	Auto	All elements	Y
direction	Visual	ltr | rtl | inherit	Ltr	All elements, but see prose	Y
display	All	inline | block | list-item | run-in | compact | marker | table | inline-table | table-row-group | table-header-group | table-footer-group | table-row | table-column-group | table-column | table-cell | table-caption | none | inherit	Inline	All elements	N
elevation	Aural	`<angle>` | below | level | above | higher | lower | inherit	Level	All elements	Y
empty-cells	Visual	show | hide | inherit	Show	'table-cell' elements	Y
float	Visual	left | right | none | inherit	None	All but positioned elements and generated content	N
font	Visual	[['font-style' || 'font-variant' || 'font-weight']? 'font-size' [/ 'line-height']? 'font-family'] | caption | icon | menu | message-box | small-caption | status-bar | inherit	See individual properties	All elements	Y

continues

Table B.1   CSS2 Property Index[1]   (Continued)

Property Name	Media	Values	Initial Value	Applies To	Inherited
font-family	Visual	[[<family-name> | <generic-family>],]* [<family-name> | <generic-family>] | inherit	Depends on user agent	All elements	Y
font-size	Visual	<absolute-size> | <relative-size> | <length> | <percentage> | inherit	Medium	All elements	Y, the computed value is inherited
font-size-adjust	Visual	<number> | none | inherit	None	All elements	Y
font-stretch	Visual	normal | wider | narrower | ultra-condensed | extra-condensed | condensed | semi-condensed | semi-expanded | expanded | extra-expanded | ultra-expanded | inherit	Normal	All elements	Y
font-style	Visual	normal | italic | oblique | inherit	Normal	All elements	Y
font-variant	Visual	normal | small-caps | inherit	Normal	All elements	Y
font-weight	Visual	normal | bold | bolder | lighter | 100 | 200 | 300 | 400 | 500 | 600 | 700 | 800 | 900 | inherit	Normal	All elements	Y
height	Visual	<length> | <percentage> | auto | inherit	Auto	All elements but non-replaced table columns, inline elements, and column groups	N
left	Visual	<length> | <percentage> | auto | inherit	Auto	Positioned elements	N
letter-spacing	Visual	normal | <length> | inherit	Normal	All elements	Y
line-height	Visual	normal | <number> | <length> | <percentage> | inherit	Normal	All elements	Y

Property Name	Media	Values	Initial Value	Applies To	Inherited
`list-style`	Visual	[`'list-style-type'` || `'list-style-position'` || `'list-style-image'`] | `inherit`	N/A	Elements with `'display: list-item'`	Y
`list-style-image`	Visual	`<uri>` | `none` | `inherit`	None	Elements with `'display: list-item'`	Y
`list-style-position`	Visual	`inside` | `outside` | `inherit`	Outside	Elements with `'display: list-item'`	Y
`list-style-type`	Visual	`disc` | `circle` | `square` | `decimal` | `decimal-leading-zero` | `lower-roman` | `upper-roman` | `lower-greek` | `lower-alpha` | `lower-latin` | `upper-alpha` | `upper-latin` | `hebrew` | `armenian` | `georgian` | `cjk-ideographic` | `hiragana` | `katakana` | `hiragana-iroha` | `katakana-iroha` | `none` | `inherit`	Disc	Elements with `'display: list-item'`	Y
`margin`	Visual	`<margin-width>` `{1,4}` | `inherit`	See individual values	All elements	N
`margin-top`	Visual	`<margin-width>` | `inherit`	0	All elements	N
`margin-right`	Visual	`<margin-width>` | `inherit`	0	All elements	N
`margin-bottom`	Visual	`<margin-width>` | `inherit`	0	All elements	N
`margin-left`	Visual	`<margin-width>` | `inherit`	0	All elements	N
`marker-offset`	Visual	`<length>` | `auto` | `inherit`	Auto	Elements with `'display: marker'`	N
`marks`	Visual, paged	[`crop` || `cross`] | `none` | `inherit`	None	Page context	N/A

continues

Table B.1   CSS2 Property Index[1]   (Continued)

Property Name	Media	Values	Initial Value	Applies To	Inherited
max-height	Visual	`<length>` | `<percentage>` | `none` | `inherit`	None	All elements except non-replaced inline elements and table elements	N
max-width	Visual	`<length>` | `<percentage>` | `none` | `inherit`	None	All elements except non-replaced inline elements and table elements	N
min-height	Visual	`<length>` | `<percentage>` | `inherit`	0	All elements except non-replaced inline elements and table elements	N
min-width	Visual	`<length>` | `<percentage>` | `inherit`	UA dependent	All elements except non-replaced inline elements and table elements	N
orphans	Visual, paged	`<integer>` | `inherit`	2	Block-level elements	Y
outline	Visual, interactive	`[ 'outline-color' || 'outline-style' || 'outline-width' ]` | `inherit`	See individual properties	All elements	N
outline-color	Visual, interactive	`<color>` | `invert` | `inherit`	Invert	All elements	N
outline-style	Visual, interactive	`<border-style>` | `inherit`	None	All elements	N
outline-width	Visual, interactive	`<border-width>` | `inherit`	Medium	All elements	N
overflow	Visual	`visible` | `hidden` | `scroll` | `auto` | `inherit`	Visible	Block-level and replaced elements	N
padding	Visual	`<padding-width>{1,4}` | `inherit`	N/A	All elements	N
padding-top	Visual	`<padding-width>` | `inherit`	0	All elements	N
padding-right	Visual	`<padding-width>` | `inherit`	0	All elements	N
padding-bottom	Visual	`<padding-width>` | `inherit`	0	All elements	N

Property Name	Media	Values	Initial Value	Applies To	Inherited
`padding-left`	Visual	`<padding-width>` `| inherit`	0	All elements	N
`page`	Visual, paged	`<identifier> |` `auto`	Auto	Block-level elements	Y
`page-break-after`	Visual, paged	`auto	always |` `avoid	left |` `right	inherit`	Auto	Block-level elements	N
`page-break-before`	Visual, paged	`auto	always |` `avoid	left |` `right	inherit`	Auto	Block-level elements	N
`page-break-inside`	Visual, paged	`avoid	auto	` `inherit`	Auto	Block-level elements	Y
`pause`	Aural	`[[<time>	` `<percentage>]` `{1,2}]	inherit`	Depends on user agent	All elements	N
`pause-after`	Aural	`<time> |` `<percentage> |` `inherit`	Depends on user agent	All elements	N
`pause-before`	Aural	`<time> |` `<percentage> |` `inherit`	Depends on user agent	All elements	N
`pitch`	Aural	`<frequency> |` `x-low	low |` `medium	high |` `x-high	inherit`	Medium	All elements	Y
`pitch-range`	Aural	`<number> |` `inherit`	50	All elements	Y
`play-during`	Aural	`<uri> mix?` `repeat?	auto	` `none	inherit`	Auto	All elements	N
`position`	Visual	`static	relative` `| absolute	fixed` `| inherit`	Static	All elements, but not to generated content	N
`quotes`	Visual	`[<string>` `<string>]+	none` `	inherit`	Depends on user agent	All elements	Y
`richness`	Aural	`<number> |` `inherit`	50	All elements	Y
`right`	Visual	`<length>	` `<percentage>	` `auto	inherit`	Auto	Positioned elements	N
`size`	Visual, paged	`<length>{1,2} |` `auto	portrait |` `landscape	inherit`	Auto	The page context	N/A
`speak`	Aural	`normal	none	` `spell-out	` `inherit`	Normal	All elements	Y

continues

Table B.1   CSS2 Property Index[1]   (Continued)

Property Name	Media	Values	Initial Value	Applies To	Inherited
speak-header	Aural	once | always | inherit	Once	Elements that have table header information	Y
speak-numeral	Aural	digits | continuous | inherit	Continuous	All elements	Y
speak-punctuation	Aural	code | none | inherit	None	All elements	Y
speech-rate	Aural	<number> | x-slow | slow | medium | fast | x-fast | faster | slower | inherit	Medium	All elements	Y
stress	Aural	<number> | inherit	50	All elements	Y
table-layout	Visual	auto | fixed | inherit	Auto	'table' and 'inline-table' elements	N
text-align	Visual	left | right | center | justify | <string> | inherit	Depends on user agent and writing direction	Block-level elements	Y
text-decoration	Visual	none | [underline || overline || line-through || blink] | inherit	None	All elements	N
text-indent	Visual	<length> | <percentage> | inherit	0	Block-level elements	Y
text-shadow	Visual	none | [<color> || <length> <length> <length>? ,]* [<color> || <length> <length> <length>?] | inherit	None	All elements	N
text-transform	Visual	capitalize | uppercase | lowercase | none | inherit	None	All elements	Y
top	Visual	<length> | <percentage> | auto | inherit	Auto	Positioned elements	N

Property Name	Media	Values	Initial Value	Applies To	Inherited
unicode-bidi	Visual	normal | embed | bidi-override | inherit	Normal	All elements, but see prose	N
vertical-align	Visual	baseline | sub | super | top | text-top | middle | bottom | text-bottom | <percentage> | <length> | inherit	Baseline	Inline-level and 'table-cell' elements	N
visibility	Visual	visible | hidden | collapse | inherit	Inherit	All elements	N
voice-family	Aural	[[<specific-voice> | <generic-voice>],]* [<specific-voice> | <generic-voice>] | inherit	Depends on user agent	All elements	Y
volume	Aural	<number> | <percentage> | silent | x-soft | soft | medium | loud | x-loud | inherit	Medium	All elements	Y
white-space	Visual	normal | pre | nowrap | inherit	Normal	Block-level elements	Y
widows	Visual, paged	<integer> | inherit	2	Block-level elements	Y
width	Visual	<length> | <percentage> | auto | inherit	Auto	All elements but non-replaced inline elements, table rows, and row groups	N
word-spacing	Visual	normal | <length> | inherit	Normal	All elements	Y
z-index	Visual	auto | <integer> | inherit	Auto	Positioned elements	N

1. CSS2 Reference Copyright © World Wide Web Consortium (Massachusetts Institute of Technology, Institut National de Recherche en Informatique et en Automatique, Keio University). All Rights Reserved. See http://www.w3.org/TR/REC-CSS2/.

HTML 4.01 Reference

Table C.1 is a listing of the HTML 4.01 elements. Sometimes, elements are erroneously referred to as tags. Use this table as a reference tool to look up elements and see how they can be used correctly in your markup. Elements that are marked Y in the Deprecated column are no longer supported in the standard. Browsers can still render them like you are used to, but it would be a good practice to stop using deprecated elements and look for alternatives.

More Resources Are Available on the Web Site

These are brief and to-the-point resources for those times when you are away from a computer that has an Internet connection. If you are on the Web and want pointers to more complete resources, check out this book's Web site at http://www.cssbook.com/.

Table C.1   HTML Elements[1]

Element Name	Description	DTD	Start Tag	End Tag	Empty	Deprecated
a	Anchor	Strict, loose	Y	Y	N	N
abbr	Abbreviated form, such as WWW, HTTP, and so on	Strict, loose	Y	Y	N	N
acronym	Points out an acronym	Strict, loose	Y	Y	N	N
address	Information on the author	Strict, loose	Y	Y	N	N
applet	Java applet	Loose	Y	Y	N	Y
area	Client-side image map area	Strict, loose	Y	Prohibited	Y	N
b	Bold text style	Strict, loose	Y	Y	N	N
base	Document base URI	Strict, loose	Y	Prohibited	Y	N
basefont	Base font size	Loose	Y	Prohibited	Y	**Y**
bdo	I18N BiDi over-ride	Strict, loose	Y	Y	N	N
big	Large text style	Strict, loose	Y	Y	N	N
blockquote	Long quotation	Strict, loose	Y	Y	N	N
body	Document body	Strict, loose	Optional	Optional	N	N
br	Forced line break	Strict, loose	Y	Prohibited	Y	N
button	Push button	Strict, loose	Y	Y	N	N
caption	Table caption	Strict, loose	Y	Y	N	N
center	<div align="center">	Loose	Y	Y	N	**Y**
cite	Citation	Strict, loose	Y	Y	N	N
code	Computer code snippet	Strict, loose	Y	Y	N	N
col	Table column	Strict, loose	Y	Prohibited	Y	N
colgroup	Table column group	Strict, loose	Y	Optional	N	N
dd	Definition description	Strict, loose	Y	Optional	N	N
del	Deleted text	Strict, loose	Y	Y	N	N
dfn	Instance definition	Strict, loose	Y	Y	N	N
dir	Directory list	Loose	Y	Y	N	**Y**
div	Generic language/style container	Strict, loose	Y	Y	N	N

Element Name	Description	DTD	Start Tag	End Tag	Empty	Deprecated
dl	Definition list	Strict, loose	Y	Y	N	N
dt	Definition term	Strict, loose	Y	Optional	N	N
em	Emphasis	Strict, loose	Y	Y	N	N
fieldset	Form control group	Strict, loose	Y	Y	N	N
font	Local change to font	Loose	Y	Y	N	**Y**
form	Interactive form	Strict, loose	Y	Y	N	N
frame	Subwindow	Frameset	Y	Prohibited	Y	N
frameset	Window subdivision	Frameset	Y	Y	N	N
h1	Heading	Strict, loose	Y	Y	N	N
h2	Heading	Strict, loose	Y	Y	N	N
h3	Heading	Strict, loose	Y	Y	N	N
h4	Heading	Strict, loose	Y	Y	N	N
h5	Heading	Strict, loose	Y	Y	N	N
h6	Heading	Strict, loose	Y	Y	N	N
head	Document head	Strict, loose	Optional	Optional	N	N
hr	Horizontal rule	Strict, loose	Y	Prohibited	Y	N
html	Document root element	Strict, loose	Optional	Optional	N	N
i	Italic text style	Strict, loose	Y	Y	N	N
iframe	Inline subwindow	Loose	Y	Y	N	N
img	Embedded image	Strict, loose	Y	Prohibited	Y	N
input	Form control	Strict, loose	Y	Prohibited	Y	N
ins	Inserted text	Strict, loose	Y	Y	N	N
isindex	Single line prompt	Loose	Y	Prohibited	Y	**Y**
kbd	Text for the user to enter	Strict, loose	Y	Y	N	N
label	Form field label text	Strict, loose	Y	Y	N	N
legend	Fieldset legend	Strict, loose	Y	Y	N	N
li	List item	Strict, loose	Y	Optional	N	N
link	A media-independent link	Strict, loose	Y	Prohibited	Y	N
map	Client-side image map	Strict, loose	Y	Y	N	N
menu	Menu list	Loose	Y	Y	N	**Y**

continues

Table C.1 HTML Elements[1] (Continued)

Element Name	Description	DTD	Start Tag	End Tag	Empty	Deprecated
meta	Generic metainformation	Strict, loose	Y	Prohibited	Y	N
noframes	Alternative content container for non frame-based rendering	Frameset	Y	Y	N	N
noscript	Alternative content container for non script-based rendering	Strict, loose	Y	Y	N	N
object	Generic embedded object	Strict, loose	Y	Y	N	N
ol	Ordered list	Strict, loose	Y	Y	N	N
optgroup	Option group	Strict, loose	Y	Y	N	N
option	Selectable choice	Strict, loose	Y	Optional	N	N
p	Paragraph	Strict, loose	Y	Optional	N	N
param	Named property value	Strict, loose	Y	Prohibited	Y	N
pre	Preformatted text	Strict, loose	Y	Y	N	N
q	Short inline quotation	Strict, loose	Y	Y	N	N
s	Strikethrough text style	Loose	Y	Y	N	**Y**
samp	Sample program output, scripts, and so on	Strict, loose	Y	Y	N	N
script	Script statements	Strict, loose	Y	Y	N	N
select	Option selector	Strict, loose	Y	Y	N	N
small	Small text style	Strict, loose	Y	Y	N	N
span	Generic language/style container	Strict, loose	Y	Y	N	N
strike	Strikethrough text	Loose	Y	Y	N	**Y**
strong	Strong emphasis	Strict, loose	Y	Y	N	N
style	Style information	Strict, loose	Y	Y	N	N

Element Name	Description	DTD	Start Tag	End Tag	Empty	Deprecated
sub	Subscript	Strict, loose	Y	Y	N	N
sup	Superscript	Strict, loose	Y	Y	N	N
table	Contains all other elements that indicate content for a table	Strict, loose	Y	Y	N	N
tbody	Table body	Strict, loose	Optional	Optional	N	N
td	Table data cell	Strict, loose	Y	Optional	N	N
textarea	Multiline text field	Strict, loose	Y	Y	N	N
tfoot	Table footer	Strict, loose	Y	Optional	N	N
th	Table header cell	Strict, loose	Y	Optional	N	N
thead	Table header	Strict, loose	Y	Optional	N	N
title	Document title	Strict, loose	Y	Y	N	N
tr	Table row	Strict, loose	Y	Optional	N	N
tt	Teletype or monospaced text style	Strict, loose	Y	Y	N	N
u	Underlined text style	Loose	Y	Y	N	**Y**
ul	Unordered list	Strict, loose	Y	Y	N	N
var	Instance of a variable or program argument	Strict, loose	Y	Y	N	N

1. HTML 4.01 Specification Copyright © World Wide Web Consortium (Massachusetts Institute of Technology, Institut National de Recherche en Informatique et en Automatique, Keio University). All Rights Reserved. See http://www.w3.org/TR/html401/index/elements.html.

HTML to XHTML Conversion Tips

Conversion tips help you convert markup in HTML to XHTML. With HTML, you can omit closing container tags, forget quotes around attributes, and generally leave a mess of things in your Web document without significant consequences. However, what if you need to share your code with browsers you haven't met yet or browsers that have yet to be written? For your Web documents to be shared correctly, you can follow a strict markup procedure. Picture XHTML as an annoying mother nagging you to pick up your clothes from the floor, sit up straight, and drink your milk. Well, XHTML is also your third grade teacher, making sure your handwriting is clean and crisp and that you play well with others. These tips will teach you everything that you need to know to please the mother and the teacher.

XHTML is less "forgiving" than HTML, but like any good teacher, she only wants the best for you. Knowing how to write proper code ensures that you will grow into a more efficient markup producer so that your page renders properly in as many browsers as possible.

More Resources Are Available on the Web Site

These are brief and to-the-point resources for those times when you are away from a computer that has an Internet connection. If you are on the Web and want pointers to more complete resources, check out this book's Web site at http://www.cssbook.com/.

Use a Valid DTD and Include Namespace

For XHTML, which requires more precise markup syntax, use the valid document type definitions (DTDs), such as the following:

- `<!DOCTYPE html PUBLIC "-//W3C//DTD XHTML 1.0 Strict//EN" "DTD/xhtml1-strict.dtd">`
- `<!DOCTYPE html PUBLIC "-//W3C//DTD XHTML 1.0 Transitional//EN" "DTD/xhtml1-transitional.dtd">`
- `<!DOCTYPE html PUBLIC "-//W3C//DTD XHTML 1.0 Frameset//EN" "DTD/xhtml1-frameset.dtd">`

Following a DOCTYPE, there must be a namespace declaration.

Here is a bad example:

```
<HTML>
```

Here is a good example:

```
<!DOCTYPE html PUBLIC "-//W3C//DTD XHTML 1.0 Strict//EN"
"DTD/xhtml1-strict.dtd">
<html xmlns="http://www.w3.org/1999/xhtml" xml:lang="en"
lang="en">
```

Inlined JavaScript and Style Sheets Should Be Free of Certain Characters

If you will have an inlined style sheet or JavaScript, avoid using these characters: <, &,]]>, or --. If you notice, that means the practice of using <!-- and --> comment tags to hide JavaScript or CSS from browsers might fail. You will need to use and link to external JavaScript and CSS files if you want to target older browsers and still be relevant to tomorrow's user agents.

Keep Only Clean Nests

As with proper coding in HTML, make sure your markup is properly nested in XHTML.

Here is a bad example:

```
<p>So there was this mafia movie about birds. Can you
<i>believe that?</p></i>
```

Here is a good example:

```
<p>So there was this mafia movie about birds. Can you
<i>believe that?</i></p>
```

Fragment Identifiers: Name and ID Have the Same Value

In XML, a fragment identifier such as #bullwhip will not be able to link to the name attribute. You will need to use id instead. However, to ensure that browsers will be able to perform the link, you might want to make name and id have the same value.

Here is a bad example:

```
<a name="bullwhip">This thing is a bullwhip</a>
```

Here is a good example:

```
<a name=" bullwhip" id=" bullwhip">This thing really is a
bullwhip</a>
```

Closing Tags Are Not Optional

Don't make the browser do the guesswork for when a container ends. If an element has a closing tag, you must include it in the markup.

Here is a bad example:

```
 <td>I really don't see an end to this prison cell.
 <td>Maybe if I run as fast as I can?</td>
```

Here is a good example:

```
 <td>Ah. Here's the end of the prison cell.</td>
 <td>Maybe if I run as fast as I can?</td>
```

All Elements Should Be Lowercase

You can still have upper- and lowercase for the values of an element's respective attributes, but you are not allowed to use uppercase or a mixture of upper and lowercases for XHTML elements.

Here are two bad examples:

```
<P>We don't design sites like our parents did…</P>
```

```
<BLOCKquote>David Siegel wrote that in 1996ish</BLOCKquote>
```

Here is a good example:

```
<p>You wrote me a paragraph of diatribe.</p>
```

Slash Empty Elements

Include a space and a forward slash before the closing bracket at the end of an empty element.

Here is a bad example:

```
<br>
<img src="bullwhip.jpg" alt="My friend with a bullwhip."
width="300" height="30">
<br>
```

Here is a good example:

```
<br />
<img src="bullwhip.jpg" alt="My friend with a bullwhip."
width="300" height="30" />
<hr />
```

Avoid Line Breaks in Attribute Values

Do not place line breaks or multiple white space characters in the values of attributes. Multiple white space characters are stripped and in their place, and one is left. The browser should convert line breaks into white space.

Here is a bad example. (Note the space between the " and Hey.)

```
<img src="cousin.jpg" alt=" Hey,

what's that over there?…

Looks like Cousin Billy with a bullwhip!" width="300"
height="400"  />
```

Here is a good example:

```
<img src="cousin.jpg" alt="Hey, what's that over there?…
Looks like Cousin Billy with a bullwhip!" width="300"
height="400" />
```

Quotes Around Attribute Values

Put quotes around the value of your attributes.

Here is a bad example:

```
<img src=this_picture_here.jpg alt=Not a good likeness.>
```

Here is a good example:

```
<img src="that_picture_there.jpg" alt="A great likeness of me.">
```

Where There's an Attribute, There's a Value

Some HTML elements contain attributes that were left to their own devices. With XHTML, you need to place the attribute name as its respective value.

Here is a bad example:

```
<hr noshade>
```

Here is a good example:

```
<hr noshade="noshade">
```

Ampersands in Attribute Values

Dealing with ampersands in the values of attributes is not really an HTML-to-XHTML conversion guideline, but it is a validation problem in HTML as it is in XHTML. Regardless, it is something to know when you're trying to validate your Web pages. Instead of an ampersand (&) in an attribute value, use the character entity, &.

Here is a bad example:

```
<a href="runaway.html?x=1&y=2">Get away from the bullwhip</a>
```

Here is a good example:

```
<a href="runaway.html?x=1&amp;y=2">Get away from the bullwhip</a>
```

Index

VOICES THAT MATTER

HOW TO CONTACT US

VISIT OUR WEB SITE

W W W . N E W R I D E R S . C O M

On our Web site you'll find information about our other books, authors, tables of contents, indexes, and book errata. You will also find information about book registration and how to purchase our books.

EMAIL US

Contact us at this address: **nrfeedback@newriders.com**

- If you have comments or questions about this book
- To report errors that you have found in this book
- If you have a book proposal to submit or are interested in writing for New Riders
- If you would like to have an author kit sent to you
- If you are an expert in a computer topic or technology and are interested in being a technical editor who reviews manuscripts for technical accuracy

- To find a distributor in your area, please contact our international department at this address. **nrmedia@newriders.com**

- For instructors from educational institutions who want to preview New Riders books for classroom use. Email should include your name, title, school, department, address, phone number, office days/hours, text in use, and enrollment, along with your request for desk/examination copies and/or additional information.
- For members of the media who are interested in reviewing copies of New Riders books. Send your name, mailing address, and email address, along with the name of the publication or Web site you work for.

BULK PURCHASES/CORPORATE SALES

The publisher offers discounts on this book when ordered in quantity for bulk purchases and special sales. For sales within the U.S., please contact: Corporate and Government Sales (800) 382-3419 or **corpsales@pearsontechgroup.com**. Outside of the U.S., please contact: International Sales (317) 428-3341 or **international@pearsontechgroup.com**.

WRITE TO US

New Riders Publishing
800 East 96th Street, 3rd Floor
Indianapolis, IN 46240

CALL US

Toll-free (800) 571-5840. Ask for New Riders.
If outside U.S. (317) 428-3000. Ask for New Riders.

FAX US

(317) 428-3280

Solutions from experts you know and trust.

www.informit.com

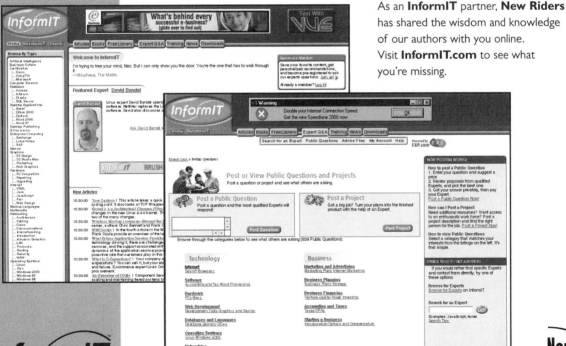

Colophon

This book was written on an Apple iBook using Microsoft Word, edited in Microsoft Word, and laid out in QuarkXPress. The font used for the body text is Bembo and Mono. It was printed on 50# Husky Offset Smooth paper at VonHoffmann Inc. in Owensville, Missouri. Prepress consisted of PostScript computer-to-plate technology (filmless process). The cover was printed at Moore Langen Printing in Terre Haute, Indiana on 12 pt., coated on one side.